STEWART LAMONT worked for twenty years in radio, television and newspapers as a broadcaster and journalist. He was born in Broughty Ferry, and studied science and divinity at St Andrews University. After working as a parish minister in Glasgow, he moved to a post with the Conference of European Churches in Brussels where he lives with his Russian wife Larisa. His books include a thriller, a study of the paranormal, and a collection of his weekly newspaper columns, as well as biographies of two seminal influences on Scotland: *St Andrew* and *John Knox*.

WHEN SCOTLAND
RULED THE WORLD

*The Story of the Golden Age of Genius,
Creativity and Exploration*

Stewart Lamont

HarperCollins*Publishers*

HarperCollins*Publishers*
77–85 Fulham Palace Road,
London W6 8JB

www.**fire**and**water**.com

This paperback edition 2002

3 5 7 9 8 6 4 2

First published in Great Britain by
HarperCollins*Publishers* 2001

A catalogue record for this book
is available from the British Library

ISBN 0 00 710000 0

Printed in Great Britain by
Clays Ltd, St Ives plc

Contents

Note: * denotes a person on whom a full article appears
elsewhere in the book.

Acknowledgements

Scots have had an impact in so many areas of activity that it is inevitable that some names and some fields of activity may have been omitted from this collection. It is also inevitable that it reflects my own priorities and limitations of knowledge. In helping to redress this, I was fortunate to have considerable assistance at an earlier stage from the historian Michael Fry, whose career in journalism has been accompanied by several books on aspects of Scottish history, the most recent being a study of Scots in Empire. I would like to express my appreciation of his contributions to the biographies, particularly in the areas of Enlightenment, politics and literature, without which the book would have fallen well short of its present scope.

The chapters on science owe much to my own interest in the subject. As a schoolboy I was enthralled by chemistry and physics, partly by my teachers David Duff and A. P. Melvin. At St Andrews University I encountered Dr D. M. Finlayson, a modern Renaissance Scotsman who helped me appreciate the importance of science, despite my defection to the divinity faculty. Later, when I moved to Glasgow, through the XIII Club I began a friendship with Professor Bill Fletcher, Emeritus Professor of Biology at Strathclyde University whose published work on famous Scots has been extremely helpful to me with this book.

I would also like to thank the Royal College of Physicians and Surgeons (Glasgow), and in particular the Librarian James Beaton for assistance with the chapter on the Scottish contribution to medicine.

Finally, I would like to thank James Catford at HarperCollins, who had the idea for this book and who has been both supportive and patient during its production.

Stewart Lamont
Brussels, April 2001

Preface

Winston Churchill was not a Scotsman but he held a seat in Parliament for Dundee up until 1922. Had he known that he was about to lose it at a General Election to an opponent who fought on a prohibitionist ticket, he might not have been so generous about the Scots, but this is what he said in a speech at that time:

> *Of all the small nations of this earth, perhaps only the ancient Greeks surpass the Scots in their contribution to mankind.*

Rather than argue with the author of *A History of the English Speaking Peoples*, I have set out to prove him right. It is, like the title of this book, at first sight a ridiculous boast that from the middle of the eighteenth century a nation of barely one million people in a damp and cold country on the periphery of Europe could exert such an important influence on the world. Yet it is not as preposterous as it sounds. Throughout its history Scotland has demonstrated an amazing ability to produce thinkers, writers, scientists, physicians and leaders far out of proportion to its size as a nation, which is still today less than one-tenth of the population of the United Kingdom.

When I set out to write this book, I knew that I could find numerous examples to support the view that Scots were significant on the stage of world history, but as the research went on, a huge number of examples bore in on me. As a result, instead of scrabbling around to find a few famous Scots to fill a book, I had an embarrassing choice and have had to be selective in the people and stories featured. The criteria I have used are simple — born in Scotland, and influential outside it.

That is why I have included so many scientists and pioneers and missed out figures like Rev. Thomas Chalmers, the social reformer, and many other Kirk ministers who had enormous influence within Scotland. There is no Lord Byron (born in Scotland), or Harry Lauder (influential as the inventor of tartan kitsch). If you are Scots you will probably want to protest about some exclusions and argue for other inclusions, and by doing so, will simply show how quintessentially Scottish you are. We have never been able to agree who the real heroes were, so why should it be possible to put them all into one book?

The story of how Scotland came to occupy this influential role is not a single story but hundreds of stories, of men (for this was an era in which the movers and shakers were predominantly male) who achieved amazing things against the odds. Some of them were born in abject poverty, others left school at twelve or were educated at home, and yet went on to push back the frontiers of knowledge in their field. Others were born with privileges but used them to create a better world. They are as varied as their stories but they have one thing in common — they were driven people, driven to go outside the boundaries in which they found themselves, whether geographical or intellectual. Call it curiosity, or a pioneering spirit, or even a divine discontent with the way things are, but it is very Scots.

Perhaps that is why so many Scots are attracted to pursuits which push back the frontiers of exploration, or science or technology. In its simplest form this impulse is to go further and faster. Is it coincidence that the first man to set foot on the moon (Neil Armstrong) was of Scots descent? Or that currently the fastest man on wheels (Richard Noble of Thrust fame) was born in Edinburgh and two world champion racing drivers (Jim Clark and Jackie Stewart) were Scots?

I do not claim such characteristics to be uniquely Scottish. There are other examples of small nations which have exercised influence far out of proportion to their numbers. The Jews and the Irish are similar to the Scots in their capacity to emigrate and integrate, while at the same time retaining their distinctive characteristics. It is tempting to add that in common with the Jews and the Irish, Scots seem to be better at achieving things outside their national boundaries than within them. Throughout the world, they are as ubiquitous as McDonalds fast-food outlets (whose founder was obviously one of us). The British Empire was dominated backstage by Scots administrators, accountants and engineers. Wherever you are in the world, a glance at the local telephone directory is liable to yield several names of Scottish origin, especially in the countries which Scots favoured for emigration such as Canada and Australia.

Their reasons for emigrating were not always positive. Lack of opportunities at home, clearances from the land, and poverty all played their part. But many were motivated by intellectual curiosity, a spirit of adventure and an international perspective, all characteristics which helped them achieve such a high success rate in whatever they did.

There are two other factors in the Scottish character which gave it force, one moral, the other educational. Scotland was ideally suited to embrace the Calvinist Reformation in the sixteenth century because it gave a high priority to morality and to learning, not simply for the elite but also for the population as a whole. George Davie called this process 'The Democratic Intellect' in his book of the same name. It was a way of thinking rather than the idea or invention of any church or philosopher. Davie calls one of his chapters 'The Humanist Bias of Scottish Science' and goes some way to explain why so many Scots scientists produced inventions. The idea is that talents, knowledge, power must be put to some use that is practical, moral and which makes the world a better place.

It could not have happened without two conditions being present: a good education system and a religious climate in which speculation and intellectual enquiry were admired and not stifled. Scotland had no Galileo. It may not have treated its scientists and thinkers as heroes, but it did not call them heretics.

I have also limited myself to a particular period when Scots influence was widely felt. Not surprisingly, it coincides with the dominance of the British Empire and the growth of the Industrial Revolution, and begins in the golden age known as the Enlightenment which provided the ideal conditions for these characteristics to flourish.

The Enlightenment Dawns

The Fall and Rise of the Scottish Empire

In 1707 Scotland entered into Union with England, then for the rest of the eighteenth century enjoyed an extraordinary cultural and intellectual flowering. As we shall see in the following pages, Scots in that period were to the fore in shaping the world we live in today.

It often used to be assumed that the Union somehow caused the Enlightenment. Or, to put it another way, the tragic and turbulent Scotland of old could not have been civilized without the benign influence spreading from England after 1707. But this always seemed an improbable, or at least an inadequate, explanation. While English influence on Scotland obviously cannot be discounted once they became one country, more emphasis is laid nowadays on what the Scots brought to the Union from their own seven centuries as an independent nation.

From the first they had formed a multicultural society. The Scottish monarchy founded by Kenneth MacAlpine in 843 itself united four peoples: the Britons who dominated the north-east of Scotland; the Scots who had originally invaded the west from Ireland; and the Angles who had infiltrated the south-east. To these

1

were later added Norsemen in the Northern and Western Isles, conquered by the kings of Scotland after the Battle of Largs in 1263 or transferred peacefully to their new allegiance upon the acquisition of Orkney and Shetland in 1469.

This mixed Anglo-Celtic kingdom vindicated its independence in a desperate struggle against the English from 1290 to 1314. One result was a further enrichment of its culture by alliance with France and by cultivation of close relations with the Papacy in Rome or Avignon. French and Latin scholarship brought the humanism of the Renaissance to Scotland. Even the Scottish Reformation could be regarded as essentially French, since it stemmed from John Calvin in Geneva.

But the Reformation also brought a reorientation of culture in a now Protestant people. Calvinist humanism, the cultivation of virtue through learning, was an interest Scots scholars shared with colleagues in other reformed nations of Europe, notably the Netherlands. English influence grew after the Union of Crowns in 1603, when James VI of Scotland became James I of England. Yet the Scots were vigilant in maintaining otherwise the independence of their church and their state.

They did so above all in the terms of the Treaty of Union with England, which gave guarantees for the cultural institutions Scots most valued, the Church, the law and the universities. The Scottish nation and Scottish culture were preserved inside the Union. Well into the nineteenth century, the life of Scotland formed a clear continuum with its past. To modern eyes, all this seems more convincing as a basis for the Enlightenment than the single influence of England.

The links between the old Scotland and the new can be gauged from the careers of the three men with whom we begin. They grew up in an independent nation and became acutely aware of the perils it faced in a world characterized by two major forces, the emergence of empires stretching out from Europe to the other continents and the consequent rapid increase in international trade. The questions they had to confront were whether a small nation like Scotland could survive in this political environment and whether indeed she should want to if she should gain economic benefits for the sacrifice of her independence. All three men had different answers for the situations they found themselves in, but the quality of their thinking continued to influence debate. After all, we are still discussing the issue of economic union and national independence today.

ANDREW FLETCHER OF SALTOUN (1653–1716)

Andrew Fletcher of Saltoun was among the first modern political thinkers, yet he failed in almost every political cause he took up. His relationship with his own country was more complex than may be suggested by his diehard resistance to its Union with England in 1707.

He came of a family of lairds in East Lothian. Gilbert Burnet, future Anglican bishop and Whig historian, was minister of the parish and acted as his tutor. Burnet later wrote in the *History of His Own Time* that his pupil had become 'a Scotch gentleman of great parts and many virtues, but extravagantly passionate'. He was notorious for his hot temper and instant readiness to fight a duel with anyone who crossed him.

Fletcher's father died in 1665, leaving him an estate and the freedom to do what he wanted. Three years later he set off on an educational tour, and he would spend most of his life wandering about Europe. His stays at home and his political career were concentrated in two quite short periods: from 1678 to 1682, when he was chosen as a parliamentary representative of his county and became a critic of royal government, and then from 1702 to 1707 when he led the doomed opposition to the Union. Otherwise he showed little interest in the Scotland which gave him the where-withal to go his own way. He loved great cities, London or Paris or Amsterdam, where he sat in public houses, acquired the raffish habit of drinking chocolate and made friends, or pottered round bookshops buying valuable volumes to send home to his library. He travelled far afield, certainly to Spain and Germany, possibly to Italy and

Hungary. He observed and talked about all that was going on, and he tried to discern beneath the everyday realities how the tide of history was running.

Sometimes he took a hand in history himself. In 1685, with exiles he met in Holland, he threw in his lot with the rebellion of the bastard Duke of Monmouth against his uncle, King James VII of Scotland and II of England. This was a foolish venture, soon crushed, and was the death of most who joined it. But Fletcher escaped because, only two days after landing in Devon, he was forced to leave again after killing the Mayor of Taunton in a quarrel over a horse. In this case his recklessness saved his life. After the Revolution of 1688 and the overthrow of the senior line of Stuarts, his forfeited estate was restored to him. But he spent much of the following decade in London, whence he encouraged the Scottish expeditions to Darien in 1698–1700.

The climax of his political career came in the last Scottish Parliament and its debates on the Treaty of Union. His long opposition to strong monarchy made him conscious of the risk that the Stuarts might come back. One way to keep them out was Union with England, which had now settled the Crown on the House of Hanover, but Fletcher's sharp mind showed him the problems of that. He hoped to find a way out of the resulting dilemmas.

One possibility was to impose what he called limitations on the King of Scots, in other words to restrict his powers. 'Since the Union of the Crowns all our affairs have been managed by the advice of English Ministers,' he said, 'and the principal offices of the kingdom filled with such men as the court of England knew would be subservient to their designs; by which means they have made so visible an influence upon our whole administration that we have, from that time, appeared to the rest of the world more like a conquered province than a free independent people.' He thought, however, that limitations would reassure the English if the Scots chose a different king of their own, while also reassuring the Scots should they decide to accept the Hanoverians after all.

Union with England would by contrast destroy rather than enhance the possibility of constitutional government in Scotland.

The two nations had different interests, and the Scots 'deserve no pity if they voluntarily surrender their united and separate interest to the mercy of a united Parliament, where the English have so vast a majority'. He did not see how a Union of the Parliaments could protect Scottish interests when the Union of the Crowns had not: 'This will be the issue of that darling plea of being one and not two; it will be turned upon the Scots with a vengeance, and their forty-five Scots members may dance round to all eternity, in this trap of their own making.'

Beneath Fletcher's nationalism lay a universal purpose. He saw the emergence of global trading and of imperialist expansion, threatening to produce the concentration and abuse of economic and political power. He proposed limitations not only within nations but also among them, with the construction of a European confederacy of regional states, none strong enough to conquer or oppress others. In the circumstances of his time this was an impractical scheme, and only today can it even remotely be contemplated. Its enduring interest lies in the ideas that led Fletcher to it, ideas about how to maintain individual or communal freedom and independence in the face of the modern world's vast impersonal forces. These remain relevant, but the immediate practical test for Fletcher was to save Scottish independence in 1707. There he failed, and he retired into private life.

WILLIAM PATERSON (1658–1719)

A pioneer entrepreneur, William Paterson helped demonstrate to his contemporaries the practical benefits that could flow from ideas of economic liberty still unfamiliar and suspect to them. He left to the modern world the basic concept of the central bank as linchpin of the financial system. His wayward but inventive vigour strained the capacities and resources of his age, yet two of his three great projects have survived into our own time, while the third has bequeathed a permanent, if doleful, memory.

He came from Tinwald, Dumfriesshire, the heart of Covenanting country, where the Scottish religious revolutionaries of the seventeenth century held out most tenaciously against oppression by the Government. Probably the young Paterson sympathized with them, for after a short time studying at Glasgow University he thought it better to quit Scotland. He went to Bristol and took ship for the West Indies. Kicking around there for several years, he made his way both as merchant and as pirate: in that swashbuckling quarter of the globe, the distinction was often unclear. Probably he visited Darien, today in Panama, situated at the narrowest point of the Americas where the strip of land formed no more than a bridge between the Atlantic and Pacific oceans. He thought it could carry the trade between the two.

On his return he went first to Amsterdam, trying to woo the venturesome Dutch with this idea. Getting nowhere, he crossed to London, but became sidetracked into something different. The Revolution of 1688 had taken place and war with France was going on. It forced the Government to borrow heavily and put a huge strain on public finances. One problem was the bad record of English kings, who had defaulted on debts in the past. So few banks or individuals felt ready to lend now. Various schemes had been aired to expand and stabilize credit but it was Paterson's, submitted in 1691, that after long delay found favour.

What he proposed was to found, under royal charter, a bank with a permanent capital which could not be wiped out by imprudent lending and bad debts. The capital was fixed at £1.2 million and subscribers were to be paid interest of eight per cent a year. They would be incorporated as the Governor and Company of the Bank of England, with power to trade in bills of exchange, bullion and forfeited pledges. Since they could never be driven out of business, their bank introduced a stability and confidence not present before in the financial system. Thus Paterson, effective founder of the Bank of England, both safeguarded the state against bankruptcy and laid the foundations for the future of the City of London as a centre of international capital.

Paterson was one of the bank's directors, but soon fell out with the rest and returned to his native land. Undaunted, he set about a second venture on the same lines, and succeeded in establishing the Bank of Scotland in 1695. Similar as it was in its origins to the Bank of England, it underwent a different evolution. Impoverished Scots lacked gold and silver, which alone were internationally recognized as money in those days. Early on, the Bank of Scotland began to extend credit to its customers, naturally secured on assets but not represented by anything material in its vaults. Soon this credit came to be represented by various kinds of paper, and then it was a short step to the invention of the banknote, the first of which was issued by the Bank of Scotland in 1713. Meanwhile, however, the Scottish state had disappeared with the Union of 1707. This was the reason why the Bank of Scotland never became a central bank like the Bank of England, but has remained a private company.

None of this exhausted Paterson's energies. Teaming up with Andrew Fletcher of Saltoun,* he revived his scheme for Darien. Scots wanted to develop their international trade. Much of this was carried on between imperial powers and their colonies, but Scotland had no colonies, and as a small, weak country saw little prospect of acquiring any. Paterson offered a way out. He said there was no need for Scots to conquer, subdue and settle territories overseas. Instead they should set up an outpost at some favourable spot, an emporium where everyone could come and trade in peace, reassured that Scotland lacked any interest in imperialism. Darien fitted the bill, or at first sight seemed to.

Paterson's plan fired his countrymen's imagination and they invested £400,000 in it, a quarter of all the capital in the country. An expedition of 1,200 Scots, including Paterson, set out across the ocean in 1698 and landed at Darien to found the settlement of New Edinburgh. But Spain protested that it lay in her territory, and England supported her. With these two great powers against Scotland, the colony was doomed, but anyway it never managed to do much trade. The conditions were awful, and many colonists died of tropical disease. Paterson buried his own wife, and only just survived himself. After a few months they had all had enough and fled the place. The whole of the money and most of the lives were lost.

Back home, Paterson actually proposed a further expedition, but nobody would listen. He had to get a job with the English secret service, and spent the next few years singing the praises of the projected Union. He stood for Parliament in the first British election and won his native county but, after some typical mismanagement on his part, the result was overturned. He looked to be a scatterbrained failure, and only later generations have appreciated the scale of his achievements at the dawn of the modern world.

JOHN LAW (1671–1729)

Young Scots who go on the razzle in London are always apt to get into trouble. Few have been in trouble so deep as John Law, who on 20 April 1694 was sentenced to death for murder. He had spent three years there living as a gambler and sleeping with other men's wives. One of these men, Edward 'Beau' Wilson, challenged him to a duel, in which he was killed by Law. The sentence was later commuted to imprisonment, and from his cell the captive managed to escape and flee the country.

In Amsterdam, at that time the main European financial centre, Law could at last benefit from the more respectable background he had from his native city of Edinburgh. He was the son of William Law, a wealthy goldsmith, a trade in which he was also accustomed to carry out such banking operations as were necessary in a primitive economy where money played as yet little part.

From Europe, John Law found time to contemplate Scotland's problems. When he came home in 1700 he set about explaining them to his countrymen, who were still reeling from the failure at Darien and the huge resulting losses. He published a tract called *Proposals and Reasons for Constituting a Council of Trade in Scotland*. Though it does not openly acknowledge any debt to William Paterson,* the ideas are close to his, and we may suppose that Law had met and spoken to him. In a sense, he sets out what Scotland might have done if Darien had been a success: the council would have co-ordinated the nation's efforts to expand its trade, while controlling credit and perhaps supervising some equitable distribution of the benefits. But since Darien had not been a success, the exercise remained academic.

Undaunted, Law elaborated part of his argument with a second tract in 1705, *Money and Trade Considered, with a Proposal for Supplying the Nation with Money*. This was more impressive. It really originated some modern ideas about credit and its distinction from capital. Law did not, by today's theories, get the distinction quite right, but he saw that it was there and that money could assume some of its actual future functions, enlarging exchanges, prompting the division of labour, fostering production, creating demand not only for goods but also for itself. He suggested a short cut to capital accumulation by the monetizing of the nation's existing assets; in practical terms, a land bank. Then, Law argued, the Scots' lower costs might even let them compete with the most successful commercial nation, the Dutch: 'By a greater quantity of money and oeconomy [sic], the Dutch monopolize the trades of carriage even from the English. Scotland has a very inconsiderable trade, because she has but a small part of the money.' The point was that Scotland need not be condemned to poverty just because she had no gold.

However brilliant the ideas, the Scots Parliament would take no notice. As the Union approached, Law went into exile again, probably because he was a Jacobite. Anyway, he disliked the English and felt more at home in France. Over there he again made his living by gambling, while pressing his theories on the great and good. He got nowhere so long as proud King Louis XIV lived, but on his death in 1715 the French realized how they had been ruined by years of his wars. They stood on the brink of bankruptcy and all ideas for regeneration were welcome. Law submitted to Philip, Duke of Orléans and Regent for the infant King Louis XV, a scheme for a state bank or central bank, not unlike the Banks of England and Scotland, to control credit and paper money. This seemed too risky to the Regent, but he did grant Law permission in 1716 to found a private *Banque générale*, with the privilege of issuing money. He ran it so well that his notes, fixed in value, rose to a premium above the official coinage, which was always being clipped or adulterated. A reliable currency benefited the state too, and the Regent issued a decree allowing the notes to be used for paying taxes.

Law never ran short of bright ideas and now he had another, which would enable ambitious colonial enterprises to be mounted without too much risk to the mother country. The vehicle would be a chartered company, like the Company of Scotland which had organized Darien or the English and Dutch East India Companies. The state would allow the company a monopoly of trade to one part of the globe but otherwise leave it alone. Law obtained a privilege for the French territory of Louisiana, stretching up the River Mississippi from New Orleans. With energetic publicity about its untold riches, he attracted enormous investments. By the spring of 1729 the shares had risen 2,000 per cent above the issue price. Law became a tycoon on a scale the French had never seen, courted by high society. The Regent appointed him Minister of Finance, though only after he had converted to Catholicism, and created him Duke of Arkansas.

But from this height his crash followed quickly. With gold and silver out of circulation, France was flooded with notes and prices rose astronomically. The Regent panicked and by another decree halved the value of the notes. All that did was produce, within a week, complete collapse of the paper currency. It cost Law his job and forced him to take refuge abroad from thousands of angry investors. He declined an offer from Tsar Peter the Great to organize the finances of Russia, but he was never able to return, as he hoped, to France. He spent his last years once more wandering around Europe and died in Venice a poor man. His flair had nevertheless touched the imagination of the French and contributed to their tradition of grandiose public policy.

As the disaster of Darien began to fade, and Scotland grew more prosperous, a new generation of thinkers emerged who were to have an influence long after their own time. Foremost among these was

DAVID HUME (1711–76)

Hume's many friends in Paris, when he was secretary at the British embassy there from 1763 to 1766, called him *le bon David*. The nickname summed up the unlikely social success of this podgy Scotsman with the funny accent and deep thoughts. He never married but he flirted blamelessly with the ladies, one of whom called him 'the most innocent, agreeable, facetious man I ever met with'.

In reality he had more interest in food. He not only ate but cooked, describing this in 1769 as 'the science to which I intend to devote the remaining years of my life. For beef and cabbage (a charming dish), and old mutton and old claret, nobody excels me.' The natural accompaniment to cuisine was conversation, practised endlessly among the intellectuals who enjoyed the hospitality at his house after his return to Edinburgh. By then he was famous enough to find a welcome anywhere but he preferred home, certainly to settling among 'the barbarians by the banks of the Thames' – a joke, but one with a barb. Hume was explosive as well as endearing.

He remains the greatest Scottish philosopher and in the top rank of all western philosophers. Profoundly original, he reached revolutionary positions all on his own, after a delicate, lonely, fatherless, introspective youth which ended with his trying in vain to work at the law and at commerce. He blossomed only on going to France for three years, which he mostly spent conversing with Jesuits at the college of La Flèche where René Descartes had been educated. Here, at the age of twenty-six, he wrote the *Treatise of Human Nature*. Published in 1738–9, it fell 'deadborn from the press', in his own words. But it was a masterpiece which changed the history of philosophy.

The book seeks to define the principles of human knowledge. Hume believed all our knowledge to be grounded in the experience of our senses. The language we use about it has meaning only insofar as it conjures up something which derives from the impressions on our senses. Ideas are memories of sensations, Hume thought, but impressions are the cause of the sensation. In other words, Hume believed that ideas were just dull imitations of impressions and complex ideas could be reduced to a sum of their parts. For example, the idea of heaven can be broken down into all the ideas associated with it, such as pearly gates and angels, and these can then be reduced to their component impressions. This radical way of thinking was seen as atheistic by many.

This leads to Hume's teaching on causality which so influenced Immanuel Kant. We pass from impressions to ideas regularly associated with them by simple force of habit, from which nothing genuine about the reality of the external world can be inferred. Morality equally arises from habits and feelings rather than from rational obedience to general principles — though we do have a natural goodwill towards one another which tends to make us happy when others are happy.

Hume had no doubt about the importance of his own work, so he was mortified when it was ignored. He turned from philosophy to topics which might have a more immediate appeal to the public. The 1740s were for him a fertile period of writing, though worldly success still proved elusive. He was turned down in 1744 for the chair of ethics at Edinburgh University, on grounds of the atheism which the selectors found in the *Treatise*. He took a soul-destroying post as tutor to a feeble-minded marquis, and was glad when a kinsman, General St Clair, rescued him with a pen-pusher's job on a military expedition to Brittany.

Meanwhile he fashioned a series of essays which became models of the genre, setting out ideas in a form easy for the intelligent layman to grasp. On politics, he argued that conditions in different countries are infinitely varied, government being justified by its utility in each context. In France an absolute but enlightened monarchy kept society in order, whereas in England the rights of the subject were being subverted by commercial elites which enriched themselves from imperial exploitation while destroying culture and liberty. On economics, he followed brother Scots William Paterson* and John Law* in moving further away from the antique delusion that wealth lay in gold and silver. Rather it lay in people and their industry, an idea which would serve the case for free trade set out in future years by his younger friend, Adam Smith.*

Hume's laborious pursuit of literary fame only paid off at last with his *History of England*, published from 1754 to 1761 in six volumes, starting in recent times and moving backwards. It was as a historian that he became best known in his own day, and indeed long afterwards, with a then novel method of bringing together political, social and literary history so as to give a broad picture of national development. He also took issue again with the Whig myth that all previous history led up to the triumph of modern England as a paragon of liberty. He debunked English heroes of the Tudor and Stuart periods, while always putting in a good word for the Scots.

This attractive man thus left a profound mark on many fields, though none deeper than on philosophy. In him above all, perhaps, the Scottish Enlightenment is vindicated as a movement which let able and original men develop themselves to the full in a stateless society. Scotland had lost her independence in 1707 yet subsequently entered on a cultural golden age, no longer held back by the bitter political and religious conflicts of the previous century. Today we still argue about how this happened, though there can be no doubt that it gave us the greatness of Hume.

It also gave the world an eccentric thinker who can, in some respects, be viewed as a forerunner of Darwin in his opinions about human evolution.

JAMES BURNETT, LORD MONBODDO (1714–99)

Lord Monboddo was best known in his own day for two of his opinions, that men had once sported tails but had since lost them, and that orang-utans were undeveloped human beings lacking only the power of speech. He seems to have taken these views quite seriously, or anyway with the magnificent unconcern of the true eccentric. To others he showed at least that the Scottish Enlightenment had a mirthful side.

It appeared all the odder in one who was in every other respect a member of the establishment. Monboddo came of that class of lawyer-lairds who ran Scotland after the Union. His home lay in Kincardineshire, and after a local education at Laurencekirk and Aberdeen he went on to the universities of Edinburgh and Groningen, in the Netherlands, where he finished his studies of Roman law. Following a conventional career at the Scots bar he became a judge in 1767, and took his judicial title from his estate.

The Faculty of Advocates, to which all those practising at the bar had to belong, was an intellectual hotbed. In particular it supplied much of the membership of the Select Society, a key institution of the Scottish Enlightenment, which met in the Advocates' Library every Wednesday for 'the pursuit of philosophical inquiry and the improvement of the members in the art of speaking'. It was a mentally adventurous age, and Monboddo's cannot have been the most outlandish ideas the society heard. After all, he kept in touch with the mainstream of European thought. He knew the works of French philosophers, of Charles de Montesquieu who stressed the influence of environment on human behaviour, and of Jean-Jacques Rousseau who believed humanity had declined from a virtuous original purity, a belief shared by Monboddo. His conclusions about the relationship between man and the apes might be regarded as a primitive theory of evolution, an anticipation of Darwinism. They were at any rate interesting enough to make him a celebrity, even in London, to which he used to ride for an annual visit till he was past the age of eighty. And they gave him there an entrée to similarly eminent figures, such as Dr Samuel Johnson, who thought him 'all paradox'.

Like many Scottish literati, Monboddo investigated his favourite topics by writing books about them, and in his case the slow accumulation of knowledge and insight was especially marked. In the end he produced two major works, *Of the Origin and Progress of Language* and *Antient Metaphysics*. Each came out in six parts, spread over the final quarter-century of his life.

Monboddo's reasoning on his pet theories can, however deluded, seem almost plausible. His view of orang-utans derived from his thinking about language. He wanted to get behind the myth of the Tower of Babel recounted in Genesis: he felt sure language originated from necessity and developed naturally, rather than as an arbitrary gift of God. Savages or infants or mutes with no command of language were still human. True marks of intelligence were rendered in behaviour rather than speech: actions speak louder than words. And Monboddo believed orang-utans, besides having a brain, larynx, pharynx and tongue like ours, were also rational creatures possessing basic attributes of humanity, as travellers in Java and Angola had discovered. The only difference was that the human attributes found no verbal form.

Monboddo's argument was that, among other things, orang-utans walk erect, they 'live in society', they 'use sticks for weapons', they 'carry on undertakings', they 'carry off negro girls' and they 'attack elephants'. Males of the species showed a sense of justice and honour in disputes with one another, while females were overcome by modesty if caught unawares in their nakedness by men with clothes on. Though nobody had ever heard an orang-utan speak, they were known to play the harp with skill and grace, so they could at least express themselves in music. Our human attainments do not always match our capacities either: if we seek to improve ourselves according to an ideal of perfectibility, we ought to accept that orang-utans might do the same. Monboddo hoped, though none had yet been seen alive in Europe at this time, that one might be brought to Scotland where efforts could be made to surmount its natural indolence and arouse a desire for learning. Attendance at Dr Braidwood's renowned classes for the deaf in Edinburgh might well do the trick.

Monboddo's *Antient Metaphysics* may sound more abstruse, but it was equally alive to issues of the day. Contemporaries took note in particular of his argument that full cultural development would only come through studies of both science and philosophy, as complementary rather than mutually exclusive subjects. Science and philosophy were indeed integrated in the Scottish Enlightenment in a way unmatched in other European countries. This was doubtless because they remained central to the curriculum in the universities, though a steady trend towards specialization would eventually break down this generalist tradition during the nineteenth century. Monboddo included in the final volume of *Antient Metaphysics* a fierce condemnation of the French Revolution, especially its attacks on religion and property. The Scottish Enlightenment had included some liberal political impulses, but from now on these tended to yield to a conservative defence of the status quo.

WILLIAM ROBERTSON (1721–93)

Every organization needs its apparatchiks. It would be going too far to say that the Scottish Enlightenment was an organization, but it did rely heavily on certain institutions — on the universities, of course, but also on learned societies and even social clubs. The whole at any rate became coherent enough to offer a useful role to men of business who made sure the right people ended up in the right places doing the right things. Of these William Robertson was the chief.

He exerted his main influence in two spheres. One was the Church of Scotland. Robertson, a clergyman himself, initially served in the rural parish of Gladsmuir, East Lothian, before moving on to the prestigious charge of Old Greyfriars in Edinburgh, where the first copy of the National Covenant had been signed. Despite that historic association, he wanted the Kirk to move away from the fanaticism he thought it represented. He feared a Presbyterian system could ultimately fall into anarchy but believed that, if it kept itself in check, it had the potential to work harmoniously with the state in maintaining social order and justifying its status as an established church. Since the congregations tended to be too enthusiastic in their religion for his taste, the key was to have their ministers chosen by someone else, contrary to Presbyterian tradition. That tradition contained alternatives, however: for ministers to be chosen by lay patrons or by the state. He formed a party called the Moderates to advocate these alternatives. With it he came to dominate the General Assembly and enforced his opinion even on parishes unwilling to accept it: some were driven into secession from the Church. But the result was to raise the standard and the status of clergymen. They were no longer to be ranting fanatics but polite and learned men welcome in any drawing room. This would make the Kirk an enlightened institution too, especially in a commitment to toleration.

But Robertson ran ahead of his constituency. In 1779, his support for repeal of the penal laws against Roman Catholics caused uproar both among the more evangelical ministers and the Scottish people. The repeal had to be abandoned, and Robertson stepped down from leadership of the Moderate party. At this point he stood defeated in his lifelong struggle against a narrow and exclusive Calvinism in Church and society.

He also served for thirty years as principal of Edinburgh University. Promoted to the post by Lord Bute,* he made this the best university in Europe, with an array of brilliant professors, intellectual pioneers abreast with learning in the rest of Europe, committed to the education which gave Scotland an elite of trained minds able to lead intellectual and social advance in their own country and elsewhere. Edinburgh thus became a centre of cultured scholarship where ideals of liberty, morality and tolerance set a global example.

Robertson was himself an academic trailblazer, as a bestselling author who negotiated publishers' advances which were huge by the standards of the time. He won fame and fortune from a succession of historical works. *The History of Scotland* (1759) first whetted public taste for thrilling episodes in the nation's past, such as the confrontation of Mary Queen of Scots and John Knox. *The History of Charles V* (1769) went further than its title suggests with an introductory 'View of the Progress of Society in Europe' which showed how historical reality matched social theories propounded by enlightened Scots. *The History of America* (1777) applied the theories to primitive peoples whose evolution was to be consummated in enlightened British rule of the colonies; unfortunately the writing was interrupted by the outbreak of the American Revolution, which the politically conservative Robertson condemned, and he thought it best to leave the book unfinished. A late work, the *Historical Disquisition on Ancient India* (1791), applied the principles again, this time to an oriental civilization.

Taken together these histories represent an expanding vision, a grand narrative comprising the emergence of Great Britain, the development of the European system of nation-states, the spread of empire in the Americas and the beginnings of empire in India. They were acclaimed for the clarity and grace of their style, for a combination of accuracy and imaginative power in their descriptions, for their evenhanded method with historical controversies and for their breadth of vision. They became bestsellers in England, France, even Russia, as well as in Scotland. The exploration of themes of power, progress and providence in history had a deep influence on the consciousness of the West. Robertson's ability to write about them arose largely from his own experience as a religious and educational leader. His advocacy of a more harmonious and integrated global order reflected his efforts to further the social and intellectual improvement of Scotland in the aftermath of the religious and political strife of the seventeenth century.

ADAM SMITH (1723–90)

One of history's ironies is that the supreme advocate of free trade, who by his advocacy changed the world, should have spent his professional life taxing traded cargoes and ended his days as a commissioner of customs. For good measure he was the son of a customs official too, who had been robbed of his previous job by the Union. Smith senior had been secretary to the court martial of the Scottish army, which vanished in 1707. After some time out of work, he reluctantly accepted a posting in the customs to Kirkcaldy, which he regarded as the back of beyond; and there his son was born.

Adam Smith himself would no doubt have relished the irony, for he well knew that human beings, let alone such a complex organism as society, could not be held within rigid prototypes. His famous book, *The Wealth of Nations*, which in modern times has sometimes quite falsely been seen as an exercise in dogmatism, formed just one part of a huge intellectual edifice which Smith meant to erect, and which would have set out a complete science of man. He had published the first part of this project, *The Theory of Moral Sentiments*, in 1759.

After getting *The Wealth of Nations* out of the way, he intended to produce an equally ambitious book on politics and government; all we can conjecture about it comes from students' notes of lectures on these subjects he gave while making his living as a freelance instructor in Edinburgh in the late 1740s, and afterwards as professor of moral philosophy at Glasgow University in 1751–64 (the happiest years of his life, he always said). A fourth book would have covered the arts. But Smith was a perfectionist, unwilling to let out of his hands any work with which he was not absolutely satisfied. Since the two later books had not been finished by the time he was on his deathbed, he ordered his papers to be burned after he had gone. All his insights, which surely have been remarkable, were thus lost to the world forever.

What remains is impressive enough. *The Theory of Moral Sentiments* presents the concept of sympathy as the explanation of how a self-interested creature such as man can set limits to his passions by virtues which arise from his sociability. The concept had already appeared in the writings of David Hume, and Smith derived it also from another source, his own teacher at Glasgow University, the Ulsterman Francis Hutcheson. The wider value of the concept as developed at the hands of these three thinkers and of others may be gauged by contrast with a leading English philosopher of the seventeenth century, Thomas Hobbes. His view of life as solitary, nasty, brutish and short amid a war of all against all justified to him an authoritarian state. The kindlier outlook of the Scots made them liberals.

Practical aspects of this liberalism are developed more fully in *The Wealth of Nations*. The quality of its analysis was enriched by a lengthy visit to France that Smith made in the 1760s, again following in the footsteps of his friend Hume. He met and talked with a group of economists known as physiocrats, whose leader, Anne Robert Turgot, was to be made a minister by the young Louis XVI. Had he been able to continue his programme of economic reforms he might have fended off the French Revolution, but he was defeated by vested interests. Significantly, these appear in Smith's work as the main enemies of progress. After returning from France, he went into virtual seclusion for ten years at Kirkcaldy. But at the end, in 1776, he was able to bring out *The Wealth of Nations*.

In this second and greater work, the emphasis changes. Sympathy does not vanish, but it yields pride of place to the rational self-interest of individuals. Smith advises that they should be left to pursue this as they wish. We can rely on the operation of an 'invisible hand', which nowadays we would identify as the free market, to ensure that their actions are brought into harmony. At any rate interference by the state, or by other vested interests, is to be avoided. It will distort and disrupt the functioning of the system, sacrificing the harmony of the whole to the partial advantage of certain participants.

The best example of this comes in the economic policy of mercantilism, common in Smith's day, which encouraged governments to beggar their neighbours by restrictions designed to hog the benefits of manufacture and commerce. It was a strategy usually pursued by big nations and the Scots, as a small nation, had suffered from it. In condemning it, Smith developed the ideas of William Paterson,* John Law* and David Hume.* Much more benefit would accrue all round, Smith said, if different nations produced what they were best at producing and traded openly with one another.

A graphic example of what he had in mind came in the disputes leading to the American Revolution, which broke out in 1776; in fact Smith called his book back from the printers to insert comments on it. He pointed out that colonial trade had been exploited by the British to maximize profits for themselves and deprive the Americans of their due. In reality this had made both sides poorer, and at length had led to armed conflict. After it was all over, and the United States had become independent, the British Government could only admit that Smith had been right. Britain then embarked on a policy of commercial liberalization which was to last through the nineteenth and into the twentieth century. So successful did it prove that the rest of the world followed. Thus began the formation of the global economy which, if with considerable interruptions, has gone on up to the present day.

HENRY DUNDAS, VISCOUNT MELVILLE (1742–1811)

Though Scotland was absorbed into the Union with England in 1707, this did not bring Scottish politics to an end. The Treaty of Union guaranteed the future existence of those aspects of the old Scotland which Scots most esteemed, the Church, the law and the schools and universities. In other words, it preserved institutions through which Scottish nationhood could still be expressed. This structure, though much altered over time, has now survived in its essentials for 300 years. The proof of its value lies in the fact that Scottish nationhood is flourishing again today as never before during that period.

At a mundane level, the national institutions have required men of business to administer them, since the job has been unlikely to appeal to anyone in London. So on the whole Scots have run Scotland. But Scots left to themselves tend to pick fights, and the country is on the whole better run by someone strong, ruthless and genial enough to unite it behind him. In the late eighteenth century, that person was Henry Dundas. From then on, Scots were also able to aspire to preferment in the United Kingdom and the British Empire. But they needed someone at the top to smooth the path for those climbing from below, to favour them without upsetting the English. Again, the person who first perfected this technique was Dundas.

He sprang from a leading family of lawyer-lairds, the Dundases of Arniston in Midlothian, who had held high judicial office since the mid-seventeenth century. Henry himself was bred to the law; he was admitted as an advocate in 1763 and then started climbing the legal ladder, as Solicitor-General in 1766 and Lord Advocate in 1775. Meanwhile, however, he was elected to Parliament, which steered his career in a different direction. In the deep British political crisis of 1783 that followed the loss of the American colonies, Dundas was instrumental in finding a way out, through the promotion to Prime Minister of a Mr Clean, William Pitt the Younger, at the time only twenty-three years old.

The two rose together. Under Pitt, Dundas at length became Home Secretary, in which post he suppressed the radical reforming movements of the day, and then Secretary of State for War, which meant directing the struggle against revolutionary France. Having meanwhile been ennobled, he was First Lord of the Admiralty in 1805, the year of the Battle of Trafalgar. Then he fell, brought down by charges of corruption in what was to be the last impeachment of a British minister. Although he was eventually acquitted, his career was over all the same. Yet he had done his work well. Other Scots had reached the Cabinet since 1707, but Dundas was the first to get there and stay there.

This was important for his country and his countrymen. He had used his years of power to consolidate political control of Scotland, mainly through manipulation of an electoral system which gave the vote to only 4,000 Scots out of more than a million. Dundas knew most of these voters. He did favours for them — jobs for the boys, tax breaks and so on — as long as they did him the favour of electing the members he wanted. He was then able to deliver at Westminster, for any purpose required, a solid phalanx of reliable support. In an age before the formal organization of political parties, this put him in a powerful position.

For loyalty from below he exchanged patronage from above. He had at his disposal all the public offices in Scotland, and because of his position in London he could dispense jobs in the British armed forces and in the colonies. Above all he was, apart from everything else, for eighteen years president of the Board of Control for India, which supervised the activities of the East India Company in the sub-continent. This was the most valuable patronage of all, for men who went out to the East and did not succumb to the climate could easily make a fortune. By the end of Dundas's life, two-thirds of British subjects in India were Scots, though Scots formed only a small minority of the population at home.

The English often grumbled to him, but he could reply that he was bringing benefits for the whole Union. He could point to the contrast with Ireland, which he also helped to bring into the Union in 1801 on the condition (which, to his dismay, remained unfulfilled) of equal rights for Roman Catholics. The Irish were therefore unwilling citizens of the United Kingdom, in part refused its blessings and in part blind to them. The result was subjection and misery. Scotland, on the other hand, became a partner of England, a partnership which remained happy and fruitful for both till the end of the twentieth century.

It demanded, though, special favour for the junior partner — which was of little consequence to England but of immense importance to Scotland, because it let Scots overcome the poverty and backwardness that had always burdened them. Through the money that flowed back from the Empire, and through eager exploitation of opportunities in international commerce, Scots enriched themselves, saw their families well provided for, rebuilt their houses and cities, improved their countryside, endowed public-spirited institutions, invested and prospered on a huge scale. Dundas succeeded in what the rulers of Scotland had hardly dared hope for in 1707, setting the country's history off on a new course. Though himself disappointed at the end of his days, he had found a future for Scotland and the Scots.

Men of Science I

Sulphur and Steam

Experimental science was taught and practised in the Scottish universities long before England or most other European countries. This was one of the reasons why Scottish scientists were in the forefront of so many discoveries. Another reason for the drive to extend the frontiers of knowledge may have been the tremendous opportunity for economic improvement which the Industrial Revolution offered, the chance for Scots to break through from their former poverty.

The connection between scientific theory and practical application proved particularly suited to Scottish minds. If science is divided into the categories of pure and applied, most famous Scots scientists can be classified under the label of applied scientists. Having discovered a new theory or principle, most of them did not simply leave the matter there; they were responsible for following through the implications and applications of their theories. Until recently the examination papers in physics of all the ancient Scottish universities were headed by the title 'Natural Philosophy', reflecting the need to bring even the principles by which the heavens were formed, down to earth in some useful way.

Since many of the pioneer scientists undertook science as a hobby rather than as a profession, their scientific work was an adjunct to the 'day job'. This was certainly true of one of the founders of modern chemistry.

JOSEPH BLACK (1728–99)

One of the by-products of the Auld Alliance between Scotland and France was a lively trade between French seaports and the east coast of Scotland. The wine of Bordeaux flowed into the port of Leith and thereafter into the mouths of Edinburgh citizens of all classes. At one end of the social spectrum it was dispensed by the wine carts which made their rounds like modern ice-cream vans, while at the other it graced the dining tables of the New Town in bottles of claret. This explains the presence of Mrs Margaret Black in Bordeaux during her confinement with her fifteenth child, who was born on 16 April 1728 and christened Joseph. Her husband John, who came from a long line of wine traders, hoped that the boy would make something of his obvious abilities and sent him to the University of Glasgow.

Joseph, much to his father's disappointment, opted for a course in arts but was eventually persuaded to look for a more practical subject. Changing to medicine, he came under the tutelage of Professor William Cullen, who had begun the previous year to give lectures on chemistry. Scottish professors, themselves multi-disciplined, took an eclectic approach to the teaching of their subject, and Cullen was no exception. During his career in Edinburgh and Glasgow Universities, he held chairs in several subjects; revised the textbooks of pharmaceutical formulae, throwing out those which were obsolete; and in 1776 compiled one of the first systematic materia medica catalogues.

Black showed such prowess in medicine that Cullen offered the boy a job as his laboratory assistant. It became not so much his hobby as his passion.

Black qualified as a doctor and stayed on at the university, where he was offered the post of professor of medicine and lecturer in chemistry in 1757 in succession to Cullen, who had gone to Edinburgh University. Nine years (and many experiments) later his old mentor Cullen retired from the chairs of medicine and chemistry in Edinburgh, and Black went east. So, apparently, did most of his students, for Black was a respected and popular teacher. It was the custom of Scottish universities to require professors to deliver lectures and students to attend them, unlike the tutorial system favoured by the universities of Oxford and Cambridge.

The chair in chemistry carried no salary, so Black subsidized his income by practising as a medical doctor, at one time numbering the philosopher David Hume among his patients.

Black's fame rests on three major contributions to knowledge. He was the first person to discover what today is best known as the greenhouse gas, carbon dioxide. Black called it 'fixed air'. He was able to identify its role in the causticization of lime, but more importantly his studies revealed it as a product of combustion, thus undermining the theory of phlogiston, the substance previously believed to be given off during combustion. Belief in the existence of phlogiston rapidly became the equivalent in the world of chemistry of believing that the sun moves round the earth.

His second great contribution was in the realm of heat. His observation that ice stays at the same temperature when melting led him to the discovery of latent heat. Latent heat is the amount of heat needed to change a given mass of a substance into another form, say a solid into a liquid or a liquid into a gas, without changing its temperature. He went on to develop a theory of specific heat, the amount of heat required to change the temperature of one gram of a substance by one degree centigrade. Black saw that the heat gained or lost by a substance depended on three factors: its mass; its specific heat and the temperature change; and that the total gained must equal the total lost. In making his observations of changes of heat he established the quantitative method of experimentation, a method whereby all the variables are measured before and after the experiment, in addition to noting any changes which have taken place.

He made his measurements with the aid of a calorimeter, his third great legacy and an invention still used to measure heat transfer today. Black's theory was that heat resembled a flowing substance (he called it 'caloric'); although this proved incorrect, it provided the basis of future developments in thinking about thermodynamics. A century later his fellow Scot James Thomson (Lord Kelvin)* was to take up the torch.

The other great legacy Black gave the world came through an inventive young man who was not one of his students but the university's instrument maker; in his spare time he made fiddles, flutes and guitars, and constructed a barrel organ for the professor. Black wrote that this was 'a young man possessing most uncommon talents for mechanical knowledge and practice with an originality, readiness and copiousness of invention'.

The young man, having absorbed Black's ideas on the latent heat of steam, was to revolutionize the world with his invention, the steam engine.

JAMES WATT (1736–1819)

Watt was born in Greenock, then beginning to benefit from new industries and trade, where his father James Watt senior, a skilled craftsman, was a leading figure in the town. James junior, a delicate lad who already suffered from the migraines and poor health which were to dog him for the rest of his life, received much of his early education at home; at school he was only bullied.

When his beloved mother died and his father's fortunes dipped, James needed to make a living. He excelled at mathematics and had inherited his father's skill in making things, but the powerful guilds which controlled the trades required seven years' training. He began an apprenticeship in London in 1754 and did well, but long hours and poor health drove him back to Scotland within a year. This time he was refused admission to an apprenticeship by the Guild of Hammermen in Glasgow because he had no local connections in the city. A job as instrument maker at the university was the result. Its intellectual climate proved a stimulus to the young man and by the time he eventually gained permission to open a shop in the Saltmarket in Glasgow, he had acquired many leading academics as acquaintances and admirers of his abilities.

Notable among these was Professor John Anderson, who one day brought him a model of a Newcomen engine for repair. This engine used steam-driven pistons to pump out water from mines but was very inefficient. Whether under the influence of the ideas he had gleaned from Joseph Black,* or whether – as the legend has it – inspired by watching the lid of a boiling kettle bob up and down under the force of steam, Watt worked away and came up with the idea of a new kind of steam engine.

But it was the model Newcomen engine which proved the catalyst. One Sunday afternoon as he walked in the park known as Glasgow Green, the Eureka moment came – the revolutionary idea of a separate condenser for the steam, which would not waste its energy by expelling it, but contain and recycle it within the system. A memorial stone now marks the spot.

With his skills, Watt was well placed to execute and build the prototype, but he needed a manufacturer. John Roebuck of the Carron Ironworks near Falkirk agreed to develop the engine for a two-thirds share after paying off Watt's loan of £1,000 from Black. While he waited for production to start on the engine, Watt went off to work as a surveyor building the Monklands Canal in Lanarkshire, but personal tragedy struck. His wife died, leaving him with two young children, and Roebuck went bankrupt. Desperate to find some new source of finance, Watt travelled to Birmingham, where he was introduced to Matthew Boulton. Boulton, impressed with Watt, bought out Roebuck's share for £1,200. A close association between the two men began at Boulton's Soho Works in Birmingham in 1774.

The engines were a huge success. Watt turned down an offer to go to Peter the Great's Russia at an annual salary of £1,000. He proposed marriage to Anne McGregor, whose father, a prosperous dyer, demanded to see documentary evidence of Watt's partnership with

Boulton. None existed — in fact, such was their friendship that none was ever set down — but Boulton appeased McGregor and Watt got his bride.

They moved to Cornwall where Watt oversaw the installation of his engine in many of the mines. He was not without his headaches, sometimes literally. 'I am plagued by the blues,' he wrote, 'my head is too confused to do any brainwork.' He had difficulty in getting the mine captains who used his engine, — 'the rudest men I have ever met in my life', — to pay royalties. But that headache was cured when William Murdoch* came into the business and took the task of collecting payments away from him. Murdoch too had a superbly inventive mind. Boulton and Watt appreciated him and the rotary governor he developed, which vastly increased the engine's efficiency; yet they overlooked their chance to share in the development of the steam locomotive and the gas lighting he had invented, and later displayed a similar blind spot over Patrick Miller's* steamship.

By this time, with the profits rolling in, Watt was a rich man and began to travel more. His gentle manner and friendly nature made him an ideal companion, as Andrew Carnegie* remarked in his biography; he was able to count Sir Walter Scott* among his close friends. His intellectual horizons were always broad and he enjoyed, through Boulton, membership of the prestigious Lunar Club (whose meetings were on Mondays closest to a full moon). Founded by the Scots doctor William Small (sometime tutor to Thomas Jefferson), its fourteen members additionally included Josiah Wedgwood, founder of the pottery firm, Joseph Priestley, the discoverer of oxygen, and Erasmus Darwin, grandfather of Charles; Benjamin Franklin was a corresponding member. The club supported the ideas of both the French and American Revolutions but itself led another change in human history — the Industrial Revolution.

Honours were heaped on Watt later in life and after his death a statue was erected by public subscription in Westminster Abbey. He gained an equally lasting memorial when the unit of power measurement known as the watt was named after him.

STEAMSHIPS: WILLIAM SYMINGTON (1763–1831), PATRICK MILLER (1731–1815) AND HENRY BELL (1767–1830)

Watt's steam engine had a revolutionary impact upon transport as well as upon industrial processes. Given the need of manufacturers to connect to their markets, it would have been natural for one of the first applications of the steam engine in transport to have been a steam-driven juggernaut plying up and down the roads of Britain. But those roads were in such poor condition in the eighteenth century that the transport system of the new industrial age developed instead along canals. John Macadam* had yet to work his magic on the roads, and the railways had yet to be developed. As it turned out, the first steam engines to be widely used in transport were in ships, and it was a trio of Scotsmen who led the way to this achievement.

The inventor of the first steamship originally set out to develop a steam road carriage. Young William Symington had the idea when he watched his father operating one of the Watt and Boulton engines at the mine where he worked, near the source of the River Clyde at Leadhills in Lanarkshire. The mine manager was so impressed that he invited the boy to Edinburgh, where his chain and ratchet model was shown to prominent academics. They encouraged him to study science, and William began as a student in 1786. He patented his engine design the following year, but soon realized that it would be impractical to run his invention on the existing roads.

Symington's fellow student James Taylor was tutor to the family of Patrick Miller of Dalswinton in Dumfriesshire and introduced the two men. Miller had amassed wealth as a merchant and banker, and retired early to devote himself to the study of navigation, artillery and agriculture. But he had also invented and patented a manually operated paddle boat. The British Government had shown no interest but King Gustavus III of Sweden gratefully accepted the prototype when it was offered to him. In return he gave Miller a gold box containing a packet of seeds; these turned out to be more valuable than their container, for from them grew a kind of turnip known as the swede, which was to transform winter fodder for Scots cattle and prevent them having to be killed off as winter approached.

Miller was prolific as an inventor. He built the first drill plough, an iron plough and a threshing machine, and was the first to construct guns with chambers; he called them 'carronades' after the Carron Ironworks in Falkirk which manufactured them, and in which he was the largest shareholder.

Miller acted quickly on Taylor's suggestion that he try out Symington's engine on his boat. In October 1788 a prototype vessel twenty-five feet long, carrying the engine on one side and a boiler on the other, chugged along on Dalswinton's lake at the sedate pace of five miles per hour. Robert Burns,* at that time a tenant farmer on Miller's estate, was placed at the event in a sketch done by the fashionable artist Alexander Nasmyth. Fired with enthusiasm, Miller built a larger boat and commissioned a suitable engine from Symington; it was built at the Carron works and achieved seven miles per hour in trials on the Forth & Clyde Canal, a key waterway across the central belt of Scotland. However, Miller was not satisfied with the engine's performance and approached Watt and Boulton to design another. Watt replied that he saw no great future for steamships and so Miller withdrew from the venture.

Symington lacked influential friends, and must have been frustrated when he heard of other (largely unsuccessful) trials elsewhere. He did not get another chance to demonstrate his steamship for a decade until Lord Dundas, Governor of the Forth & Clyde Canal, commissioned him to produce a steam-driven paddle steamer to pull barges. Symington had patented a new design, one that was to become standard on paddle steamer engines, of a piston-rod guided by rollers, with a connecting rod to a crank on the paddle wheel. In 1801 the *Charlotte Dundas* had river trials and in 1803 a second version of the boat successfully pulled two barges for twenty miles along the canal, to the delight of all present. Among them was the American artist, engineer-inventor Robert Fulton who, with a

Watt and Boulton engine, launched his own vessel *Clermont*, which went from New York to Albany in thirty-two hours in 1807.

Dundas helped to procure Symington an order for six more boats from Lord Bridgewater, an English waterway baron, and it looked at last as if he would get his reward. Then a double blow struck. The directors of the Forth & Clyde Canal voted to ban paddle-power because of the damage that wash from the boats would do to canal walls, and the six further boats were cancelled when Bridgewater died.

Bankrupted by the venture, Symington was forced to sell his assets for scrap and appeal to the state for funds as the inventor of steamships. He received £150, not enough to prevent him dying in penury in London in 1831. Taylor, the go-between, was a little luckier. His widow was awarded an annual pension of £50 for his part in the invention of steam navigation.

By then others had taken up the development of steamships. Henry Bell, born at Torphichen in West Lothian, had long been watching Symington's efforts. After working as an engineer in London, he returned to Scotland in 1790 and was present at the trials of the second *Charlotte Dundas* in 1803. By 1808 he moved to Helensburgh on the Clyde, where his wife ran the public baths and adjacent hotel. Bell's passion to build his own paddle steamer resulted in the launch in 1812 of the *Comet*, which provided the first steamship service in Europe at the time, running 'by the power of air, wind and steam' between Glasgow, Greenock and Helensburgh. Like Symington, Bell discovered that steamships found little favour among the conservative minds in the Royal Navy and the Government, despite endorsement by none other than Lord Nelson ('My Lords and Gentlemen, if you do not adopt Mr Bell's scheme, other nations will, and in the end vex every vein of this empire. It will succeed and you should encourage Mr Bell').

Bell was not an inventor, nor even an exceptional entrepreneur, but his contribution to maritime history is important because of what followed in his wake. He began the glorious tradition of Clyde pleasure steamers which plied the picturesque stretch of water from

Glasgow and the industrial towns along the River Clyde out towards the sea in the west. More importantly, he started a process which led to shipbuilding and the Clyde becoming identified with one another. Between 1810 and 1980, it is reckoned that over 30,000 ships of importance were built on the tiny stretch of water called Clydeside, among them in 1840 *Britannia*, the wooden paddle ship which sailed from Liverpool to Halifax, Nova Scotia in twelve days, and in the twentieth century the three great Cunard liners, the *Queen Mary* and the *Queen Elizabeth I* and *II*.

WILLIAM MURDOCH (1754–1839)

There are a number of parallels between the life of William Symington* and that of another William whose true potential was never realized or rewarded in the way that he deserved. William Murdoch, like Symington, was encouraged by his father (a miller and tenant farmer at Bello Mill in Ayrshire) to be both proficient with his hands and inventive with his mind. As a boy he had illuminated a cave near the mill by gaslight obtained from heating coal in an old pot, an early signal of his later achievement in developing a system for lighting buildings and public areas by gas. Murdoch never claimed to have invented the process but he was responsible for making it a practical proposition.

Murdoch was ideally suited to the machine age. Through his father's business connection with Roebuck he was able to get an introduction to Boulton, and arrived at the Soho Works looking for a job. The tall stove-pipe hat he was wearing dropped on the floor with a clang and Boulton was immediately impressed when he discovered the young man had turned it on his own lathe. His prodigious talents soon became evident when he invented a device which made the engine go twice as fast and opened up rotary motion using steam power. He made other modifications to Watt's engines, as well as inventing the oscillating engine, a rotary engine, cast-iron cement, and a steam gun. He devised a lift driven by compressed air, which he used to ring bells in his own house, and a system for sending small objects through a tube exhausted by an air pump.

Murdoch was an ideal protégé for Watt but there are indications that the older man was less than generous, even jealous, in his dealings with the younger. The two could not have been more different in character. When Murdoch took over dealing with the Cornish mine captains who were slow to pay their dues, Watt was relieved; he found it difficult to stand up to these hard men who despised incomers. But Murdoch won their respect, defeating one of them in a fist-fight and showing considerable courage whenever he plunged into cold water in dangerous conditions to repair pump engines which had broken down. His status was secure after he married a Cornish girl, Ann Paynter, and he now called himself Murdock to make it easier for the Cornish miners to pronounce his name.

Soon there were attempts to lure him away from Watt and Boulton. They responded by giving him a cash payment, although it was nowhere near what he could have got if he were to set up in opposition. For he now had something to sell, in the shape of the locomotive he had been building in his spare time. Finished in 1784, it was powered by one of Watt's engines and resembled a tricycle. A steam carriage followed and the loyal Murdoch approached Watt and Boulton with his plans. Watt reacted peevishly: 'William should do as we do and apply himself to the business in hand.' The real reason for Watt's disgruntlement was revealed later when he wrote: 'I did not like that a scheme of mine which I had revolved in my mind for years and hoped at some favourable time to bring to perfection, should be wrested from me, or I should be impelled to go in as a secondary person.' He agreed reluctantly to let Murdoch develop a prototype, but the deadline and conditions imposed were so stringent that the hard-pressed Murdoch was unable to meet them and gave up the idea in 1786. It was not until sixteen years later that Richard Trevithick produced the first practical steam carriage in Britain. Was it mere coincidence that he spent his early life in Cornwall, the place where Murdoch's prototype fiery chariot had hissed around the countryside?

Murdoch turned his inventive talents to the creation of gas lighting in the dark evenings at his home in Redruth. In 1791 he extended the kind of apparatus he had used as a boy; by the following year he was able to produce enough gas to light his home and offices along more than twenty yards of pipe, and even to supply a gas lantern with which he used to walk home across the moors at night. In 1794 he tried to persuade Watt that a patent should be taken out, but Watt was busy trying to renew his own engine patents.

Murdoch returned to work at Soho from Cornwall in 1798 and successfully mounted a public demonstration of his system, while other offices began to adopt gas lighting. Watt still did not see the potential. By the time he came round to the idea and authorized gas lighting for the whole Soho Works in 1805, it was too late for Murdoch to get a patent. Already a contract to light London by gas had been given to a company managed by one of his former apprentices.

Watt and Boulton never fully appreciated Murdoch's talents; although they asked him to join them among the creative minds of the Lunar Club, he was never invited to join them as a Fellow of the Royal Society, either in London or Edinburgh. After the deaths of Watt and Boulton in 1809 and 1819, their sons continued to run the business. They gave Murdoch a more respected status than their fathers had accorded him, but it came too late for him to share the fame of Watt or the fortune of Boulton. The loyal lieutenant retired in 1830 at the age of seventy-six and was buried nine years later beside his patrons in Handsworth churchyard.

Before we leave the subject of steam, we meet an extraordinary Scot who embodied all the virtues and expertise of science and the arts, and possessed a lively sense of humour to bind them together. This Renaissance man of the nineteenth century was ...

JAMES NASMYTH (1808–90)

The autobiography of James Nasmyth gives a fascinating insight into what it must have been like in the golden age of Edinburgh when the New Town was being built, Robert Burns was holding court in a tavern in the High Street and Walter Scott was in his pew at Greyfriars Kirk. Nasmyth is able to tell the story at close hand since his grandfather helped build the New Town, and his father painted the best-known portrait of Robert Burns. According to legend, this extraordinary family, whose members were adept in both art and technology, got their name from one of its members who was given shelter from the marauding Douglas border clan by a blacksmith. When the pursuers entered the smithy, the nervous quarry pretended to use his hammer, but to such ill effect that a Douglas soldier spotted the ruse and cried 'Ye're nae smith!'

The Nasmyth crest carries a hammer but James Nasmyth preferred to invert the family motto, which translates as 'Not by art, but by the hammer'. The inventor of the steam hammer instead made technology into an art form: his machines were oil paintings and his engineering drawings works of art. He advocated that 'the correctness of the eye' should be an essential part of the school curriculum: 'Drawing is the Education of the eye. It is more interesting than words. It is graphic language.'

His principle for engineering was that 'The eyes and the fingers — the bare fingers — are the two principal sources of trustworthy knowledge in materials and operations the engineer has to deal with.' This he learned from his father Alexander, who had designed a lightweight iron bridge which resembled a bow and strings, and had invented a form of silent riveting achieved by squeezing the rivet; the latter was born out of the necessity to avoid using a hammer, the sound of which would disturb the neighbours.

James Nasmyth left school at twelve and went to London as an apprentice to the engineering toolmaker Henry Maudslay for two years before moving to Manchester in 1831. There he started a foundry near to the Bridgewater Canal, which was then under construction. Familiar with Miller's problems in getting the Forth & Clyde Canal Company to allow his paddle ships to pass along their canal because of damage to the walls, Nasmyth came up with an ingenious solution. It involved the barges pulling themselves along by means of large chains suspended on either side of the canal, like the rails of a funicular into which a wheel turned by the engine engages its cogs. The creation of wash in the canal could thus be avoided. But the directors of the canal remained intransigent.

His greatest invention, the steam hammer, came in 1839. One of these was used by Isambard Kingdom Brunel to make the prop shaft for his steamship *Great Britain*, but the British Admiralty preferred to stick with screw-type shafts. Nasmyth moved on to develop other steam-driven machine tools, including a pile driver, a planing machine, a hydraulic punch and lathe. The description of his inventions at the end of his autobiography, accompanied by his impeccable drawings, is a book in itself.

At the age of forty-eight he was a wealthy man. Retiring to devote himself to astronomy, he produced accurate drawings of the willow-pattern craters on the moon before the astronomer Herschel announced their discovery, and in 1874 published a book, *The Moon as a Planet, a World and a Satellite*, as well as a study showing how solar alignment had influenced the design of the pyramids. Truly, Nasmyth was a man in whom we catch the inner beauty that drives invention, and whose life's work was to render the vision of the eighteenth-century engineers into the machines of the nineteenth century.

CHARLES MACINTOSH (1766–1843)

Chemistry fascinated many of the brightest minds of the late eighteenth century. Charles Macintosh had a head start in the subject; his father was a manufacturer who used chemicals in his business.

When Charles entered the family firm it was involved in the production of cudbear, a dye for silk and wool produced by soaking a species of lichen from the Highlands in vats with ammonia and lime for two weeks.

The process depended upon a supply of ammonia of proper quality and young Charles devised a unique system for obtaining it. Before sewage systems were installed in Scottish cities, those living on the top floor of tenements would dispose of their urine by emptying the container into the street out of an open window, shouting 'Gardyloo!' to warn anyone below. Macintosh recruited squads to go from door to door around Glasgow to collect the urine instead, paying a penny per gallon for as much as 3,000 gallons a day. He was careful to give his men hydrometers so they could check that his suppliers were not watering down the product.

Ammonia was distilled from the liquid, and with it a variety of shades of dye could be made from the cudbear. Unfortunately stocks of lichen were not so renewable; the Scots supply was soon exhausted, sending Macintosh to Scandinavia to secure a different species. He persuaded the King of Sweden to lower export duty on the lichen, but its price nevertheless rose steadily from £3 to £45 per ton. So, shrewd businessman that he was, he found a product which his customers could more easily afford. By exploiting commercially a process already in existence, he was soon managing to produce another dye of excellent quality by dissolving calcined blood, hooves, hair and rags in potash and sulphuric acid. When iron sulphate was added, crystals of Prussian blue emerged from solution, and this Macintosh was able to sell at a tiny fraction of its previous market price.

In another display of his combination of entrepreneurial skill and scientific knowledge, he set up a highly successful factory to produce alum from coal shale by treating it with alkali. Vegetable dyes require a fixer and there was none better than alum, a complex aluminium salt which can be used in tanning hides, purifying sugar and hardening tallow. It is also a waterproofing agent, but Macintosh was to make history by finding an even better waterproofing substance — rubber.

Although Joseph Priestley had noted the chemical composition of rubber, it remained limited in its use since no successful solvent could be found with which to make it more workable. Macintosh, in his constant search for new sources of ammonia, was by 1819 distilling ammonia from left-over tar bought from the Glasgow Gas Company. During his distillation experiments he produced naphtha, already well-known for its properties as a solvent, and it worked the necessary magic to dissolve the rubber. He gave some to the professor of surgery in Edinburgh to make rubber gloves with, but had his eye on a more commercial application. Added to cloth in a kind of sandwich, the naphtha/rubber mix penetrated the fibres; when the naphtha evaporated, he was left with waterproof cloth. Thus was born the garment that still bears his name – the macintosh – which he patented in 1823.

One of Macintosh's lesser-known discoveries is bleaching powder. Chlorine had been discovered in 1774 and its bleaching power documented in the mid-1780s by a French chemist. James Watt,* having learned this on a visit to France, passed the knowledge to his father-in-law, who was a bleacher and became the first in Britain to use chlorine in bleaching. The downside of the process was that strong fumes of chlorine were emitted. When Macintosh came across the process in use at the St Rollox factory of Charles Tennant in Glasgow, he suggested passing lime through the liquid, thus creating the more manageable chemical compound chloride of lime, or bleaching powder. The patent was registered in Tennant's name, but Macintosh must take the credit for a chemical which has been repackaged in hundreds of ways since its discovery.

He also spotted that chloride of lime might be an effective remedy for the spread of disease. In 1804, long before Pasteur and his theory of how disease is spread, Macintosh wrote to the War Office proposing the use of the powder to stop the spread of contagion. No one took him up. Macintosh himself was too busy researching other discoveries to take the matter further. His rubber process was now being used to make not only waterproof clothes but inflatable goods such as cushions, pillows and beds. It made his fortune and he took as a partner Thomas Hancock, who is credited with the invention of vulcanized rubber.

But Macintosh's fertile mind was still at work. In 1825 he patented a process for converting iron into steel. It was not a commercial success, but James Beaumont Neilson (another Scot), creator of the hot blast process for steel production, acknowledged its value when he assigned a share of his patent to Macintosh, the alchemist who turned water into gold.

SIR DAVID BREWSTER (1781—1868)

David Brewster was in some ways like the stereoscopic images with which he experimented — in order to get the full picture, two images need to be put together. One is of a quarrelsome man of strong religious convictions who opposed the theory of evolution. The other is of a man of wide interests who numbered the likes of Sir Walter Scott and the painters Alexander Nasmyth and J.M.W. Turner among his friends, and who was yet terrified of speaking in public. Brewster's importance as a scientist lies in his studies of the properties of light (particularly its polarization by biaxial crystals) but he is chiefly remembered as the inventor of the kaleidoscope. It is less well known that he invented a new version of the stereoscope, and encouraged the artist David Octavius Hill (1802—70) to use photography as an aid to his painting, with the result that he became one of the pioneers of this new way of making pictures.

Born at Jedburgh, Brewster was a child prodigy who had constructed his own telescope by the age of ten. He went to Edinburgh University the next year, and after completing his divinity studies was licensed as a minister of the Church of Scotland, but opted instead for a career in science.

Some Properties of Light, his first paper, was published in 1813 and others quickly followed. His work on the polarization of light by crystals led to Brewster's Angle being named after him. This is the angle between the entry and emergence of light from a prism at which the maximum degree of polarization occurs, and it is still used in the design and construction of lasers. He was made a Fellow of the

Royal Society in 1815. He often adapted, improved and invented instruments to assist his research and one of these was the kaleidoscope. The invention was patented in 1817 and his *Treatise on the Kaleidoscope* appeared in 1819. The device quickly became a popular toy. Brewster himself suggested it might be employed to design carpets.

Later in life Brewster managed to produce another invention which caught the public imagination. His studies in early photography led him in 1849 to develop the lenticular stereoscope, which he used to produce a 3D image. When an example of the device was put on display at the Great Exhibition at Crystal Palace in 1851, Queen Victoria was fascinated by it, and it became a popular item in Victorian drawing rooms.

Brewster was deeply involved in the early days of photography. He favoured the calotype photographic process pioneered by his friend Fox Talbot, over the daguerreotype which used silver on a glass plate. The calotype was much cheaper and, unlike its rival process, allowed copies to be made from the negative. His book on stereoscopic photography, *The Stereoscope, its History, Theory and Construction*, became a standard work on the subject, although marred by its personal animosity towards his fellow physicist Sir Charles Wheatstone (1810–70), who had actually discovered the process of stereoscopy. Brewster's disputatious streak led one colleague to remark that 'Nobody ever had dealings with him and escaped a quarrel.'

He always said he did not want an academic post because the students would distract him from research. But in 1839 he accepted a sinecure, the position of principal of St Salvator's and St Leonard's Colleges at St Andrews University. To the dismay of his new colleagues, he set out to make something of it by championing a programme of reform in the university. When, on the formation of the Free Church of Scotland in 1843, he joined it, the other professors moved to depose him, on the grounds that all holders of academic offices were required by law to be members of the established Church of Scotland. Although the rule had grown obsolete, it was only after a long legal battle that it was abolished. In 1859 Brewster left St Andrews to become principal of Edinburgh University.

As well as being an energetic researcher he was a prolific writer, who edited a number of scientific journals and composed a biography of Isaac Newton. He founded the British Association for the Advancement of Science and had the distinction of being awarded all three principal medals of the Royal Society for his optical research. Yet despite the eminent position he attained, he never lost his fear of public speaking.

JOHN LOUDON MCADAM (1756–1836)

The Roman Empire was famed for many achievements, among them the superb system of roads which covered its territory. Every legionary was trained in the craft of roadmaking and carried the necessary tools. With the retreat of the Romans from Britain had begun a decline in the condition of Britain's roads that continued throughout the medieval period. At the beginning of the Industrial Revolution the roads of Britain, and especially Scotland, were no better than dirt tracks, and much worse when it rained.

It may come as a surprise to discover that the inventor of modern roadmaking methods, John McAdam, neither invented nor used 'tarmacadam', the road material which bears his name. It is perhaps even more surprising since his uncle through marriage was Admiral Archibald Cochrane, Earl of Dundonald, who first distilled tar from coal and used it as a wood preservative and sealant in the Navy. The use of the term 'tarmacadam' derives from the name of a company formed in 1901 by E.P. Hooley, the county surveyor of Nottingham, who had noticed the binding effect of a burst barrel of tar on a road surface for which he was responsible. Shortened to 'tarmac', it points us back to the man whose methods helped bring Britain's roads out of the Middle Ages.

McAdam came from Ayrshire. Emigrating to America, he married a prosperous heiress, prospered in his own career as Crown Commissioner for Naval Prizes, and inherited from his uncle William a considerable fortune. Unfortunately things then started to go wrong. William's estranged widow claimed the estate, and by 1783 Britain had lost America. The family moved back to its roots in Ayrshire. McAdam purchased the estate of Sauchrie near Maybole where he spent fifteen years. They were not wasted. During that time he perfected a technique of making roads. He was appointed a deputy lieutenant of the county and after war with France broke out in 1793 he found himself raising a regiment against possible invasion. In moving it around he realized how urgent was the need for better roads.

Since 1767 Britain had operated a Turnpike Act which allowed local landowners and authorities to extract tolls from travellers for the upkeep of the roads. In reality little of the money was put to good effect, the rest being pocketed or squandered. McAdam became a kind of freelance consultant and was asked to improve the road system around the strategic port of Bristol. His formula for roads was simple. They should consist of a ten-inch layer of stones, preferably of granite (each less than six ounces in weight and less than two inches in diameter). Under the pressure of traffic, the stones would compact to form a mass impervious to water. To assist drainage, a camber three inches high would be made in the middle of a road eighteen feet wide.

McAdam forbade such commonly used materials such as earth, clay or chalk because they absorbed water and cracked when the frosts of winter arrived. His method involved the use of a ring to test that the hard stones were not too large. Previously he had told his men that they should use their own mouths as sizing tools. As the story goes, he once rebuked a foreman for using stones which were too big; when the man opened his mouth to reply, he revealed an excessively large mouth with no teeth!

There were too many vested interests at work for the road system to be integrated and efficient, but road trusts were developing all over the country and McAdam argued that roads needed the oversight of official commissioners and trained surveyors; the task should not be left to the workmen on the site. McAdam assumed an almost missionary role in road development and was overwhelmed with calls for advice, but never charged fees for giving it. In his old age he petitioned the government to recognize his work and after much debate he was awarded £2,000. Three sons followed him into the roads business; James was appointed surveyor-general of British roads in 1837 and knighted, an honour his father had declined on the grounds that he was too old and infirm. Between 1816, when John took up his role at Bristol, and 1861, when his grandson William died, it is reckoned that eleven McAdam kinsmen in three generations were surveyors of turnpike roads. Inevitably that brought charges of nepotism, but it also draws attention to the role the family played in transforming the road system of Britain.

We turn now to another Scots engineer, a man with whom McAdam had disagreed sharply over whether roads over soft ground required 'bottoming', i.e. a paved foundation, but one who left his own mark upon the landscape of Britain.

THOMAS TELFORD (1757–1834)

Thomas Telford was born in a mud-walled thatched shepherd's cottage near Langholm, Dumfriesshire. With the death of his father shortly afterwards, his mother struggled to support her son by farm labour until Thomas was old enough to join her in the fields. Apprenticed as a stonemason, by the age of twenty-four he had acquired enough knowledge to try for a job with one of the bigger architects in London. He got there by volunteering to ride a horse which a neighbouring landowner was sending to the city. Through this arrangement he met Sir William Pulteney, who invited Telford to restore his home at Shrewsbury Castle. The job led in 1787 to his appointment as surveyor of public works in Shropshire, where he built a new infirmary, a county gaol, a church and a bridge over the

Severn. Between 1790 and 1796 he built forty road bridges. Rising at five a.m., he would work through till supper at nine p.m. and read poetry until he fell asleep (his favourites were Burns and Milton). Despite his intense workload, he never forgot to send money back to his mother and for the support of Andrew Little, a friend from youth who had trained as a surgeon but had since become blind.

His first big commission was the Ellesmere Canal, begun in 1793, linking the River Mersey with the Dee at Chester and the Severn at Shrewsbury. He took as his assistant another Langholm lad, Matthew Davison, who thereby joined a team which was in the next twenty years to complete most of the outstanding engineering projects of that period. A spectacular aqueduct carried the canal across the Vale of Llangollen in a cast-iron trough 11 feet in width, over seventeen spans along 1,000 feet at a height of 127 feet. The opening ceremony in 1805 established Telford as the star of the engineering world.

While the canal was under construction, Telford was asked to undertake a survey of the Highlands by Pulteney and others, who were trying to rebuild the social structure destroyed by the Jacobite rising of 1745–6 and the subsequent exodus of population. In 1801 and 1802 Telford surveyed up the west coast and down the east. He concluded that the poor communication system cut off the Highlands from participating in the new industrial age and made suggestions as to how to improve it. The government responded by handing him two huge new commissions. The first was to build the Caledonian Canal, linking north-east to south-west Scotland through the Great Glen. The other was to improve the existing road system, building 928 miles of new roads, upgrading 280 military roads and erecting 1,200 new bridges along the way.

By 1822 the first boat passed through the Caledonian Canal which Telford had finished at a cost of £1 million, with twenty-eight locks taking the boats through some of the bleakest terrain in Britain. Four years after work had begun, Telford went to Sweden in response to an invitation from the King to help plan the Gotha Canal, which was to link the North Sea with the Baltic. In Sweden he was enthusiastically welcomed by Count von Platen, the driving force behind the project, who had already completed fifty-two of the 105 miles of canal required. The two men became good friends. Telford, despite his humble origins, was at ease socially and later in life, with more time on his hands, hosted bachelor dinner parties at his Westminster home. He left Sweden with a knighthood and turned to his next project – the route to Dublin.

The problem this time was that the road from London to Holyhead, whence the ferry departed, passed through the most mountainous region of Wales and then crossed the Menai Strait to the island of Anglesey. Telford surmounted both of these obstacles, and his suspension bridge over the Menai Strait is thought by many to be his greatest engineering achievement. The poet Robert Southey, a friend and regular dinner companion, called him 'Pontifex Maximus' and the 'Colossus of Roads'.

There is a monument to Telford at Westkirk, Langholm, but memorials to his self-taught engineering genius remain all over Britain. The Dean Bridge in Edinburgh, St Katherine's Dock in London, and the draining of the Fen country, are but a few of his achievements. He did not wish to be buried in Westminster Abbey, where there is a statue of him in the east nave, but he was an only child who never married; there was no next of kin to object, and so that is where his body lies.

The Scottish contribution to road transport does not end with McAdam and Telford. Although their roads opened up new possibilities for travel, to ride over them on wooden, metal or (at best) solid rubber tyres was literally a shaking experience. That is until the pneumatic rubber tyre was developed by

JOHN BOYD DUNLOP (1840–1922)

Dunlop did not actually invent the pneumatic tyre. That honour belongs to another Scotsman, Robert Thomson (1822–73) from Stonehaven, who registered the patent in 1846 after it was successfully tested in London. Nothing came of the idea, which was abandoned because it was too expensive for common use. Thomson went on to patent a fountain pen in 1849 and a steam traction engine in 1867, but he is seldom credited with his inventions.

The same might be said of a blacksmith from Keir in Dumfriesshire named Kirkpatrick Macmillan (1813–78), who in 1842 invented the first bicycle (actually a tricycle), with front-wheel steering and the rear wheels driven by pedals. He had tested the device, which had solid iron tyres, by setting off to ride to Glasgow, a distance of eighty miles, arriving two days later with a very sore bottom. Alas, he did not take out a patent and so his machine was widely copied.

Johnny Dunlop, the young son of John Dunlop, owned one of these machines, and his father, in search of a device to make his own journeys around the countryside a little more comfortable, had the idea of making a rubber tyre to use with it. The son of a farmer at Dreghorn in Ayrshire, Dunlop's health was too sickly for him to become a farmer himself, so he trained as a vet and moved to practise in Belfast in 1869. His first attempt at tyre production utilized a rim of wood, covered with inflated rubber protected by a canvas strip. It proved highly effective.

The next step was to fit all three of Johnny's wheels with pneumatic tyres. Once that was done, the young lad was able to leave his pals far behind and Dunlop persuaded the captain of the Belfast cycling club to use his tyres in a proper race. He won easily, to cries from the onlookers that there must be a demon in his machine. When Dunlop explained the trick he was cheered by the large crowd, and he lost no time in trying to patent his invention.

At first he had to overcome the problem of Thomson's patent of 1846, but he was able to show that his own design included rims and valves, which the Thomson tyre did not. He went into partnership with W.H. Du Cros, a wealthy paper merchant, to form the Dunlop Rubber Company. Du Cros's enthusiasm for the new product knew no bounds. But he fell foul of the penny-farthing bicycle sellers who saw their product threatened by the new device, being on more than one occasion refused entry to premises dealing in penny-farthings and once finding himself surrounded by an angry mob of penny-farthing users.

This zeal also cost him his partner, ending John Dunlop's involvement with the product which has ever since been associated with his name. The incident which brought about the separation was the appearance of an advertisement for Dunlop tyres showing an elderly man, with a long white beard and eyeglass, speeding on his bicycle through the Belfast streets. This was none other than Dunlop himself, who had taken up cycling in his retirement and was extremely annoyed to find himself advertising his own product. He was so offended by Du Cros's cheek that he resigned from the company and had nothing more to do with it. While the company went on to become an international force, Dunlop lived out his retirement in Dublin, where he had bought a draper's shop.

THOMAS GRAHAM (1805–69)

Born in Glasgow, Graham was the son of a prosperous manufacturer who had it in mind that he should become a minister of the Church of Scotland. Thomas entered Glasgow University at the age of fourteen and soon came under the spell of chemistry. The professor of chemistry was then the notoriously grumpy Thomas Thomson, who nevertheless showed immediate respect to Graham after the boy asked an extremely pertinent question. Thomson was demonstrating the ability of liquids to absorb gases when Graham suddenly said, 'Don't you think, Doctor, that when liquids absorb gases, the gases themselves become liquids?' It was the start of a long fascination with gases which eventually made him the leading chemist of his age.

After receiving his MA from Glasgow in 1826, Graham went to Edinburgh before returning to Glasgow in 1830 as a professor of chemistry, then accepting the chair of chemistry at University College, London in 1837. He remained there until 1854 when he was appointed Master of the Mint, an honorific post once held by Isaac

Newton. Most of its holders treated the post as a sinecure, but Graham took it so seriously that he ceased all his researches for several years while he devoted himself to reorganizing the operation of the mint. Perhaps to discourage others from repeating this example, the post disappeared on his death in 1869.

But it was as a physical chemist that Graham is chiefly remembered and his textbook *Elements of Chemistry* was widely used throughout Europe. He founded the Chemical Society of London in 1841, a model for others around the world, and after the death of John Dalton in 1844 he was generally acknowledged as Britain's leading figure in chemistry. His main contributions were in the diffusion of gases (Graham's Law, which links the rate of diffusion of gases to the inverse of the square root of their density, is named after him). He also did work on the absorption of gases by charcoal, and was the first to observe that the metal palladium is able to absorb large amounts of hydrogen gas at low temperatures. Exposing palladium to the atmosphere produces heat and the discharge of the gas.

Graham was the outstanding pioneer of colloid chemistry. Colloids are solutions in which are dispersed particles so small they cannot be separated out by filtration or gravity; rubber is a colloid, as is gelatine. Graham was the first to use the term colloid, along with other related terms such as gel and sol. He recognized that 'colloids and crystalloids appear like different world of matter ... but in nature there are not abrupt transitions and the distinctions of class are never absolute'.

He also discovered the formulae of the three phosphoric acids.

But some of his chemical investigations would have done credit to Sherlock Holmes. In 1837 he published an article on how to detect whether coffee (then an expensive import) had been adulterated with vegetable substances. He pointed out that enough alcohol is produced during breadmaking to ignite a flame, and used to demonstrate this fact spectacularly by using the flame to ignite gunpowder.

One of his students from his Glasgow days found another way of lighting up a room. He was ...

JAMES YOUNG (1811–83)

Professor John Anderson, he who brought the model engine to James Watt's instrument-making premises in Glasgow with such fateful results, also played an important role in launching the career of another Scots inventor. He had provided in his will for a foundation called the Andersonian University (now Strathclyde University) for the purpose of making scientific education available to artisans. In 1830 it numbered among its students David Livingstone,* who was studying medicine, Lyon (later Baron) Playfair, and James Young, who had been apprenticed as a carpenter and cabinet-maker to his father at premises nearby.

Young attended the lectures of Professor Thomas Graham* and became so adept in chemistry himself that within a few years Graham was employing him as a deputy. It was on one occasion during this period that Young demonstrated a galvanic battery, which he had designed, to two young boys named Thomson who were destined to become eminent scientists themselves. The younger brother, William, was the future Lord Kelvin.*

When Graham left Glasgow for London in 1837, Young followed him and, after marriage the following year, found work in north-west England in the chemical industry. In 1847 he received a letter from his student friend Lyon Playfair, now professor of chemistry in the Royal School of Mines, who had married the daughter of a Derbyshire industrialist. Near to a mine owned by her family at Alfreton, a spring had been discovered which disgorged about 300 gallons of naphtha per day. It looked like thin treacle and after one distillation yielded a colourless liquid which burned brilliantly. Playfair's in-laws were not equipped to develop it and he offered Young the opportunity to do so. Playfair had noted that a fraction of the oil turned cloudy in cold weather, rather like the 'earth oil' from Burma which Christianson in Edinburgh had extracted as a solid and named 'petroline', or the paraffin which Reichenbach in Germany had obtained from beechwood tar.

Young approached his employer Charles Tennant, but the

Alfreton oil was not a big enough enterprise for his company. However, he did not stop Young going ahead on his own with the aid of the works chemist, and soon afterwards oil for lubrication and illumination purposes was produced. But Young needed other sources as Alfreton was drying up. He thought (wrongly) that the oil must come from coal distilling in sandstone and set to work to distil coal as Murdoch* had done. Although oil is in fact produced by the compression of marine plants over millions of years, his mistake did not matter; it was the process which carried him further. In 1850 he took out the patent for a process of extraction he called 'cracking', which is still used today for the thermal splitting of paraffin hydrocarbons into simpler molecular forms.

It was then that Hugh Bartholomew, another old student friend from Andersonian days, manager of the Glasgow Gas Works, came up with the suggestion that Young might use cannel coal, a tarry substance then plentiful in mid-central Scotland, which had been used to light the Isle of May lighthouse in the Firth of Forth since 1635. It worked so well that Young gave up his job at Tennants and set up a plant at Bathgate near to the cannel coal supplies. It turned out a range of hydrocarbon products, including oils for lighting and lubricating, solid paraffin and candles. Young's success led to accusations that cannel coal was not coal at all and therefore not covered by his patent. Another objection was that paraffin wax existed before his patent; this was perfectly true, but Young was able to show that his process had turned it from a laboratory curiosity into a commercial product and he won his cases. He visited America in 1869 to collect the substantial royalties due to him from the many manufacturers using his process. Realizing that the crude oil wells which had come on stream in America would eclipse his modest source of cannel coal, he set out to find alternative sources of oil for the process.

He found them in the shale deposits of West Lothian, and these revived his fortunes for a number of years. But the discovery of crude oil in America was the beginning of the end for Young's method. He retired in 1870 and devoted himself to philanthropy and cruising in his yacht *Nyasa*, named in honour of the territory in Africa explored by his friend David Livingstone, whose later expeditions were financed by Young. His acumen for chemistry was undimmed in his later years. Noticing that the bilgewater in the metal hull of his yacht was acidic, he added caustic soda to neutralize it in order to prevent rusting, an idea which was swiftly taken up by the Royal Navy.

Young was buried in Inverkip churchyard on the west coast, where he worshipped, but his monuments are in West Lothian — the pyramids of shale, now grassed over, which remain from his mines, and the smoking stacks of the BP oil refinery at Grangemouth which took over from his enterprises. A different kind of oil is refined there, but it is cracked by the same process that Young pioneered on his way to becoming the world's first oil baron.

SIR WILLIAM RAMSAY (1852–1916)

Our last chemist is almost as unknown today as were the chemical elements which he discovered in the late nineteenth century. Everyone is familiar with helium gas. It fills weather balloons and has a host of other uses. Neon is another gas the name of which has passed into the language from its use in fluorescent lighting tubes. Krypton and xenon may not be so well known, but together with the others they form a series in the periodic table of chemical elements known as the 'inert gases'. And they were all discovered by Ramsay.

The nephew of the geologist Sir Andrew Ramsay, William studied chemistry at Glasgow, then completed a doctorate at Tübingen in Germany. A series of swift promotions saw him move successfully from Glasgow to Bristol, then to the chair of inorganic chemistry at University College, London in 1887, where he remained until his retirement in 1913.

Ramsay had been working on the oxides of nitrogen when he deduced that a previously unknown gas must exist in the atmosphere. Another eminent chemist, Lord Rayleigh, had come to the same conclusion. The two men continued to work in their separate laboratories but communicated their experimental results to each other almost daily. At a meeting of the British Association in August 1894 they announced the discovery of argon.

While seeking sources of argon among minerals, Ramsay discovered helium in 1895. Then, by deductive logic of which Sherlock Holmes would have been proud, he looked at Mendeleev's periodic table of chemical elements and worked out the missing links which brought him to the discovery of neon, krypton and xenon in 1898.

Although it seemed of little importance at the time, when working in 1903 with the renowned chemist and physicist Frederick Soddy, he noticed that helium was present in the emanations of radium, as part of the radioactive decay which was soon shown vividly in the cloud chambers of physicist C.T.R. Wilson.* Ramsay was awarded the Nobel Prize for Chemistry in 1904. In his era the frontiers between chemistry and physics began to blur, as study of the physical properties of substances merged with exploration of the forces underlying the structure of matter.

PLOUGHSHARES AND PERCUSSION CAPS

The litany of invention which poured out of Scotland from the eighteenth century onwards, had enormous impact on the world of *agriculture*:

Rev. Patrick Bell (1800—69) invented the reaping machine which evolved into the combine harvester.

Sir Hugh Dalrymple (Lord Drummore) (1700—53) invented the system of hollow pipe drainage, which allowed waterlogged land to be dried and brought large areas into agricultural production.

Andrew Meikle (1719—1811) invented the threshing machine.

James Small (1730—93) invented the iron plough, which brought immediate improvements over the existing wooden apparatus.

James Paterson (1770—1840) lived in Musselburgh at a period when the fishing industry along the coast of East Lothian benefited from his process for making fishing nets by machine (which is still in use).

However, some inventors were more attracted to pistols than ploughshares:

Patrick Ferguson (1744–80) was born in Pitfour, Aberdeenshire and was posted as a military officer to America during the revolutionary war. He invented the breech-loading rifle, capable of firing at least seven shots per minute. The weapon helped the British to win the Battle of Brandywine in 1777, but Ferguson himself was killed in the Battle of Kings Mountain in South Carolina three years later.

Rev. Alexander Forsyth (1769–1848) was fond of shooting game but the damp Scots climate made the use of flintlock guns somewhat unreliable. He invented the percussion cap, which ignited an enclosed charge when struck by a hammer, and from his invention was developed the bullet.

COLOSSI OF ROADS

Thomas Telford was not alone in his efforts in bridge building:

Sir William Arrol (1839–1913) was responsible for two bridges which were the most substantial in the world when they opened, and which are still in use today. The first is the distinctive cantilever rail bridge over the Forth at Queensferry, and the second is the Tay Railway Bridge which replaced the structure destroyed in a storm. He also worked on Tower Bridge in London.

Sir William Fairbairn (1789–1874) was born in Kelso in the Scottish Borders. He became an engineer and introduced tubular steel as a construction material, which proved to be much stronger than solid steel.

Sir Robert McAlpine (1847–1934) left school at the age of ten to work in a coal mine. He went by the tough-sounding nickname of 'Concrete Bob' because of his use of concrete in the building and civil engineering firm he founded. He also pioneered labour-saving machinery in the construction industry and built roads, public buildings and, notably, Wembley Stadium.

John Rennie (1761–1801) was from Phantassie, East Lothian and began his career as a land engineer. He went on to build docks the whole length of Britain from Wick to Torquay, including the famous London and East India Docks, and in London built three famous bridges, Southwark, Waterloo and London Bridge (the third now having been re-assembled in Arizona). He was accorded the honour of burial in St Paul's Cathedral.

Finally, a trio of inventors who supplied tools which made the task of construction engineers easier:

Thomas Drummond (1797–1840) was a surveyor who eventually became Secretary of State for Ireland and insisted to absentee landlords that 'property has its duties as well as its rights'. He pioneered railway development in Ireland but is remembered for his invention of the Drummond Light, a kind of heliograph which made it possible to observe points more than sixty miles distant and was adapted for use in lighthouses.

James Beaumont Neilson (1762–1865) invented the hot-blast oven, which greatly reduced the amount of coal required to smelt iron ore. This evolutionary leap in the efficiency of the iron industry came at just the right time to match the needs of the railway and shipbuilding industries.

Sir Dugald Clerk (1854–1932) invented the two-stroke Clerk Cycle Gas Engine in 1877 and went on to become a leader of engineering research during the First World War.

FAR-SEEING SCOTS

As well as exploring the earth, Scots have contributed to mapping the heavens both as astronomers and inventors. The inventor of the reflecting telescope was **James Gregory** (1638–75) and the first person to measure the distance of a fixed star was **Thomas Henderson** (1798–1844). The star in question was Alpha Centauri but Henderson was beaten to publication in 1839 by the astronomer Bessel, although the two men eventually met and became good friends. Henderson, born in Dundee, was a lawyer's clerk but his passion for astronomy led him to become Her Majesty's astronomer at the Cape of Good Hope in South Africa, where he logged over 60,000 observations before returning to Scotland as the astronomer royal.

His successor in the post, **Charles Piazzi Smyth** (1819–1900), was known as the 'Peripatetic Astronomer' as he travelled around the world in search of better viewing conditions. Industrial smog in cities had made observations difficult even before public lighting systems were introduced. He eventually founded an observatory on the site of what is now the Las Palmas Observatory in the Canary Islands. Smyth was also a pyramidologist and his theories on the Pyramids as an astronomical tool incurred controversy in his lifetime, but his legacy to Edinburgh was the instigation of the 'One O'Clock Gun' which often startles unwary tourists when it is fired daily from the castle ramparts.

North America

A Symphony of Scots in the New World

Scots have been involved in North America from the first settlement in Nova Scotia in the 1620s, followed later in the seventeenth century by others in New Jersey and South Carolina. Since then a constant traffic in people and goods across the Atlantic (for the great part in Clyde-built ships) has continued, and as recently as 1980 the US Bureau of Census recorded 5.3 per cent of the population (some 12.2 million people) as being of Scots descent. But it was in the formation of both the United States and Canada that Scots influence was most acutely felt.

Scots Americans may not have such a high profile as Irish or Jewish Americans, but have they played an influential role right from the beginning of the history of the United States. Sixty-one per cent of US Presidents have had Scottish blood in their veins. Nine of the thirteen Governors of the newly created United States of America were Scots.

So many significant Americans have had Scottish ancestry that this section will confine itself to those who were actually born in Scotland. We begin with someone whose influence was felt in the period that led up to the creation of the United States of America.

ROBERT DINWIDDIE (1692—1770)

Rather than follow in the footsteps of his father, a prosperous merchant, Robert Dinwiddie embarked on a career as a colonial administrator, first in Bermuda, then in 1737 over Pennsylvania and the southern colonies of British North America. His post entitled him to a seat on the Virginia Council, where he swiftly gained a reputation as a zealous (some might say officious) administrator, ready to assert the royal prerogative.

It brought him promotion to Lieutenant-Governor of Virginia, at a time when the conflicts which became the French and Indian War were beginning to flare up on the state's borders.

A firm advocate of British expansion to the west, he sought the help of native Americans and the other British colonies in the struggle against the French. Favouring the use of a regular army over the less reliable militia, he promoted an able young officer named George Washington to lieutenant-colonel in 1754.

Dinwiddie left office at his own request in 1758 and returned to London, exhausted by the pressures of the war and a controversy of his own making, which arose when he tried to impose a tax for land patents in Virginia. The affair, known as the 'Pistole Fee' dispute, centred on the legality of imposing taxes on colonial subjects; as such, it was a precursor of the argument that led to the American Revolution.

Our next Scot was a supporter of the Revolution, not only in his own right but through those whom he taught. Among his students were a future president and vice-president, nine cabinet officers, twenty-one senators, thirty-nine congressmen, three Supreme Court justices and twelve state governors.

He was ...

REV. JOHN WITHERSPOON (1723–94)

Witherspoon was born at Gifford in East Lothian and became a parish minister in Beith, then in Paisley. He was the leader of the evangelical party in the Kirk but also an adherent of the Common Sense philosophical school of the Scottish professor Thomas Reid and others, and he believed reason would lead most people to share his moral and theological positions. This proved, however, to be untrue of the Kirk, where the evangelicals were not in the ascendancy. In 1768 he emigrated to America to become president of the College of New Jersey (later known as Princeton University). At first he declined the job since his wife was reluctant to leave Scotland, but he was persuaded a second time. He imported many Enlightenment themes to the curriculum at Princeton, and despite his own strong opinions, showed no desire to protect his students from ideas with which he disagreed.

This quality of tolerance was matched with a sense of humour. By night he suffered from insomnia, which resulted in a tendency to nod off after dinner. While a member of the New Jersey legislature, he unsuccessfully proposed that its daily sessions should end before dinner, remarking: 'There are two kinds of speaking which are very interesting – perfect sense and perfect nonsense. When there is speaking in either of these ways I shall engage to be all attention, but when there is speaking, as there often is, halfway between sense and nonsense, you must bear with me if I fall asleep.'

There was no danger of anyone falling asleep through Witherspoon's own speeches. His bushy eyebrows, large nose and ears gave him a striking appearance and his voice in the pulpit was melodious. His sermons, delivered without notes, were 'loaded with good sense and adorned with elegance and beauty of expression', but were far from flowery. A certain visitor, admiring his well-tended garden, noticed that the preacher grew only vegetables. 'Doctor, I see there are no flowers in your garden,' he remarked. 'No, nor in my discourses either,' replied Witherspoon. His oratorical abilities played well at Princeton, which, despite its burgeoning reputation, suffered from financial problems, and Witherspoon undertook regular preaching tours which raised funds for the college. His legacy was that Princeton played a unifying role within American Presbyterianism, but even more important was his emphasis upon the need for a well-educated clergy.

The only ordained clergyman to sign the Declaration of Independence, he encouraged his graduates to become 'ornaments of the State as well as the Church', but there was no question of the state running the church or vice versa. Over the question of how the church was to relate to the state in the newly independent United States, he played a key role. Instead of adopting the European model in which a particular religion or church was established by the state, the US decided to opt for total separation of the two. The relationship is sometimes called the Jefferson Wall, after Thomas Jefferson, who is credited with its invention, but clearly Witherspoon's ideas were influential in founding, from the outset, religious pluralism in the American nation.

His openness to those from other Christian traditions came from his admiration and respect for some of the founding fathers of American faith. In a sermon in May 1776, he argued that the hand of Providence was to be seen in the assembling of different groups in America who had been driven out of their own countries:

> Some of the American settlements ... were chiefly made by them as they carried the knowledge of Christ to the dark places of the earth, and continue there in as great a state of purity as is to be found in any Protestant church in the world. Does not the wrath of man in this instance praise God?

The word 'Americanism' was coined by Witherspoon, but in his speech on 4 July 1776 at the signing of the Declaration of Independence he also showed deep patriotism:

> There is a tide in the affairs of men, a nick of time. We perceive it now before us. To hesitate is to consent to our own slavery. That

noble instrument upon your table, which ensures immortality to its author, should be subscribed by every pen in this house. He that will not respond to its accents and strain every nerve to carry into effect its provisions is unworthy of the name of freeman.

For my own part, of property I have some; of reputation more. That reputation is staked, that property is pledged on the issues of this contest and although these gray hairs may soon descend into the sepulcher, I would infinitely that they descend thither by the hand of the executioner than desert at this crisis the sacred cause of my country.

Witherspoon did not descend for another eighteen years into the 'sepulcher' he occupies today in the presidents' lot in Princeton Cemetery. During that time he played an active role in college, church and state. He served first in the Congress in New Jersey, then in the Continental Congress, until 1782 when peace seemed assured and American independence had been guaranteed. During the years of the war of independence he had served on the secret committee on the conduct of the war and the board of war in 1778. His own son James was killed at Germantown, but that was not the only shadow in his later life. His last years were clouded by financial difficulties in the college, the death of his wife in 1789, and gossip over the 'scandal' when he remarried a twenty-four-year-old widow in 1791. Witherspoon became totally blind in 1792 and died two years later, but he gave America a vision.

JAMES WILSON (1742–98)

One of the signatories of both the Declaration of Independence and the US Constitution, and the architect of the US Supreme Court, James Wilson preferred to remain out of the limelight. A stickler for legal principle, he nearly did not put his name to the Declaration of Independence because of his scruples that the Middle States, which he represented, were divided on the issue and that therefore he did not have a clear mandate to sign. By finally agreeing to endorse the Declaration, he broke the deadlock in which the Pennsylvania delegation found itself. His signature made sure that it opted for independence.

Born in Scotland in 1742, Wilson received his education at the universities of St Andrews, Edinburgh and Glasgow. At the age of twenty-three he set sail for the New World; aided by letters of introduction, he obtained a job there as a tutor with the College of Philadelphia, which shortly afterwards conferred upon him the honorary degree of Master of Arts. Attracted to law as a profession, he was admitted to the Philadelphia bar in 1767 and set up in practice in Reading the following year. He married Rachel Bird, who bore him six children, and began to build for himself a promising practice, as he personally handled nearly half of the cases which were brought to the county court.

As the years went by, he identified himself more and more with the colony in its battles with the British Government. He fought with the weapon he knew best, legal argument. In 1774 his essay on the 'Nature and Extent of the Legislative Authority of the British Government' was distributed to members of the first Continental Congress and caused quite a stir. He was the first to articulate in legal form the claim that the British Parliament could have no jurisdiction over the American colony since there was no representation in Parliament for Americans, an argument reduced by others to the catchy slogan 'No taxation without representation'. The statement that 'all members of the British Empire are distinct states, independent of each other, but connected together under the same sovereign', which appears in the Declaration, is a clear indication of how influential his arguments were.

As a member of the Pennsylvanian Provincial Congress in 1775 he made a passionate speech on the possibility of an unconstitutional act being made by Parliament. Here, in embryo, is the principle of judicial review, the American system in which acts passed by government can be checked against the constitution which was to evolve in the Supreme Court.

During the next years he was a member of the Continental Congress and the Constitutional Convention, where a fellow delegate described him thus: 'Government seems to have been his peculiar study. All the political institutions of the world he knows in detail, and can trace the causes and effects of every revolution from the earliest stages of the Grecian commonwealth down to the present time.'

Wilson spoke throughout his career of the need for parliaments to contain a full representation of the people they governed. Only then could national government be strong and at the same time command respect. This led him logically to consider the problem of poor representation, which was plaguing Congress at the time. He spoke against representatives who did not take their roles seriously enough and stayed away in their home states, neglecting their responsibilities in the national congress and making efficient government almost impossible. There was a prime illustration of this in 1783, when American diplomats sent back to Congress the final version of the Treaty of Paris, designed to end the war between Britain and America. A quorum of nine states was needed to ratify the treaty, but there seemed little hope that this would be achieved. Weeks passed and there was even an attempt to convene Congress in the bedroom of a sick delegate in order to get approval before the long-awaited treaty was confirmed.

In 1789, Wilson became professor of law at the University of Pennsylvania and in the same year, associate justice of the Supreme Court, the institution he had helped create; but his performance here was less prophetic and original than his early career had promised.

We turn now to another of America's early heroes, but one who fought with a sword rather than a pen.

JOHN PAUL JONES (1747–92)

When Jones ran through one of his sailors with a sword, the career of the man whom Thomas Jefferson later described as 'the principal hope of America's future efforts on the ocean' was nearly ended before it had begun. Naval historians have never been able to agree about Jones. Was he patriot or pirate? Swashbuckler or self-serving gangster? Hero or hardman?

His early years point to the less flattering analysis. Born in the gardener's cottage on the Arbigland Estate, Kirkbean in Dumfriesshire, as plain John Paul, he was apprenticed to sea at the age of thirteen before getting his first command (the brig *John*) at the age of twenty-one. He was at first involved in slave ships but quit what he called 'the abominable trade' and began to make his fortune with other cargoes, such as sugar from the Caribbean. He was arrested and brought back to Scotland to stand trial for the murder of a sailor he had ordered to be flogged, but was able to produce witnesses who testified that the man had died not of his wounds but of yellow fever while on another ship.

In 1773, with his ship *Betsy* in Tobago, he decided he would invest the money set aside to pay the crew for shore leave in a return cargo. Mutiny was in the air. When the ringleader attempted to go ashore Jones drew his sword; the man lunged with a club, whereupon Jones ran him through. 'The greatest misfortune of my life' was how Jones later described the incident in a letter to Benjamin Franklin, claiming that he had immediately offered to give himself up, only to be urged by his friends to flee to America to avoid the fury of the dead sailor's associates.

Luck was with him. His brother, a successful tobacco planter in Virginia, had died leaving John as his heir. He began with the intention of rescuing his riches and setting up as a farmer, but he also seized the chance to reinvent himself. Adding 'Jones' to his name, he began to build a new identity. With America on the brink of war, and the smell of the sea still in his nostrils, he accepted a commission as a lieutenant in the navy of the Continental Congress.

At first he seemed to want to offend neither side as his ship flew the Grand Union flag (half American and half British), but he soon learned that there were greater rewards in being an American patriot.

In the custom of the times, under his authority of command, he took enemy merchant ships as prizes and was thus able to exist without salary throughout his career in the US Navy, rising quickly to captain. His skilful seamanship and cool courage quickly earned him the reputation of a naval hero.

In 1778 he persuaded the French to return a thirteen-gun salute, the first recorded instance of the Stars and Stripes being recognized by a foreign power. The French entered the war the same year. But his promises to recruits that they would make their fortune from prize booty were less easy to deliver. Returning to his ship in the French port of Brest after a love affair with the wife of a wealthy merchant in Paris, he faced a furious crew who wanted to be paid. Jones thought quickly and proposed a raid.

His target was Whitehaven, the small port on the Solway Firth from which he had sailed as a boy. It yielded little in the way of booty, so he conceived the more audacious plan of kidnapping the Earl of Selkirk from nearby St Mary's Isle and holding him to ransom. Alas for the raiding party, the Earl was not at home, so they took the family silver instead. It is reported that the Countess of Selkirk complained to a Mr Craik that 'your late gardener's son, born in your grounds, has returned as a buccaneer and the great villain has taken the family silver'. The new Jones, who had pretensions to be a gentleman, was later ashamed of the action and sent back the silver.

It was little wonder that after these raids the British viewed him simply as a pirate; but officially he was now Commodore Jones, commander-in-chief of the American fleet, and wore a 'Scotch bonnet edged with gold' above his dress uniform. His greatest hour came on 14 August 1779 off Flamborough Head, when, Jones engaged the far superior British frigate *Serapis*. Jones's ship, the *Bonhomme Richard*, was so badly damaged that the captain of the *Serapis* asked if Jones had struck his flag — the signal of surrender. A midshipman rose to do so, whereupon Jones shot him, shouting the famous words, 'Sir, I have not yet begun to fight!' He went on to win the battle against the odds.

Jones was now a hero. Congress thanked him and Louis XVI presented him with a sword. His reputation grew, partly through 'chapbooks', the forerunner of comics, one of which portrays Jones shooting the unlucky midshipman. He never married, but went on to win many female hearts in Paris after the Revolutionary War while he was negotiating prize money claims. In 1788 he came to the attention of the Russian Empress, Catherine the Great, who had ambitions to annex Constantinople and control the Black Sea.

His third incarnation as Kontra Admiral Pavel Ivanovich Jones did not last long. He had gambled that this career move might enable him to come back at the head of the new American navy, but it was not to be. Despite success for his squadron in the Dnieper River region of the Black Sea, he gained little credit for his efforts. His assumption of seniority among the four Russian admirals in the Black Sea had provoked them to close ranks against him. Forced to leave Russia, in 1790 he returned to France but died in Paris in 1792 before his ambition could be achieved.

Short in height ('little Jones', Jefferson called him), fastidious in his dress, he had the vanity of a Napoleon and no doubt something of the same ruthlessness. The pirate image and the rough, tough early life add to the portrait of a harsh, unsophisticated man. Yet there was another side to Jones, which he had acquired during his controversial career. Intense about his honour and his duties, this uneducated Scots son of the soil taught himself to be a gentleman.

This side to his character is shown in his correspondence with the naval authorities on the duties of a naval officer:

> *It is certainly for the interest of the service that a cordial exchange of civilities should subsist between superior and inferior officers, and therefore it is bad policy in superiors to behave towards their inferiors indiscriminately, as tho' they were of a lower species. Such a conduct will damp the spirits of any man. Cheerful ardor and spirit ought ever to be the characteristic of an officer — for to be well obeyed it is necessary to be esteemed.*

That kind of management theory gave Jones the status of a prophet at the US Naval Academy, where midshipmen for generations were required to memorize his dicta, such as: 'The credit of the service depends not only in dealing fairly with the men employed in it, but on their belief that they are and will be fairly dealt with' or 'None other than a Gentleman, as well as a seaman, both in theory and practice is qualified to support the character of a Commissioned Officer in the Navy, nor is any man fit to command a Ship of War who is also not capable of communicating his ideas on paper in language that becomes his rank.'

In 1905 his body was brought back from France and his remains placed under the Grand Staircase in Bancroft Hall at the Naval Academy, Annapolis, Maryland where it lay until 1913, inspiring the parody song 'Everybody works but John Paul Jones! He lies around all day, body pickled in alcohol.' In 1913 his casket was moved to the crypt of the Academy's new chapel where he is revered as founder of the US Navy.

The classic American dream is to go from rags to riches in one generation. There is no better example of its fulfilment than

ANDREW CARNEGIE (1838–1919)

Andrew Carnegie was no ordinary rich man. At one point reputed to be the wealthiest man in the world, he gave most of his worldly goods away before he died. He believed that it was a law of nature for wealth automatically to accumulate in the hands of a few, but that those few had a moral duty to use it for the common good. The epitome of the self-made man, he held the principle of inherited wealth to be extremely pernicious; if millionaires were selfish enough to keep their wealth, the state should take it away from them by taxation when they died.

Carnegie was born in 1838 in Dunfermline, where his father, William, was a struggling cottage weaver. Although the family were poor, Andrew was cherished, his parents telling him he should only go to school when he so wished. Fortunately Robert Martin, the local 'dominie' or schoolmaster, enticed him to school at the age of eight and gave him the first penny he ever earned for reciting a Burns poem. The boy also showed early entrepreneurial skill by allowing his schoolfriends to have one of his rabbits named after them if they undertook to feed them.

The family were invited by one of Mrs Carnegie's sisters to join her in America, where more opportunities existed than in Scotland, and in 1848 Andrew embarked with his parents for Pittsburgh, Ohio. Living in the poorest quarter, like other immigrants they used the network of ethnic contacts and Andrew began as 'bobbin-boy' in a Scots-only mill. Soon he was in a factory which made the bobbins, run by another Scot. The literacy and numeracy he had acquired won him a clerical job. Promotion to a telegraph office followed. He attended evening classes and devoured the library of the philanthropic Colonel Anderson, who made his 400 books available every Saturday to any poor boy who wished to borrow them. When the new railway to Philadelphia opened, the Pittsburgh superintendent, Thomas Scott, appointed Carnegie, then only sixteen, as his personal assistant. The young man once averted a strike by relieving the leaders of their jobs, an early taste of his tough attitude to labour relations.

By the time he was twenty-four he succeeded Scott, who had shrewdly taught his protégé that it was better to accumulate shares in the new railways than salary. It was the rapid growth of Carnegie's stock that provided him with his first venture capital. His fierce appetite for learning provided him with a thorough knowledge of the railways, telegraphy and bridges which were fast shrinking America. He spotted that iron bridges would soon replace the wooden ones which were incapable of carrying the new heavy locomotives and carriages, and created the Keystone Bridge Company and Union Iron Mills with Thomson and Scott.

The diminutive Carnegie (he was five feet three inches tall) still hankered for Scotland and hoped to be made American Consul in Glasgow. He once wrote, 'What Benares is to the Hindu, Mecca to the Mohammedan, Jerusalem to the Christian, all that Dunfermline is to me.'

Fortunately for him, he didn't get the job. But a trip to Britain produced a deal with Henry Bessemer, whose new process for making steel from pig-iron was to revolutionize the raw materials of construction. The process demanded iron ore low in phosphorus; Carnegie ensured he was ahead of the competition by finding a cheap supply for his new steel mill, boosting his fortune further as steel production expanded by persuading his workers to take stock instead of higher wages (and shrewdly retaining a fifty-five per cent holding for himself).

Carnegie's success was built on several factors additional to his personal qualities of fierce determination and willingness to take risks. His accountancy and stock control expertise enabled him to keep a tight rein on all that was happening in his enterprises. New technology enabled him to more than double the output of his furnaces; Carnegie was fanatical about what today is called R&D, and ploughed much of his early profit back into developing more efficient production processes.

Carnegie was a ruthless businessman. He relied on loyal lieutenants and partners whom he rewarded with shares in the business, but if these men proved not to be up to the job they were soon forced out.

If the railway companies offered a deal which did not suit him, he would threaten to build his own railway in opposition, and he usually got his own way — but at the price of popularity.

In 1892, when he broke a strike, the *St Louis Dispatch* wrote: 'Three months ago Andrew Carnegie was a man to be envied. Today he is an object of mingled pity and contempt.'

After years of wheeling and dealing, a yearning to bring something positive to the world drove him in the last twenty years of his life. In 1901 he sold out all his interests in Carnegie Steel to J.P. Morgan for $480 million, and as they shook hands Morgan remarked, 'Mr Carnegie, I want to congratulate you on being the richest man in the world.' But far from being content with that title, Carnegie went on to preach what he called 'The Gospel of Wealth'. He laid out three choices for the disposal of wealth. First, rich men could leave it to their families. Like many self-made men, Carnegie was less than ecstatic about the hereditary principle, as he saw too many instances of wealthy families who squandered their riches or were cursed by them. Second, wealth could be bequeathed after death, but he had little trust that the wishes of the deceased would be followed.

His conclusion was that the duty of the man of wealth was to set an example of simple living, to give all his riches away and become 'the sole agent and trustee for his poorer brethren ... doing for them better than they would or could do for themselves'. Carnegie became the living embodiment of his own philosophy; by the time of his death in 1919, he had given away $325 million. He had paid for 7,689 church organs, over 1,000 of them in Scotland. Most of his benefactions went to building libraries and to education. The Carnegie Foundation in the USA today is heavily involved in education and peacebuilding charities. He heartily approved of death duties:

> *Of all forms of taxation, this seems the wisest. Men who continue hoarding great sums all their lives, the proper use of which for public ends would work good to the community, should be made to feel that the community, in the form of the state, cannot thus be deprived of its proper share. By taxing estates heavily at death, the state marks its condemnation of the selfish millionaire's unworthy life.*

Carnegie was no saint. Despite his words about simple living, he bought an estate at Skibo Castle in Scotland for his wife Louise, and could not resist throwing himself into politics, using his money to support Gladstone and the British Liberal Party and expressing his republican and pro-Irish Home Rule views through the many newspapers he owned.

But in many of his radical opinions, 'The Star-Spangled Scotchman', as novelist William Black called him, showed himself to be a man ahead of his times; he was not afraid to make controversial benefactions to causes he believed noble, such as the university for black Americans at Tuskegee, Alabama. Equally, when Woodrow

Wilson asked him to donate a college stadium for American football, a sport he did not much care for, he gave the college a boating lake instead, prompting Wilson to remark, 'I asked for bread and he gave me water.'

ALLAN PINKERTON (1819–84)

The episode which more than any other tarnished Andrew Carnegie's* reputation was the Homestead Strike. His ally in breaking it was an equally tough and determined Scot, Allan Pinkerton, who had emigrated to the United States in 1842 from Glasgow, where his father had been a sergeant of police. His departure followed his involvement in radical protest and his subsequent career showed that revolutionaries often make the best secret policemen. His gravestone describes him as a 'friend to honesty' and a 'foe to crime' but others were less kind, calling him self-righteous and bull-headed. Yet Pinkerton claims a special place in history as the inventor of that American archetype, the Private Eye – the nickname for private detectives was derived from the Pinkerton logo, which showed an all-seeing eye. He has an even greater claim to fame as the founder of the American Secret Service.

When he first arrived in America, Pinkerton was apprenticed as a cooper, making barrels in Kane County, Illinois. One day, while collecting wood from an island, he stumbled on a gang of counterfeiters who were using the place as a hideout. He succeeded in rounding them up, and this bold act led to his election as deputy sheriff; he went on to hold the same post in nearby Cook County. Preferring less conventional methods than he was able to use as a sheriff, he resigned in 1852 to form the Pinkerton Detective Agency.

The Pinkertons, as his men came to be called, operated undercover, sometimes infiltrating the organizations they were investigating, recording evidence in code in their little black books. Two outstanding successes guaranteed them fame. In 1861 they foiled an attempt in Baltimore to assassinate the president-elect, Abraham

Lincoln, on the way to his inauguration. Then, in 1866, they recovered $700,000 stolen from the Adams Express Company and arrested the thieves. The former incident marked the beginning of their contract as the first US Secret Service. Pinkertons also went undercover in successfully combating the notorious Molly Maguires, an Irish mafia who had gained control over the Pennsylvanian coalfields and were terrorizing the workers.

During the Civil War, Pinkerton again proved he was the ideal man for the Secret Service. He himself assumed the identity of E.J. Allen and his men were highly successful in monitoring the movements of Confederate troops. After the war, in 1877, Pinkerton's organization was hired to perform the more controversial and equally dangerous work of strike-breaking. His attitude is perhaps best conveyed in the title of a book which he wrote the following year, *Strikers, Communists and Tramps*.

With hindsight we might find it difficult to share Pinkerton's view of strikers at that time as subversives and criminals. The men worked twelve-hour days, seven days a week, some for as little as fifteen cents per hour. Of the 3,800 workers at Carnegie's Homestead Mill, only 800 belonged to the Amalgamated Union; the rest were bottom-of-the-pile immigrants. But these too supported the strike, out of desperation and because Carnegie and Frick went too far in their cost-cutting. The Amalgamated Union had been recognized after a previous strike a few years earlier, but Carnegie now removed recognition while cutting the minimum weekly wage from $25 to $22. The atmosphere which the Pinkertons met was already red-hot with resentment. The tough tactics which had gained them success in breaking other strikes simply resulted in inflaming violent protests in which four Pinkertons were killed.

Although the conflict at Homestead Mill happened eight years after Pinkerton's death, the event did nothing for the reputation of either man. Carnegie lived to redeem his reputation by becoming a public benefactor, while Pinkerton is less of a hero to posterity. In many ways this complex character ranks as the J. Edgar Hoover of the nineteenth century.

Zeal such as Carnegie showed in his business dealings, or Pinkerton in his pursuit of strikers, gives an edge to the frontier spirit when it comes to building a new country. But it is often shown at its worst in religion, as we shall see in the story of the man who gave America its National Park system.

JOHN MUIR (1838–1914)

America's most renowned naturalist and conservationist, John Muir looked and sounded like an Old Testament prophet. A congressman who joined him in his campaign against the building of a dam in the Yosemite Valley remarked, as Muir declaimed his opposition to the project, 'With him, it is me and God and the rock where God put it.' There was something fanatical about Muir, but his zeal was sublimated into reverence for the created order rather than harshness towards his fellow creatures.

Unfortunately, with his father Daniel it was the opposite. Daniel Muir was a prosperous grain merchant in Dunbar, whose attraction to Puritan forms of religion led him to emigrate to America after he came under the influence of the Campbellites, a sect named after the Scots father and son who founded it in Ohio in 1807. The family moved to a farm in Wisconsin in 1849. John had a harsh childhood, tempered by his mother's gentle influence but tyrannized by his father's strict attitudes, which were summed up in his remark when John fell ill with pneumonia that 'God and hard work were by far the best doctors'. The boy was whipped regularly and allowed no 'frivolous' books, but read avidly at a neighbour's home the travels of Mungo Park* and the Romantic poets, who awakened his reverence for nature.

Muir had an inventive mind; often he would rise before dawn to get time to himself, which he used to construct an array of devices such as barometers, thermometers and combination locks. He took these to the state fair at Madison in 1860, and was rewarded with a place at the University of Wisconsin. There he was introduced to theories of glaciation and the Ice Age by Dr Ezra Carr, and developed a passion for Wordsworth's poetry. Mrs Carr became his mentor, almost a mother figure in his life from then on. Still bent on being an inventor, he found a job in an Indianapolis machine shop in 1866 which he held until a dramatic incident changed his life a year later. A file pierced his eye, blinding him, and the other eye went blind in sympathetic shock. His sight returned after a month but he saw this as divine providence. 'From this time I bade adieu to all my mechanical inventions, determined to devote the rest of my life to the study of the inventions of God.'

In 1868 he walked 1,000 miles to the Gulf of Mexico and sailed to Cuba, then crossed Panama and returned to the west coast. But it was the Sierra Nevada and Yosemite that captured his imagination, 'the most divinely beautiful of all the mountain chains', which he called the Range of Light. Living in a log cabin, he explored the region, writing a journal and regular letters to Mrs Carr, who encouraged him to publish and sent him a stream of influential visitors. Apart from an interval during which he married and raised two daughters while running his father-in-law's fruit farm, nature became his great cause.

Through a series of articles in *Century* magazine, Muir drew attention to the devastation of mountain meadows and forests by sheep and cattle. With his editor, he campaigned for the creation of a National Park; in 1890 the first was created at Yosemite by an Act of Congress. Muir was involved subsequently in the establishment of Sequoia, Mount Rainier, Petrified Forest and Grand Canyon National Parks. The publication in 1901 of *Our National Parks* led to a visit to Yosemite from President Theodore Roosevelt; there, amid the forest, he and Muir laid the foundation of his innovative conservation programmes. But despite his influence and the inspirational quality of his writings (over 300 articles and ten books), Muir was unable to stop the building of the Hetch-Hetchy Dam in his beloved Yosemite in 1913 to supply water for San Francisco. He died a year later of double pneumonia.

Muir had flourished away from the baleful glare of his father, but through his life he had kept a regular correspondence with his mother, sending her pressed flower specimens, copies of his writings and seeds for her garden. In his relationships with nature and the women who were close to him he had managed to cultivate her gentle good humour, reserving the evangelical zeal he derived from his father for a more pantheistic gospel in which he managed 'to do something for wildness and make the mountains glad'.

Our final Scottish American is also credited with making his mark upon the land, but in a very different way.

JAMES WILSON (1835–1920)

'He was a canny Scot, a delightful associate, thoughtful, genial and thoroughly loyal,' said President William Howard Taft of the man who, as US Secretary of Agriculture, set records which have never been equalled for tenure of office and achievement. Wilson was born within a few miles of the land which Robert Burns* had farmed in Ayrshire, one of fourteen children who emigrated with their parents to Tama County, Iowa in 1852. He farmed, taught as a schoolmaster, was elected to the Iowa state house in 1867 and then pursued a career in state politics and as a professor of agriculture at the state university until President McKinley appointed him Secretary for Agriculture in 1897.

His friendship with another Scottish American, Henry Wallace (father of a previous Secretary of Agriculture), may have helped him get the position. He also had close friendships with other Scots, such as Andrew Carnegie* and Governor William Hoard of Wisconsin (founder of *Hoard's Dairyman* magazine). Hoard, Wallace and Wilson met regularly to share wit, Burns's poetry (which Wilson often quoted to make a point) and a glass of whisky. Of such was the Scottish mafia made.

Wilson, known as 'Tama Jim' to distinguish him from an Iowa senator of the same name, was a staunch Republican, fond of saying that he would admit there might be good Democrats but he had as yet failed to find one. Unsurprisingly, such opinions did not play well with Democrat Woodrow Wilson, who ended his sixteen-year tenure when he was elected President in 1912.

But Wilson's record under the three previous Presidents, McKinley, Roosevelt and Taft, all of them Republicans, was impressive. He revolutionized American agriculture, extending the influence of his department into research, soil conservation, reforestation, plant disease and insect control, and even into weather forecasting, improvements to rural roads, and the inspection of food. The effect was to give the United States the lead in agricultural science throughout the world.

Tama Jim's monuments are the research facilities at Beltsville, Maryland which are among the best in the world, and the classic colonnades of the huge complex which today houses the department he once headed.

Possibly the most bizarre tale of the colonial era in North America is that of **Peter Williamson** (1730–99), later nicknamed 'Indian Peter', who qualifies for the title of 'the one who got away'. Unlike many Scots who travelled to America, he went there forcibly, kidnapped in his native Aberdeenshire and sold into slavery. Captured by Cherokee Indians, he escaped to join the army and was again captured and imprisoned, this time by the French. He eventually returned to Edinburgh where he became a successful businessman, publishing the first street directory of the city and setting up a postal service. Rubbing shoulders with the Edinburgh lawyers who were the senders and recipients of much of his mail gave him the impetus to launch a legal action against officials in Aberdeen for permitting the slave trade, which he duly won.

His story reminds us that in the eighteenth century the frontiers in North America had yet to be defined. The French, the Indians and the British formed a triangle of interests in what is now called Canada. It was a Scotsman who played a crucial role in achieving British dominance in Canada. He achieved it by two amazing pieces of exploration, yet confessed himself satisfied with neither.

SIR ALEXANDER MACKENZIE (1764–1829)

Mackenzie, born in Stornoway in the Western Isles, came to America with his father at the age of twelve after the death of his mother. Anxious to escape the war of independence, the pair migrated north to Montreal, loyal to the British and dominated by the fur trade to which it was the gateway in the north-west of Canada. His knowledge of Gaelic was useful for conversing with the numerous Gaelic speakers who had come to Canada, well equipped as they were by genes and upbringing to cope with the hardships of Canadian winters. But he had to learn French to become a *bourgeois* or boss of the guides and traders who transported the furs from the north where they were acquired.

He also had to acquire, 'after the fashion of the country', an Indian wife, without whom he would have been helpless for clothes or shelter.

Mackenzie took easily to the trade and was soon making a good income. He bought into the North-West Company, becoming the rival of another equally ambitious young Scot, Simon McTavish (1750–1804); each was intent on making his fortune. Mackenzie's plan involved charting a way through to the Pacific Ocean, which would give the ambitious traders access to the markets of China.

In 1788 he discovered and charted Canada's largest river, the 2,500-mile stretch of water which reaches up to the Arctic Ocean and is now called Mackenzie River, one of eleven physical features in British Columbia and the North-West Territories named after him. Yet for all that, Mackenzie called it 'The River of Disappointment' because it had not taken him to the Pacific. He gained permission to go back to Europe to improve his navigational skills. On his return he set off down the Peace River, and on 14 May 1793 his party emerged in pelting rain at the Pacific Ocean. But once again there was a bittersweet taste. The route was unsuitable for canoes, for it involved carrying them overland in several places to complete the journey, and therefore the sought-after river route which would have offered easy access to the coast was denied to Mackenzie.

He had taken a considerable quantity of money to trade with the Russians he hoped to meet at the journey's end and his efforts did bear some commercial fruit, giving the North-West Company a huge lead over their rivals, the Hudson's Bay Company.

Mackenzie wrote up his adventures in a best-selling book, *Voyages*, which outsold demand in English and German, and with his fur interests was soon one of Canada's wealthiest men. He had something of Carnegie's combination of toughness and tenderness about him. He could reduce an Indian trapper to tears, but made sure the Indian 'wife' he left behind and her children were well looked after. Quarrels were bitter when they came, and the jealous McTavish saw that they did: Mackenzie founded his own company, which tried unsuccessfully to take over the Hudson's Bay Company. He never adopted Canada as his country, once saying, 'I think it unpardonable in any man to remain in this country who can afford to leave it.' And leave it he did, returning to live in Scotland. He became a friend of the Prince of Wales, the darling of fashionable parties, and was eventually knighted.

He bought an estate named Avoch on the Moray Firth but his latter years were clouded by ill-health and he died there in 1829. A few years earlier, in 1812, Napoleon had paid him the compliment of studying the detailed descriptions of rivers and terrain in his books as a means of planning an overland reconquest of Canada for the French, but decided to invade Russia instead.

WILLIAM LYON MACKENZIE (1795–1861)

British settlers began to make their way to Canada after 1763, when France finally gave up all claim to the country. First came demobilized soldiers, then loyalists fleeing the American Revolution. The province of Quebec or Lower Canada remained largely French-speaking, but Upper Canada, today the province of Ontario, steadily filled with English-speaking pioneers. Among those who came to these lands round the northern shores of the Great Lakes were many thousands from Scotland, and Canada has ever since been a favourite destination of Scots seeking their fortune overseas. So heavy was this early immigration that the life of Canada in many respects seemed to replicate the life of Scotland, especially in religion and politics. From Montreal a large, wealthy colony of Scottish businessmen running the fur trade sustained a Tory party as corrupt and reactionary as the one ruling Scotland, while frustrated radicals in the rest of the country raged in vain against it.

Among them was William Lyon Mackenzie, who as a young shop-keeper in Dundee had read the literature of liberty and become a strident activist in local reforming circles. A crucial year in his life was 1820, which saw severe economic recession in Scotland accompanied by outbreaks of violence. In Dundee the authorities moved against known trouble-makers, and Mackenzie decided to get out altogether. He emigrated to Canada. Here he took to a different career in journalism, soon making a name for his fierce attacks on the arrogant Tories. Elected assemblies existed at this period in Upper and Lower Canada, but they lacked real power. Without reference to them, a Governor-General sent from Britain appointed all public officials, who could not be called to account by the representatives of the people. In his articles Mackenzie liked to dwell on the contrast between this situation and that just across the border in the United States, to all intents and purposes a full democracy.

Through his journalism, and eventually as an editor, Mackenzie became well known enough to get elected to the assembly of Upper Canada, besides becoming Mayor of Toronto in 1834. He reached these positions only in the face of fierce opposition from the Tories, marked on both sides by libellous insults and sometimes by worse: on one occasion young ruffians broke into Mackenzie's offices, removed his presses and hurled them into Lake Ontario. After his election, the tame Tory majority in the assembly sought grounds for disqualifying him from membership, and he was voted out again. But his constituents kept re-electing him till he was allowed to sit.

It proved almost the last straw for Mackenzie that progress was still blocked in Canada while in Scotland, after a long agitation, the

Reform Act of 1832 finally extended the right to vote beyond the narrow elite of 4,000 people who had enjoyed it since the Union. With his emigration he had in effect given up hope of change; now in the supposedly freer life of the colonies he ended up with fewer rights than if he had stayed at home. Mackenzie had so far been an advocate of moral force in politics, of seeking reform through persuasion. Henceforth he moved towards physical force, advocating resorting to violence if the authorities would not respond to legitimate demands.

As the colonies often offered refuge to the disaffected, there were many Canadians ready to cast off British rule and perhaps throw in their lot with the United States. They were not all radicals or republicans either. Some of Montreal's tycoons favoured this course because they saw their future markets as continental rather than transatlantic. Mounting discontent over a variety of grievances in Canada led to actual rebellion in 1837, which received some illicit help from across the border, though the outbreak was easily suppressed. Mackenzie had been hot-headed enough to place himself at the head of the rebels in Upper Canada, but almost at once he saw the game was up. With the empty gesture of declaring himself chairman of a provisional government, he fled to the United States.

The consequence was that the Government in London at last realized Canadian problems had to be taken seriously. It sent Lord Durham over to investigate them. With his report of 1840 he recommended a transition to responsible government, that is to say, with ministers answering to elected representatives. This was introduced over the next decade, at the end of which Mackenzie felt safe enough to return. He was re-elected to Parliament, no longer the firebrand he had been in his youth, but reconciled to a Canada under the Crown. Even so, he has remained a patron saint of Canadian nationalism. For another century, Canadians would remain loyal to the Empire, but the memory of Mackenzie was always there to remind the British that this loyalty could not just be taken for granted but had to be earned through mutual respect. In the twentieth century the memory became embodied in his grandson William Mackenzie King, the Prime Minister who dominated three decades of the country's politics till the 1950s, with an outlook at times critical of imperial power as an obstacle to Canada's full independence. It has now been gained without affecting the old friendship with Britain, and the flow of Scots across the ocean continues to this day.

The Scots-born immigrants to Canada were particularly influential in developing communications across the North American continent through the different media of railways and journalism. Many, like Lyon Mackenzie, ended up in politics. Another example is **Charles Herbert Mackintosh** (1843–1931), MP for the city of Ottawa and the editor of several newspapers. One of the better known Canadian newspapers today, the *Toronto Globe*, was founded by **George Brown** (1818–80), whose family moved in 1837 from Scotland to America where his father founded the *British Chronicle*. In 1843 George Brown visited Upper Canada and saw the opportunity to start a newspaper there. The *Globe* was born and it provided a launch-pad for Brown's career in politics as a Liberal. He championed the cause of confederation and was a member of the coalition government which achieved it, but later resigned.

Brown was an ally and friend of Canada's first Liberal Prime Minister, **Alexander Mackenzie** (1822–92), who may be distinguished as the one without the knighthood (having refused the honour three times). Mackenzie was born in Logierait in Perthshire and came to Canada at the age of twenty. He worked as a builder in the family business before becoming editor of the *Lambton Shield*, a reform newspaper. The peak of his political career came between 1873 and 1878 when he led Canada's first Liberal Government. It came to power when the Conservative administration came to grief over a scandal concerning the Canadian Pacific Railway. Mackenzie was caustic in his censure of his predecessor, calling him 'a drunken debaucher'. The subject of this scorn was Canada's first premier who held power during this formative period in Canadian history.

SIR JOHN MACDONALD (1815–91)

Sir John Macdonald was born at Dornoch in Sutherland, and emigrated young to Canada. He became active among Canadian Tories, who in many ways formed a continuation of the old Scots Toryism long after it had been hounded from power by political reform at home. He helped his party adapt to the more popular forms of government which emerged in the provinces of Canada during the mid-nineteenth century, and became convinced that a confederation of them all was the right way to face the future. In former times, Toryism had essentially been a defence of privilege. Instead, Macdonald made it his job to see that in this vast stretch of territory, reaching from the Atlantic to the Pacific Ocean, and from the Great Lakes to the Arctic Circle, all the leading interests would be given their stake in a new structure. Being an intelligent and ingenious charmer, a pragmatic conservative burdened by no great weight of principles, he was the right man to bring the confederation into being in 1867. He served much of the rest of his life as Prime Minister.

The task was to build a nation and, as a Scot, Macdonald knew the concept of nationality could not be clear-cut. Scots of his time had concentric loyalties, to Scotland, Britain and the Empire. This sense of concentric loyalty helped him in his own tortuous task of bringing together the disparate provinces of British North America. Certain interests had had to be squared before he could even embark on forming the confederation. Macdonald needed to carry the radical opposition and despite their personal and political animosity, he and fellow Scot George Brown* managed to achieve it through a coalition government. He also had to defer to the commercial elite of Montreal, again largely Scottish, by adopting a protectionist programme permitting infant Canadian industries to grow till they could compete fully in a global system of free trade. Macdonald did not stand alone among the world's statesmen of his day in sensing that pure economic liberalism was probably passing its peak. His version of Scots Toryism also shared its passion for economic improvement, infinitely heightened by the technological capabilities of the Victorian era. Perhaps the most prodigious of all feats by Scots who exploited them were the Canadian transcontinental railways, built with Macdonald's support as a means of binding the nation together.

It had been clear all along to Macdonald that Canada needed a federal constitution on the American model, not centralized government on the British model. He gave guarantees for the particular interests of the provinces, knowing the French felt themselves under pressure from the English-speaking majority. But Macdonald, while elaborately deferring to Quebec's sensibilities, also recognized in the Britishness of the provinces one basic element of any conceivable common identity. It was not just a matter of foiling the United States to preserve imperial authority in North America. Thus far disaffection in Canada had taken on an anti-British colour. This was the reason why the provinces had been given responsible government. To his radical countrymen, Macdonald stressed that an equal if not greater risk to Canadian interests came from the Americans, which must be countered by unity and by a concerted effort to develop the West before they seized it. This could be, and has been, defined as negative nationalism: British Canadians were to build, along with the French, a more ordered and stable society than the liberal experiment in the United States. Negative or not, Canada would grow increasingly conscious of it.

Having retained her British allegiance, Canada had to redefine her working relationship to the Empire. Macdonald believed Canadians were loyal to it, so he felt he could go quite far in asserting difference, not only in internal but also in external policy: for instance, he insisted on having a High Commissioner in London to press his own views there, rather than relaying them in the traditional way through his Governor-General and the Colonial Office. On the other hand he showed a cautious interest in the sort of ideas for imperial federation that Lord Rosebery* was promoting. In the first place this meant co-operation over trade and defence, but Macdonald always entered the caveats that any proposals had to be acceptable to colonial opinion. Notions of a supreme Imperial Parliament were not acceptable. In 1886 the crisis over Irish Home Rule made many wonder whether it might be resolved in an imperial framework, under just such a Parliament charged with the care of joint interests, leaving the domestic affairs of British territories under subordinate legislatures in them. Macdonald rejected this, saying Ireland should be content with the same status as Scotland. This may seem inconsistent with his claims for Canada. But as a pragmatist, he saw that any worldwide commonwealth must allow scope for gradations in the relationship of the dispersed parts to the whole, as he had allowed it inside his own confederation. The Canadian case was different from the Scottish case because needs and aspirations were different in each, although preserving allegiance to the Crown remained common to both.

The great Canadian railway linking the country from east to west can be credited to two Scots. The main credit usually goes to

DONALD SMITH, LORD STRATHCONA (1830–1914)

Donald Smith, born at Forres in the north-east of Scotland, had a knack of turning up at significant moments in Canadian history. As a youth he left to join the Hudson's Bay Company, which held a chartered monopoly of the trade, mainly in furs, over the northern half of North America, though one now under challenge from various rivals. The company was run by and largely recruited from Scots. Smith rose to be manager of operations in Labrador on the Atlantic coast and then the company's senior official in Canada. The confederation of 1867 threatened its future too, because an overland link between British Columbia on the Pacific Ocean and the other founding provinces in the east entailed settlement of the west. This region the company had kept empty, because tilled land yielded no furs. But it did not seek to stand in the way of political development, and sold its rights to the federal government.

In turn that created a problem in Manitoba, peopled by the Métis, a community of mixed blood, French-speaking and Roman Catholic, which had relied on the company for protection and employment.

They did not wish to join the confederation. In 1869 a band under their leader Louis Riel seized Fort Garry, now Winnipeg, and declared a provisional government: if the Canadians wanted this territory, they would have to fight for it. Luckily the Métis still trusted the company, and Smith was sent to negotiate with them. He clinched a deal with Riel and in the depth of winter the pair held a public meeting at the fort, addressing a crowd of 1,000 for five hours in the open air in a temperature of twenty degrees below zero.

They seemed to have stilled the people's fears and paved the way for a peaceful solution. But then a sudden outbreak of violence and bloodshed between Métis and local supporters of Canada threatened to burst the new confederation apart, since it divided French-speakers and English-speakers. The Prime Minister, Sir John Macdonald,* kept cool, mixing firmness with conciliation. In July 1870 a royal proclamation annexed to Canada the whole of North America above the 49th parallel. Macdonald then received delegates from Manitoba to draw up terms of entry into the confederation. He gave the Métis the guarantees they wanted for their religion and language. At the same time he assembled an expeditionary force of militiamen and a few British regulars, which in August advanced on Fort Garry. Riel did not stand and fight but fled into the United States. His rebellion collapsed, yet he had vindicated his people's rights, and the agreement he reached with Smith stood.

The Canadian Government launched, within a decade, policies for settlement of the west. In thirty years a fertile belt 200 miles deep along the American border was colonized. But it still had to be bound physically together. This led to one of the great engineering feats of the Victorian era, construction of the Canadian Pacific Railway. It was the brainchild of Smith's cousin, George Stephen, who exchanged his dreary life as a draper's apprentice in Aberdeen for the promise of the New World and made the fortune that would raise him to the House of Lords as Lord Mount Stephen. Smith, whose career inside the Hudson's Bay Company had elevated him into Canada's commercial elite, formed the syndicate to finance the project. The odds were formidable, and the syndicate almost went bankrupt. It had to be saved by an official subsidy together with lavish grants of land along the planned line, twenty-five million acres in all, which were sold to settlers while the directors awaited the inevitably slow returns. The railway was due to be completed by 1881, but not till four years later did Smith drive in the last spike at Craigellachiea in the Rocky Mountains, named after a village in Scotland.

From 1889 to 1914 Smith was Governor of the Hudson's Bay Company, in effect ruler of the desolate North-West Territories beyond the area of settlement in Canada. In his time its ways of life, with Indians living as before, exchanging furs from animals they hunted for goods from the company, scarcely changed. He continued to draw most of his officers from the thrifty, hard-working sons of northern Scotland, who indeed still man the company today. From 1896 he doubled as Canadian High Commissioner in London, with the title of Lord Strathcona.

Smith now took a hand in enterprises elsewhere. Lack of oil in the British Empire had become a worry, since this was a seaborne empire, carrying its commerce in merchant ships and protected by the Royal Navy. Oil came only from Scotland, from the deposits of shale in West Lothian, from Burma, where oil had been struck by a Glaswegian company, Burmah Oil, and from one or two other places. American production already far outstripped British production. The great hope was the Middle East, where Burmah Oil prospected and made a strike on the Persian Gulf. The Shah insisted on having a separate corporation formed to exploit his resources. In 1911 the Anglo-Persian Oil Company was set up, only to be restructured in the First World War, when the British Government acquired a big stake in it. It then became British Petroleum. At the outset it might better have been dubbed Scoto-Persian, since at least half its early directors came supplied by Burmah, while its inaugural chairman was Smith, in his last great venture before his death.

The final Scots Canadian in this North American section can most certainly be said to have changed the world, for he was the inventor of standard time zones.

SIR SANDFORD FLEMING (1827–1915)

Fleming was born in Kirkcaldy in Fife and emigrated to Quebec at the age of seventeen. He worked as a surveyor in Montreal, Ottawa and Halifax and was eventually given charge as surveyor of the greatest project of the time, the Canadian Pacific Railway. Fleming also promoted the first postage stamp for Canada and a trans-Pacific telegraph cable linking Vancouver with Australia.

As he set about his task of completing the Canadian Pacific, he realized that the timetable for such a railway would be a nightmare. Midday was judged to be the moment when the sun was directly overhead, which meant that noon in Kingston struck twelve minutes later than in Montreal and thirteen minutes sooner than in Toronto. At each station the travellers would be required to adjust their watches to local time, an interminable process on a trans-Canadian journey.

Fleming came up with the idea of establishing a system of universal time which would apply from Halifax to Victoria, but also from Paris to New Delhi. He divided the globe into twenty-four hourly zones; within each of these zones, the time would be the same everywhere. It was a simple and practical solution, but it proved much more difficult to persuade governments to put it into practice.

There were those who argued that it was 'communist' in its intent, and others who thought that it was contrary to the will of God, who had set the sun on its course. But Fleming persevered. His crowning moment came at the International Prime Meridian Conference, which took place in Washington DC, and the system came into being on 1 January 1885, earning him the title 'The Father of Standard Time'. Queen Victoria knighted him on the occasion of her Diamond Jubilee in 1897 and he went on to serve as Chancellor of the Queen's University in Kingston, Ontario. Today his memory lives on mainly through the college in Ontario which bears his name, yet without his initiative the world would be a much more confusing place.

Men of Science II

Electricity and Ether

In the latter half of the nineteenth century the Industrial Revolution moved into its second phase. The first had been accomplished by the application of mechanical inventions which produced major advances in the technology of heavy industry and gave Britain one of the world's most modern economies. Meanwhile Scottish scientists were turning their minds to the next stage of the process, which involved more penetrating analysis of the nature of matter with the purpose of manipulating it for practical ends. Here was the continuing drive for applied science which we noted in Part I as being distinctively Scottish. But it also contained an assumption that the universe worked according to certain principles, and that behind it all there was a unifying theory to be discovered. That was certainly the belief of the most decorated scientist of the nineteenth century:

WILLIAM THOMSON, LORD KELVIN (1824–1907)

The discoveries of Kelvin, one of the most respected scientists in the world during his lifetime, helped to lay the foundations of modern physics. He was not actually born in Scotland but, the fourth of seven children, in Belfast, where his father, of Scots origin, taught mathematics. The death of his mother when he was six drew William and his brother James closer to their father, who eagerly shared with them the most advanced mathematical theories of the time, some not yet taught in British universities. The appointment of their father as professor of mathematics in Glasgow resulted in these child prodigies matriculating at the university at the ages of ten and eleven respectively. Both boys went on to become professors of science there, but it is William the world remembers, under the name of Kelvin which he took as his title on being ennobled in 1892. The unit on the absolute temperature scale is named the Kelvin in his honour.

An early influence on Kelvin was *The Analytical Theory of Heat*, a work by the French mathematician Jean-Baptiste Joseph Fourier which described by a series of equations the flow of heat through a solid object. Kelvin was the first to realize that Fourier's equations could be applied to other forms of energy flow, such as fluids in motion or electricity flowing through a wire. At the age of sixteen he wrote a paper defending Fourier against his critics.

After Glasgow, Kelvin went on to Cambridge University, then worked in Paris at the laboratory of Henri-Victor Regnault. There he gained practical experience as he gradually formulated his ground-breaking theories of the ways in which heat and electricity are related and the interchangeability of forms of energy. In 1846 the chair of natural philosophy (i.e. physics) at Glasgow became vacant and his father easily persuaded his colleagues to invite his son to fill it. Kelvin remained at Glasgow until he retired in 1899 at the age of seventy-five, despite several tempting offers to go elsewhere.

As much action man as academic, he won several medals for rowing at Cambridge and participated in the hazardous transatlantic cable-laying operation, becoming an influential consultant on the project. It was a unique test of his equations on the flow of heat through solids, and they proved to be accurate in describing what would happen when current was passed through a telegraph cable stretched over 3,000 miles.

The chief electrician of the Atlantic Telegraph Company disputed the results but Kelvin's views eventually prevailed, the company adopting a telegraphic receiver patented by him in 1858. The device, called a mirror galvanometer, worked by the movement of a coil between two magnets attached to a mirror, which in turn deflected a beam of light on to a scale. Later modified as the siphon recorder, it came to be used on most of the telegraphic cables in the world. Knighted in 1866 for this work, his participation in engineering consulting firms during this boom era for telegraphy made him a wealthy man, with an estate near Largs and a 126-ton yacht. His yachting excursions resulted in a number of inventions: a type of compass, a form of analogue computer for measuring tides, and sounding equipment.

Kelvin's great legacy was in bringing together the latest developments in heat and electromagnetism. His whole career (like Einstein's a century later) was guided by a belief that the various theories about matter and energy were converging towards a single, grand unified theory – one by which all forms of energy could be tied together by mathematical formulae – even if such a theory might never be attainable. James Joule in 1847 advanced a hypothesis suggesting the interconvertibility of heat and motion. This met powerful resistance from his peers because it undermined the belief that heat was a substance (Joseph Black's caloric) rather than a form of dynamic energy. In 1851 Kelvin defended Joule's thesis in a paper with the title 'On the Dynamical Theory of Heat', which also contained his version of what became known as the second law of thermodynamics (this states that no heat engine can have an efficiency of 100 per cent because it is impossible to convert heat totally into mechanical work), one of the fundamental laws of physics.

He made a less distinguished contribution to the debate over Darwin's theory of evolution. At fifteen he had produced his highly original mathematical 'Essay on the Figure of the Earth', in which can be found the source of many of his ideas throughout his life. This led him to calculate that more than a million years ago the earth's temperature and the heat of the sun were much greater; the resulting environment would have been entirely different from that required to sustain Darwin's hypothesis. Published at the height of the evolution debate, Kelvin's views incurred the wrath of T.H. Huxley, the distinguished biologist and leading proponent of evolution; moreover, his calculations of the age of the earth and sun were very inaccurate, although he was correct to argue that any theory of geology or biology had to accord with the laws of physics.

He was also wrong about powered flight. Shortly after the first flight took place in 1908, General Baden-Powell asked his opinion of the new development. Kelvin wrote in reply, 'I have not an atom of faith in heavier than air machines. The future of air transport lies with balloons.'

His scientific partnerships with Joule, Tait (professor of physics at Edinburgh) and renowned German physicist Hermann von Helmholtz helped push forward the frontiers of science. Kelvin also helped shape the ideas of a fellow Scot who eventually surpassed him in significance, and ranks with Newton and Einstein among the great scientists of all time.

JAMES CLERK MAXWELL (1831–79)

There are similarities between the early lives of Kelvin and Maxwell. Both came from families with a scientific background and showed an amazing aptitude for mathematics as boys; both held to a strong religious faith throughout their lives; both lost their mothers at an early age (Maxwell when he was nine) and had a close relationship with their fathers which was far from the Victorian stereotype. But while Kelvin went happily off to university at the age of ten, Maxwell's father preferred to have his son's company at home at Glenlair, their country home in Galloway, and employed a sixteen-year-old tutor who beat James, whom he judged to be stupid. James developed his own method of dealing with this bully, and would on occasion mischievously produce a live frog from his mouth. Despite his unkind treatment he retained fond memories of his childhood home; later in life he returned to Glenlair as often as he could, to enjoy the life of a country gentleman.

At first he did not fare well at Edinburgh Academy where, as a late starter, he was a target for bullying. His strong Scots accent was mocked and he received the nickname 'daftie' from boys who mistook his thoughtful manner for stupidity. His considered air may have sprung from his short-sightedness, which was eventually rectified by spectacles. Yet despite such a discouraging start, by the time he was fourteen he had discovered mathematics and was able to write a paper thought good enough to be read to the Royal Society of Edinburgh.

Professor James Forbes, the man who did the reading on his behalf and who held the chair of natural philosophy at Edinburgh University, gave the boy the run of his private laboratory, there being no practical classes for undergraduates in physics at that period. During his student days at Edinburgh, a family friend took him on a visit to the scientist William Nicol, inventor of the Nicol Prism, a device by which geologists were able to analyse polarized light. Young James received a present of two prisms from Nicol, and he treasured them all his life.

Forbes and Nicol had sensed in Maxwell the potential which he now began to realize. Having moved to Cambridge University he began to interest himself in electromagnetism, and graduated with a first. In 1855 Maxwell applied for a professorship at Aberdeen University in order to be closer to his father, who had fallen ill, although by the time he took up the post in 1856 his father had died. At the time there were two colleges, Marischal and Kings, within Aberdeen University; Maxwell held the chair in Marischal. There he took the opportunity to introduce practical classes for his students and to begin research on the theory of gases. His brilliance was demonstrated by his proof (for which he won the Adams Prize from

Cambridge) that the rings of the planet Saturn were composed not of gas but of particles of matter.

He married the daughter of the college principal in 1858 and the couple spent the long vacations at Glenlair. It is possible that either of these factors may have been politically detrimental to his position in the university, for when the two Aberdeen colleges were amalgamated the following year (a move which Maxwell supported) it was the Kings professor who was appointed to the joint chair. Maxwell was out of a job. Passed over by Edinburgh for a vacant post in favour of an old classmate, P.G. Tait, he found himself at King's College, London in 1860, where he spent five highly productive years.

During this time he drew together his research in electricity and magnetism, expressing his theories in four simple equations now known as Maxwell's Equations. They provided a theoretical framework in which electricity, magnetism, light and X-rays were drawn together. All were seen to be waves and forms of energy. Together with radio waves they formed part of an invisible world which we now take for granted but which was yet to be revealed to people of the nineteenth century. Maxwell not only sensed this invisible world, he proved its existence by mathematics. To him alone belongs the credit for the most significant discovery of nineteenth-century science — the synthesis of electricity, magnetism and light.

He unravelled another link in the chain of the electromagnetic spectrum when he brought optics and light into his scheme. He was first to identify that the human eye has three kinds of receptors (to red, blue and green light) and that deficiency in one of these leads to colour blindness. His research also led him to take the first colour photograph. The crowning achievement for Maxwell's electromagnetic theory was his prediction as early as 1864 that an oscillating circuit would be the source of waves which would travel in free space at 3×10^8 metres per second, a rate equivalent to the speed of light; although this was not verified until 1887 by Heinrich Hertz.

In 1865 he returned to Glenlair, seeking time to look after the estate and complete his *Treatise on Electricity and Magnetism*. He regularly met and corresponded with Tait in Edinburgh and Kelvin in Glasgow, treating the latter as a mentor and freely acknowledging his debt to him. But Kelvin's theories on their own would not have carried physics forward into the twentieth century.

In 1871 Maxwell was recalled to Cambridge to become the first professor of experimental physics. He oversaw the setting up of the Cavendish Laboratory (donated by William Cavendish, Duke of Devonshire) and promoted research (including his own on gas movement) which established it a centre of excellence in physics. But tragedy struck in 1879 when cancer of the colon claimed the life of this outstanding genius.

Maxwell's discoveries about the nature of electromagnetic radiation opened up a whole new universe. The fruits of his theories were the invention of the telephone, fax, radio, radar, and television — all but one of them invented by Scotsmen.

ALEXANDER GRAHAM BELL (1847–1922)

The inventor of the telephone was not a physicist but made his first attempt at a 'speaking machine' by means of a deft exercise in zoology. Bell grew up in Edinburgh and after leaving school at the age of thirteen, spent a year with his paternal grandfather, then professor of elocution in the University of London. His father, Alexander Melville Bell, also taught elocution and when his son returned home, he challenged the boy to see if he could invent a voice machine. Bell senior knew that the boy had already shown some inventive ability, producing a device for de-husking cereal that employed rotating blades.

Alexander dissected a lamb's larynx obtained from a local butcher, noting the position of the vocal cords and building a model in which mechanical organs replaced them. By blowing through a tube linked to this, he was able to produce sounds. Then an Edinburgh schoolteacher called Philip Reis showed him another device he had made which he called a 'telephone'. It consisted of two boxes containing metal knitting needles, connected by electric wires fed from a battery. When someone spoke or played music into one box, the needle in the other vibrated, giving off a similar sound. But neither Bell nor Reis rushed to take advantage of the potential of the device at that time.

Instead Bell embarked on a career teaching deaf girls by means of a system invented by his father called Visible Speech, which employed symbols to represent words and letters. This had been developed for Bell's mother, who although profoundly deaf was able to play the piano by attaching her hearing tube to the sounding board. The Bell family suffered in addition from a more serious malaise — tuberculosis, which had claimed the lives of both Alexander's brothers. Bell was now showing symptoms. Believing the less polluted air of Canada would be better for his health, he decided to emigrate there. His parents, anxious not to be parted from their one remaining son, accompanied him.

Bell had already been acting as assistant to his father and stood in for him on several occasions. Being thereby eligible to apply for a teaching post himself, in 1872 he was appointed professor of vocal physiology at Boston University. Like his father, Bell fell in love with a deaf girl who later became his wife. The name of Bell's wife-to-be was Mabel Hubbard, and he began to experiment with instruments which might enable the deaf to hear. Dissecting a human ear obtained from the mortuary, he set out to construct an artificial ear using a magnet and a coil of electrified wire which could carry sounds to a similar device at the other end of a length of wire. On 2 June 1875, Bell and his assistant Thomas Watson tried to make it work without electrifying the wire with a battery on the lines of Reis's 'telephone'. With Watson in a downstairs room at the receiving end, Bell, from the attic of his house, uttered the famous words: 'Mr Watson, please come here, I want you.' A few moments later Watson appeared, shouting 'I could hear you!'

Bell registered a patent for his device on 14 February 1876. Having no business expertise, he sought the help of Mabel's father, who suggested putting the new invention on show at the Philadelphia Exhibition. The 'telephone' excited scant interest until the arrival of a group that included Kelvin,* fresh from laying a transatlantic cable, Professor Hendry, inventor of the electric bell, and the Emperor Pedro of Brazil, who had been one of Bell's pupils in Boston. When Pedro tried out the device he leapt with excitement, crying 'Great heavens! The thing talks!' A successful public demonstration followed in which Bell was stationed in Salem while Watson stood in Boston beside an organ that blared out 'Auld Lang Syne' and 'Yankee Doodle Dandy'. The crowd in Salem were ecstatic at what was effectively the first broadcast of music.

Mabel and Alexander, married in 1877, were accompanied on their honeymoon to England by the prototype telephones. Londoners were treated to a demonstration of telephony outside Bow Church; there passers-by in the street could pay a penny to say 'How do you do?' to a man on top of the steeple who would reply, 'Very well, thank you.' Queen Victoria tried out a model in her Isle of Wight retreat; so enthralled was she that she had a land-line telephone installed between there and London, by means of which an organ recital was relayed to her.

The telephone caught the public imagination in many countries. On returning to the United States in 1878, Bell found that New Jersey already had a system with 100 subscribers. Despite competition and litigation, the Bell system remained supreme, making him a fortune.

He went to live in Nova Scotia, where he became interested in the new sensation of powered flight, sponsoring the first flight by Canadians in 1908. In 1915, the first coast-to-coast telephone link in America was opened. Bell and Watson were at either end of it, but this time Watson replied to his superior's request to come and join him by saying, 'Thanks for the invitation, boss, but it would take me a week now.'

The irony of Bell's telephone is that the person for whom he created it, was never able to use it. Mabel remained stone deaf all her life. It is often assumed that the invention of the fax machine came long after that of the telephone, but in fact the fax was invented, by a Scottish clockmaker, over thirty years before Bell registered his patent.

ALEXANDER BAIN (1811—77)

Bain was born in 1811 in Watten, right at the northern tip of Scotland. After hearing a penny lecture at the age of twelve he decided that science was for him. Since his parents lacked the means, and he was far from the centres of learning, he trained as a clock-maker in Edinburgh and migrated to London to the district of Clerkenwell, then famed for its watches and clocks.

His first patent, in January 1841, was for an electric clock worked by an electromagnetic pendulum and later that year he registered another, in conjunction with Lieutenant Thomas Wright, RN, for a means of controlling railway engines remotely by electricity by turning off the steam, and giving signals. It included a significant departure from the 'moving needle' telegraph of Wheatstone. Instead of pivoting the needle by an electrified coil, Bain suspended a moveable coil which the current crossed, between the poles of a fixed magnet, in a similar way to Kelvin's* siphon recorder.

In 1844 Bain produced his next invention – a device for measuring the speed of ships using electric current produced by vanes revolving in the water behind the ship. At the same time he outlined a device for sounding the depth of the sea by means of electrical signals, and another which would set off a fire alarm when the mercury in a thermometer had risen sufficiently to complete an electrical circuit.

By 1846 Bain had returned to live in Edinburgh and it was here that he patented his greatest invention – the 'chemical telegraph', the prototype of the modern fax machine. Recognizing that the telegraph systems then in operation were slow because they involved mechanical actions such as the tapping of keys or the movement of a beam of light, he reckoned that the process of information transfer could be speeded up if the signal currents could be made to inscribe a mark on a band of travelling paper. The sending machine scanned an image or text line by line, emitting an electrical signal which was at one strength if it encountered ink and at another if it found only white paper. At the other end the receiving machine did the same in reverse, except that the electrical signal made a mark on chemically treated paper (a solution of ammonium nitrate and potassium prussiate which turned blue when the current passed through it).

The problem of co-ordinating the movements was solved by synchronizing pendulums which moved in unison so that the electric scan made at the sending end was echoed by the movements of the electric 'pen' and paper at the other.

The Italian inventor Giovanni Caselli developed a version called a pantelegraph, involving eight-foot pendulums; this in 1860 sent 282 words in fifty-two seconds from Paris to Amiens. In the hands of Edison, Bain's method was demonstrated to Kelvin at the Centennial Exhibition in Philadelphia, operating at a rate of 1,057 words in fifty-seven seconds. It was cumbersome but still much faster than the Morse method, which could only manage forty words per minute.

Bain's method was used in England on the lines of the Old Telegraphic Company. In the USA it was taken up by Henry O'Reilly, but Samuel Morse succeeded in raising an injunction against it on the slender grounds that the paper was covered by his patent, and the Bain chemical telegraph was confined to the Boston–Montreal line.

Unhappily for Bain, it was not until the 1920s that the rotating drum method of facsimile transmission was widely used in sending pictures for newspapers, and only from the 1970s was the process used in offices.

In 1847 Bain produced an 'orchestrion', which employed a perforated piece of paper to play wind instruments in the same way as a pianola, and another device to play keyed instruments at a distance by means of electric current. But his capacity for invention seems to have become exhausted after his earlier reversals. He received a considerable sum for his creation of the chemical telegraph and went to America, but there lost most of his money. Returning to live in Hammersmith in 1852, he fell gradually into ill-health and poverty. Kelvin and others obtained a Civil List pension for him of £80 per year, though he was living in such obscurity that at first he could not be tracked down for payment to be made.

In his latter years he resided in Glasgow, where heart problems and paralysis in his legs caused him to be put in a Home for Incurables at Kirkintilloch. He died there on 2 January 1877 and was buried in the Old Aisle cemetery. By this time he was a widower, although he had a son in America and a daughter living in Europe. Bain's story is a tragic one. His fertile and inventive mind triumphed over his poor upbringing and lack of education to produce a series of precocious inventions, but they are largely unknown even in his native land. Unlike our next inventor, who achieved fame if not fortune from his invention, Bain was fated to enjoy neither.

Broadcasting has made the world a smaller place, and two of the greatest figures in the development of radio and television were from a small corner of Scotland. What is more, they were both sons of Presbyterian ministers and they studied engineering at the same time in the Royal Technical College in Glasgow, which we met earlier under its previous title of Andersonian University and which is now Strathclyde University. In another twist of fate and coincidence, it fell to one of these men, John Reith,* to reject the invention of the other.

JOHN LOGIE BAIRD (1888–1946)

The career of the inventor of television began somewhat bizarrely. On graduating in 1914, Baird was given a job as an assistant mains engineer with the Clyde Valley Electrical Company. Upon the outbreak of the First World War he volunteered for active service but was rejected because of his poor health. He also suffered, literally, from cold feet. Employing his spare time to valuable effect, he developed his first invention, the Baird Undersock — 'keeps the feet warm in winter and cool in summer' — made by impregnating cotton socks with borax.

But his ill-health forced him to seek a better climate than the West of Scotland. Sock profits financed a move to Port of Spain in the West

Indies. The island was heavy with fruit and Baird decided to produce jams and chutneys for sale. Unfortunately his 'factory', where the fruit was mixed with sugar cane and boiled, proved to be a magnet for millions of insects. On one occasion Baird was seen fleeing the premises clad only in his trousers as the creatures rained down on the sticky cauldron. He packed his wares into crates and arrived back in London, where he tried unsuccessfully to sell them from a small shop in Lupus Street.

His next venture was Baird's Speedy Cleaner, a soap for cleaning floors. This enterprise foundered soon after a mother used the product on her baby's bottom; the child's skin, turned angry red and the woman even angrier. Baird moved to Hastings on the south coast, low in spirits and funds. While living there he invented a glass razor blade and a pair of shoes with pneumatic soles. The former nearly severed an artery and the latter had such bounce they almost propelled him over the cliffs at Hastings.

Baird liked to joke about his failures, but he was remarkably secretive about an idea for transmitting images electronically which came to him as he walked on those cliffs.

His room at 8 Queens Arcade became a jungle of boxes, wires and valves and eventually he succeeded in transmitting a shadow of a cardboard box across the room. At this time several experimenters in different parts of the world were trying to achieve the same result, but Baird was the first to make a working device. Elated, in better health and with the help of investors, he was able to move his operations to an attic in Frith Street, London in 1925, and mounted a three-week demonstration of his television at Harrods department store, for which he was paid £60. He approached the Marconi Company, who replied they were not interested.

There was a more positive reaction to his demonstration at the Royal Institution in January 1926; it was followed by a test transmission between Frith Street and the BBC radio studios at Savoy Hill. Soon he was able to move to more spacious premises near Leicester Square, founding a company called Television Ltd with £500. He also produced 'Noctavision', through which, by means of infra-red light, he was able to transmit pictures of people sitting in total darkness. In 1928 he produced colour television at a demonstration in Glasgow using his system of rotating discs with spirals of holes covered by blue, red and green filters. The discs were aligned so that the holes allowed through the necessary beam of red, blue or green light in order to produce a picture. He even managed the same year to make a short-wave transmission of a television picture to the USA and send another to a ship, the *Berengaria*, in mid-Atlantic.

To exploit the invention, Baird International Television was launched with capital of £1 million and Baird was made managing director. The BBC had begun transmissions in 1928; thirty people who had bought Baird receivers were able to tune in. Synchronization of the sound and picture had been a problem, but it was overcome by 1930 when Gracie Fields sang during the first synchronized transmission. Baird scored another success with a big-screen version of television, erecting in a cinema, the London Coliseum, a screen of ground glass behind which were 2,100 light bulbs. In 1932 he televised the Derby from Epsom racecourse. Now famous and prosperous, he married the daughter of a South African diamond merchant and set sail for America to launch his television system.

It was then that Baird's fortunes received three significant setbacks from which he was never to recover. The first was the failure of television to take off in the USA; television had started there in 1928 but by 1933 had closed down because of its inability to cover large distances and consequently to attract enough advertising. The second was the resistance to television of the BBC's Director-General, John Reith, Baird's erstwhile fellow student, who was yet to be persuaded that it had a future. By the time the BBC had realized it would need to embrace television, a third and formidable threat to Baird's dominance of the field had manifested itself.

The problem was a technical one. Baird's system scanned pictures mechanically employing 204 lines per image. An alternative system developed by Marconi-EMI used a cathode-ray scanning system which gave 405 lines per image. In 1934 the two systems were set against each other. The British government committee charged with choosing between them proposed that for two years the two systems should have alternate weeks of transmission and the BBC should then decide which one to adopt. Baird lost.

The tragedy for Baird was that his system could produce colour and even stereoscopic images, and Marconi's could not. He remained in business through Gaumont cinemas, who showed his colour transmissions on large screens during the late thirties. His receivers were selling well but in 1939 television was stopped in Britain when war broke out. Baird resisted offers from America, continuing to work on a high-definition colour television receiver which could project a picture on to a large screen. He met the objections to his mechanical scanning system by developing a two-colour (blue/green and red) cathode-ray system. With this he transmitted a picture of a dummy dressed in pink and blue to a group of journalists in 1944, a generation before colour television became available in Britain. Unfortunately Baird died in 1946 before he could realize the potential of his invention. It was only much later that the significance of his role in the development of television was truly appreciated.

JOHN REITH, LORD REITH (1889–1971)

Although an engineer by training, John Reith will be remembered not for any technical advance he brought to the field of broadcasting but as the patriarch of public service broadcasting through the BBC, the institution which has served as a model for broadcasting organizations since its inception in 1922. The word patriarch properly catches the Old Testament flavour of this complex and flawed man whose energy and passions were as often channelled into petty hatreds, jealousies and lusts as they were into defending the independence of the institution he helped to create.

Reith held the principle that broadcasting should exist to promote education and the arts, and to inform the public on a basis which was free from commercial pressures, propaganda needs or audience figures. Born in Stonehaven the son of a Free Church minister, he stood well over six feet in height, cutting an awesome figure as he pursued this doctrine with tyrannical zeal. For him it had the force of a moral principle. His favourite quotation was from Kant: 'the starry heavens above me; the moral law within me', but sadly a governor summing up his sixteen-year reign at the BBC was nearer the mark when he said, 'Reith was one of those who never grow out of the illusion Carlyle denounced so passionately: the illusion that the world was made for them.'

Reith's early years were dominated by a friendship with Charlie Bowser, a boy nine years his junior whose parents lived near his father's manse in Glasgow. This love (for no other word can describe the torrent of infatuation, jealousy and hatred towards Bowser which were preserved in his private diaries) holds as much a key to his character as anything which emerged during his long public career. Charlie followed him into the army in the First World War. Reith became engaged to Muriel, the girl Charlie had been courting. Bowser accepted this, but Reith decided he must find a girl for his friend and then proceeded to have jealous rages over Bowser's impending marriage, eventually breaking with him but returning obsessively in his diary to the subject of Bowser long into old age.

These pre-Freudian passions seem not to belong to the twentieth century, but they are further complicated by the series of love affairs with younger women which Reith had throughout his career. Yet this was the same man who asked applicants for jobs at the BBC in the tone of a Grand Inquisitor if they accepted the 'fundamental teachings of Our Lord Jesus Christ', who demanded that female members of staff resign on marrying, and who dismissed male employees if they divorced their wives. Reith was as maniacal and self-contradictory as King David in the Book of Samuel.

Wounded in the head in the First World War, he had a taste of bureaucracy in munitions work for the British Government in the USA before returning to be general manager for the engineering firm of Beardmore's in Coatbridge. In both jobs, Reith's views were that others did not conform to his exacting standards. He resigned from

Beardmore's in 1922 in disgust when orders he believed he had been promised did not materialize and the firm looked like having to close.

In London, seeking another job, he saw an advertisement for a general manager of the BBC and wrote to Sir William Noble, chairman of the appointing committee, 'I am an Aberdonian and you probably know my family ...' Reith was appointed and in the political turmoil of the twenties, his instinct to avoid partisan commitment and defend his own interest proved to be an advantageous policy. It kept the BBC above the fray in the fraught atmosphere of the General Strike in 1926 when the Government was pressing to take control of the news. Winston Churchill wrote, 'I first quarrelled with Reith in 1926 over the General Strike. He behaved quite impartially between the strikers and the nation. I said he had no right to be impartial between the fire and the fire-brigade.'

Reith's ego occasionally got in the way of his impartiality. A newsreader had the election results snatched from him so that Reith could read them himself. When the man tried to point out that listeners were ringing in to complain they could not hear him, he was fired for his trouble. Life under Reith was never dull. Although tyrannical, he did succeed in making the BBC an important patron for creative arts when it could have become a vehicle simply for entertainment and news. His other great achievement was to win the right for the BBC to control foreign language and overseas broadcasting on the same impartial basis as the domestic services, although it was funded by the Government. The BBC World Service still enjoys that status today.

As the thirties ended and war loomed, Prime Minister Chamberlain called Reith in and pressed him to move on. His mania was hardly satisfied by a succession of jobs such as chairman of Imperial Airways, then (during the war) successively Minister of Information, Transport and Works, none of which he said ever 'stretched' him. He hoped to be made Viceroy of India or ambassador to the USA but no offer came.

Reith fought against the introduction of commercial broadcasting, designed to break the monopoly of the BBC in the mid-fifties. He passed the sixties in bitterness, at his daughter Marista's marriage to a Kirk minister, inveighing against changes at the BBC (he described *Juke Box Jury* as 'evil') and complaining that his potential had not been used. At his death he left an estate of only £76 net, £6,155 gross for the long-suffering Muriel. Their son Christopher renounced the title, but the word 'Reithian' remains in the dictionary, defined as 'the responsibility of broadcasting to enlighten and educate public taste'.

ROBERT WATSON WATT (1892–1973)

Historians of the Second World War mostly agree that the Battle of Britain in 1940 was crucial, and that had the German air attack not been successfully repelled, Britain would have lost the war early on. The greatest credit rightly belongs to the Spitfire and Hurricane pilots, 'the few' who intercepted the enemy squadrons, but it must be shared with the inventor of the device which enabled them to know where and when to head the Luftwaffe off.

That device was radar. Its inventor, Robert Watson Watt, was born at Brechin in Angus and studied engineering at Queen's College, Dundee, then part of the University of St Andrews. After graduating in 1912, Watson Watt was offered an assistantship by Professor William Peddie, whose work in radio waves was of particular interest to the young man. The principle that objects could be tracked by bouncing radio signals off them was already known, but no one had been able to apply it effectively. On taking a post at the Royal Aircraft Factory at Farnborough in 1915, Watson Watt investigated the use of radio in tracking thunderstorms and assisting aircraft to avoid them. He needed a means to display the radio signals visually and hit upon the idea of using cathode-ray oscilloscopes for this purpose. Unfortunately these did not become widely available until 1923.

The following year Watson Watt moved to work in Slough where the Radio Research Station had been formed. In 1927 it merged with the National Physics Laboratory and he became superintendent of the establishment at Slough, then in 1933 he moved to head a new radio department at Teddington. H.E. Wimperis in the Air Ministry knew that Britain at the time was severely under-equipped in military terms and asked if Watson Watt could look into the possibility of developing a 'death ray'.

Watson Watt and his assistant Arnold Wilkins soon realized that the energy levels required to 'microwave' the crew of an aeroplane flying thousands of feet away were unattainable. Instead, in a paper of February 1935 entitled 'The Detection of Aircraft by Radio Methods', they came up with a less dramatic suggestion. The problem was how to avoid the strong outgoing radio signal overwhelming the weaker echo coming back, and how to separate the two. Watson Watt solved this partly by pulsing the outgoing signal so that the echo was received in the 'gaps between pulses'. He engineered a rotating scanner to catch these echoes and display them via a cathode-ray oscilloscope, which turned the weak signals into blips of light. Within a month Sir Henry Tizard, the new head of a committee set up to oversee scientific developments in air defence, had organized a secret demonstration of the technique using the BBC's short-wave transmitter at Daventry to track and detect a Heyford bomber. After a successful trial, in 1936 Watson Watt moved to Bawdsley Manor near Felixstowe to head a team to develop the device. A chain of radar stations along the east and south coast of England (Chain Home and Chain Home Low) were completed in time for the outbreak of war in 1939.

Knighted for his efforts in 1942, Watson Watt was content to live quietly in retirement and did not seek public recognition. After the war, the Government showed their gratitude for his invention with a payment of £50,000. Had it been peacetime and had he patented his secret weapon, he would have been a millionaire.

Our final physicist is synonymous with the device he invented and acclaimed for the part it played in advancing particle physics, a science which has done much to enlarge our understanding of matter and energy.

CHARLES T.R. WILSON (1869–1959)

When Charles Wilson was presented with the Nobel Prize for Physics in 1927, his mind went back to the moment he stood on the summit of Ben Nevis, Scotland's highest mountain, in the late summer of 1894. Awestruck by the beauty of the coronas and 'glories', or coloured rings which surrounded the shadows cast on the clouds and mist, he decided at that moment to try to reproduce those effects in the Cavendish Laboratory in Cambridge where he worked.

Wilson was the son of a farmer at Glencorse near Edinburgh (within sight of the research unit which recently developed Dolly, the first cloned animal). His father died when he was four and the family moved to Manchester, where he went on to study at Owen's College (now the University of Manchester) with a view to becoming a physician. Instead he followed in the footsteps of another Owen's student of a decade earlier, J.J. Thomson (himself later to make an important contribution to particle physics), by taking up physics at Cambridge where he graduated in 1892. His attempts to recreate the weather of Ben Nevis in a jar led to the creation of the cloud chamber which is named after him and which the father of the atom, Charles Rutherford, described as 'the most original and wonderful instrument in scientific history'.

Wilson produced a vessel in which he could, by means of a piston, rapidly expand and thus cool water vapour; the vapour would condense on any particles present, making them visible. He had deduced that the few drops which appeared time and again as he expanded a volume of moist, dust-free air might be the result of condensation on nuclei, possibly ions in the atmosphere. In 1896 he illustrated this with X-rays, then newly discovered. It fitted in with the discovery by J.J. Thomson and Rutherford that air was made conductive by the passage of X-rays. Wilson's prototype device showed this as tiny condensation tracks in the chamber. His teaching responsibilities after 1900 prevented him from developing the chamber as he wished, but in 1911 he was the first person to see and photograph alpha and beta particles and electrons as they appeared in his device as 'little wisps and threads of clouds'.

The Wilson cloud chamber was involved in many of the breakthroughs in atomic physics. As splitting the atom became commonplace, it was the means by which many of the new particles contained in its nucleus were seen for the first time. Electrons, protons and the component parts of nuclear fission all had their distinctive tracks. The more bulky the particle the larger the trail it left. Later, when it became possible to accelerate atomic particles and force them to collide, the splinters and sub-particles which resulted could be viewed and photographed for later study as they emerged into the cloud chamber as tiny trails, each with its significant 'fingerprint'.

Wilson himself was awarded the Nobel Prize in 1937 jointly with A.H. Compton for their discovery of the Compton effect, in which an electron absorbs a photon, forming an intermediate particle which then splits apart into an electron and photon of different wavelength. CTR, as his friends and colleagues called him, went on to make further studies in thunderstorm electricity and carried out many observations on atmospheric electricity not far from his birthplace in Glencorse. He retired to live near there at Carlops when he was eighty and would travel into Edinburgh by bus to lunch with fellow physicists until his death at the age of ninety.

5

Writers

Pens Mightier than Swords

Scots love to express themselves in song and poetry yet, in one of the many Scottish paradoxes, their greatest contributions to literature have come in prose: in the novel and in a vast body of readable nonfiction, ranging from journalism to what we now call the social sciences. This corpus of writings in its turn reflects the disparities of the national character. It often shows a profound and passionate love of place, of people and of history. It can create a brooding sense of magic and mystery which is tempered by an inborn scepticism. Esteem of status and talent need not contradict a strong belief in the merit of each individual, however humble. Much Scottish literature shows also a reverence for the communal, more often on a local than a national scale, and this furnishes it, even when the writers were Tories (as many were), with a democratic essence. Calvinist religion taught Scots about the folly of humanity and the fleeting nature of worldly things, yet some writers were astute men of affairs accumulating wealth and property like any crass materialist.

The past is alive for Scots, and the best authors have made it alive for their readers, yet they usually remained men of their times, with the ideas, aims and hopes of their fellows. Their vision may be blurred by a streak of wildness and anarchy, yet not wholly at the cost of clarity and logic. Their poetry, like the turbulent history of the country, is often sorrowful, yet they offer sound common sense too. These oppositions within Scottish culture have gained mythic status, though it must be conceded that masculine, rational, logical, material values have had the upper hand in shaping it, to the detriment of the feminine, imaginative, intuitive and spiritual values. It is thus an imbalanced culture, but one which has not lost sight of its inherent alternative, always hovering somewhere in the background in an attachment to family, community and landscape. We begin with Robert Burns, where this side of things comes to the fore. It may signify a gradual change in national temper that modern Scots take him as being, of all their writers, the most representative of themselves.

ROBERT BURNS (1759–96)

At the opening, or reopening, of the Scottish Parliament in July 1999 one of the most memorable moments arrived when the singer, Sheena Wellington, performed the traditional version of Robert Burns's 'A Man's a Man for A' That'. Till then it had been a day of joy in the sunshine, of admiration for the pageantry or of curiosity about the refurbished interior of the Assembly Hall in Edinburgh. But suddenly all that ceased and those present, even those watching on television, felt themselves face to face with some essence of Scottishness over which a veil is usually drawn, since Scots are not a race at ease with their emotions. The message was of the brotherhood of man, of the trifling nature of outward differences when we are all the same inside. It brought home to the spectators that this was what they wanted their new Parliament to be about, and for this they wished the Scots to regain their place among the nations. Hearts surged and tears came to many eyes.

It remains to be seen whether political realities will match the hopes awakened at that moment, but it did confirm Burns's place in the affections of the nation — not that this needed much confirmation. In the whole of English-speaking civilization there is no other who approaches his position as the people's poet, one adopted by ordinary men and women as their own, seeing their experience reflected in his verse so that he becomes part of their lives. A poet's reputation is normally determined either by his peers and similar literary persons, who nowadays find little of interest in Burns, or else in the modern world inevitably by academics, who exhibit a similar indifference even though he is without doubt the best British poet between Alexander Pope and William Wordsworth. None of this in any way diminishes the acclamation of Scots for Burns. Nor is it empty acclamation, because they also read him, learn him and recite him. Wherever three or four of them are gathered together, there is bound to be one who has a poem or several poems of Burns off by heart — the whole of *Tam O'Shanter* is by no means uncommon. Many more will know his lovely, simple, moving songs, either written by himself or rescued from the peasant society around him which was about to descend into dissolution. And every year on his birthday, 25 January, Scots remember him with public recitation of his poems and public performance of his songs, however far they may be from the hills of home.

The greatest Scottish poet of the twentieth century, Hugh MacDiarmid,* found this idolatry distasteful. He could never make up his mind if he really liked Burns. He was an intellectual, whereas Burns was instead a creature of pure feeling. MacDiarmid thought this a deficiency, to be blamed ultimately on the decay of the Scottish mind since the Union. Yet, for better or worse, Burns's fullness and directness of feeling, without hypocrisy or bathos but to the exclusion of almost everything else, are what make him the people's poet (something MacDiarmid, to his chagrin, never became). Burns is foremost a poet of affection and love, often directly of physical love, because he can render the pleasure of the fleeting moment. And his affection may extend beyond old friends, drinking companions or rustic eccentrics, beyond human beings altogether to a horse or a dog, to a mouse or a louse. Burns is also aware of serious matters, though.

He had had Calvinism drummed into him (without its making much impression), he knew about the tragic history of Scotland, he was stirred by the French Revolution: all these he turned, one way or another, into poetry. But nothing could be more unlike religious or political poetry as we otherwise understand it. What count with Burns are the feelings aroused in him by the stimulus of facts and ideas, not the facts and ideas themselves. His reaction to theology is to proclaim that it matters not a fig to him if the church tries to fix a straitjacket on errant human nature, that he would rather take the devil's part and proclaim his joy in the world of the senses than accept as a snare and a delusion the delight he has felt there. He could turn without a blush from nostalgia for the Jacobites to praise for the Tree of Liberty, celebrating two diametrically opposed political movements because they appealed alike to his generous nature. He had politics of a sort as simple as his emotions, politics based on belief in the natural right to freedom of the individual. What he did not have, because it could distort and crush, was an ideology. Those modern Scots who try to give him one have got him wrong.

Perhaps he is finally so attractive as a poet because he is so attractive as a man, a poor fellow who suffered hardship, sickness and early death, yet who never gave up. He was often worried, even fearful, yet he does not give the impression of being deeply unhappy. Great men do not always need a long life. In his thirty-seven years he achieved much, and he must have known this: not only his own poetry, but also the recording of a vast archive of Scottish song, preserved in James Johnson's *Scots Musical Museum*. He transcended the limits of his own condition, and to many Scots it must still seem that he helps them to transcend the limits of theirs.

Burns's contemporary Michael Bruce (1746–67), the Loch Leven poet, died young before his promise was fulfilled. His legacy was many of the Scottish Paraphrases (hymns based on passages of the Bible), such as 'O God of Bethel', which are still sung in churches. Another contemporary was James Hogg, known as the Ettrick Shepherd, later a friend of Sir Walter Scott,* remembered now not so much for his poetry as for the dark novella *The Rise and Fall of a Justified Sinner*, which dealt with the same themes that R.L. Stevenson* explored in *Dr Jekyll and Mr Hyde*. But one poet did enjoy greater fame than Burns in the latter half of the eighteenth century, although few know of him today. He was the author of an epic poem which was the talk of drawing rooms throughout Europe at the time.

JAMES MACPHERSON (1736—96)

The sense of being at the extremity of things, of living in an outpost of civilization, has been a constant in the modern Scottish psyche. During the eighteenth century this sense was fed by the fact that half of Scotland remained, at least in the estimation of the other half, primitive. Two rebellions arose in the Highlands in this period, and at the height of the Scottish Enlightenment the clansmen had only just been subdued. Lowlanders regarded these brother Scots with a mixture of fascination and horror.

But that was the making of more than one literary man who came from the borderland between culture and barbarism. Among them was James Macpherson, born on the fringes of the Highlands at Kingussie, who was to renew his contact with the primitive in later life in another quarter of the globe, as secretary to the colonial Governor of Florida from 1764. Scots often befriended Indians on the frontier, and Macpherson travelled among them. But, finding little to admire, he advocated that they should be subdued by armed force. After a couple of years he quarrelled with his employer and went home.

In his absence he had grown famous all over Europe for his poetry, which up to then had failed to make him any money and had sent him to seek his fortune in America. Macpherson had regarded himself as a poet from his early years. While still a student at Aberdeen University, he began composing a long and rather turgid work called *The Highlander*. His professor there, Thomas Blackwell, had written a *Life of Homer* arguing that the greatest epic poetry was always written in societies passing from barbarism to civilization. Macpherson hoped to exploit that.

In 1759 he happened to go on holiday to Moffat, the little spa in Dumfriesshire. There he met one of the young literary lions of the Enlightenment in Edinburgh, John Home, himself the author of a tragedy called *Douglas*, at the premiere of which had arisen the famous cry, 'Whaur's yer Wullie Shakespeare noo?' The pair got talking of Gaelic poetry and Macpherson claimed to have some examples. He translated them for Home, who was impressed and sent copies to various critics. They, too, felt full of admiration, indeed excitement. Macpherson hardened up his story: these were extracts, he said, from an epic poem 9,000 lines long which an old man in the mountains of Lochaber had off by heart. But it would be desirable to get a manuscript. Macpherson's new friends commissioned him to go and find one.

He whetted their appetite in 1760 by publishing his *Fragments of Ancient Poetry Collected in the Highlands*. Then he set off for the north with his cousin, Ewan Macpherson, himself a Gaelic poet and more fluent in the language than James. They did find manuscripts, and copied down ballads recited to them. James took all the papers to Edinburgh and sat down to knock them into shape. Before the year was over he brought out *Fingal, an epic*, alleged to have been created by Ossian, a bard of the third century who was also son of Fingal, the Scottish counterpart of the Irish hero Finn.

The work caused a huge sensation. Ossian's poem became the most famous of the eighteenth century, in Scotland and beyond. To Scots it proved that they had a corpus of ancient poetry as rich as any and, more to the point, older than English literature. But the English were less susceptible to its charms (along with David Hume* who, while impressed at first, said Macpherson must produce his sources to establish the poem's authenticity). In particular Dr Samuel Johnson branded it a fraud. This was difficult for Macpherson to refute. There were, and are, Gaelic poems referring to Ossian, but none like the Greek *Iliad* or the German *Nibelungenlied* setting out the whole legend. And Macpherson did have his manuscripts, though none with this actual poem in them. Before long, it was being widely concluded that he had forged the Ossianic epic. Macpherson published another poem, *Temora*, more original and less successful, but his literary career had reached its end.

That reckoned without the reaction in Europe, where Ossian took off and was soon translated into several languages. Sophisticated Europeans viewed it as an unsuspected elemental substratum of western culture which gave a vital stimulus to the birth of the Romantic movement. It had arrived just in time, as weariness set in with Enlightenment philosophy. Its greatest admirer was the Emperor Napoleon, who took an Italian version with him on all his campaigns, and eventually into exile on St Helena. He liked it so much that he had his palaces in Paris and Rome decorated with enormous murals of scenes from the epic, notably one where Ossian welcomes home the ghosts of dead heroes. Given this immense popularity, the poem's authenticity did not really matter. Modern scholarship is anyway inclined to take a more generous view than the early critics. There was nothing but fragments for Macpherson to collect and a conjectural reconstruction of the whole poem, which probably had existed in oral form in the distant past, was not in itself an illegitimate use of the material. If we discount the English preju- dice of the time against Scotland, and especially against the least civilized part of Scotland, Macpherson deserves credit for his work.

SIR WALTER SCOTT (1771–1832)

The fourth chapter of Sir Walter Scott's *The Heart of Midlothian* is dramatic. It is set in Edinburgh in 1736, after the condemnation of Captain Porteous, commander of the City Guard, for opening fire on spectators to maintain order at an execution. As a result he has in his turn been sentenced to death, but now he gets a reprieve which arrives from London just when he is about to be led to his doom. Scott creates an uneasy sense of foreboding as he describes the crowd in the Grassmarket breaking up, disappointed of a death on the scaffold there.

The author at this point is preparing our minds for one of the most famous scenes in literature, when Porteous is dragged that night from the Tolbooth and hanged by the mob nevertheless. Scott reinforces this pause in the action by focusing on a group of citizens climbing back up the West Bow into the city. We walk along with them. We hear their voices. Of course they speak Scots. One utters a sentence often quoted to sum up the political predicament of Unionist Scotland: 'I ken, when we had a king, and a chancellor, and parliament-men o' our ain, we could aye peeble them wi' stanes when they were na gude bairns — but naebody's nails can reach the length o' Lunnon.' Being ordinary folk, they do not spend long on the great issues of the time and soon return to concerns of their own.

Two of them are bores: Saddletree, a shopkeeper learned in the law, and Butler, a schoolmaster who constantly corrects his Latin. They wrangle without listening to each other over pedantic points of syntax and statute. Eavesdropping, the reader can observe how Scott captures the stubborn disputatiousness of his countrymen, although he softens it here into relative amiability. But then, watching more closely, the reader may catch darker clouds flitting across this scene.

These people are not just blinkered in a comical kind of way. They are actually callous and indifferent to the drama of life and death in the midst of which they find themselves. They complain at wasting money on good seats for an execution which has not taken place. Somebody recalls how her own granddaughter might have been shot dead when Porteous opened fire, because little children like to creep close to the scaffold at a hanging. Or again, perhaps all this is not so much callousness and indifference as the fortitude and resilience with which Calvin's God has endowed his Covenanted people, able to laugh at fate because they are sure they can brave it.

The range to be found even in the most prosaic pages of Scott is one of the main reasons why he is starting to come back into fashion again after long neglect. Internationally famous in his own lifetime and for several decades afterwards, he suffered in the twentieth century a rapid decline in reputation. He was too turgid for the modern reader and his interests were too outdated, even in his native Scotland – perhaps especially in his native Scotland, where he could be readily dismissed as a prosy old Tory. But that was in a world and a Scotland more certain of their values than is now the case.

At the turn of the millennium, Scots especially are living through a period of helter-skelter change of which the outcome is unknowable. Other countries may be reasonably sure that ten years on, even while things may move along, they will look fairly much as they do today. Scots have not the slightest idea how their country is going to look in ten years' time. The conceivable extremities vary from dingy province to harebrained republic, though more pleasant possibilities do exist in between. Scott lived through such a period too, though of course the pace in his day was very much slower. But there is hardly one of his Scottish novels that does not begin with something like the formula that opens *The Heart of Midlothian*:

> *The times have changed in nothing more than in the rapid conveyance of intelligence and communication betwixt one part of Scotland and another. It is not above twenty or thirty years...*

An acute sense of movement lies behind them all, together with a fear of crashing which Scott constantly struggles to overcome. We have a revolution in electronic communications whereas he had the first Industrial Revolution, turning Scotland from a nation of feudal lords and peasants into one of capitalists and workers. We have devolution whereas he had political change in the opposite direction, with radicals intent on destroying whatever the Treaty of Union had preserved of the old Scotland and instead pursuing anglicization, in the Whig conviction that England meant progress and Scotland meant reaction.

A man of his time, Scott loved some aspects of progress: he lit up with gas-lamps the antiquarian make-believe of Abbotsford, the country house he built for himself in the Borders south of Edinburgh. He hated other aspects, and was reduced to tears in warning his

Whig friends (despite being political foes, they remained good friends) that little by little their well-meant reforms would destroy everything that made Scotland Scotland. Out of that particular thought he was deeply moved by an impulse to save Scotland, a difficult enterprise because the heritage of the Scottish past was already being enfeebled and fragmented around him.

The task he set himself culminated in the visit of George IV in 1822, the first time a reigning monarch had set foot on Scottish soil in nearly two hundred years. This visit reinvented Scotland, forging an image of the nation which for better or worse has proved permanent, blending the bravery and romance of the Highlander with the good sense and loyalty of the Lowlander. Scotland in the past had so often been torn apart or had torn herself apart. In the imagination, or even in fantasy, she might become immune to this destruction and self-destruction. That was what Scott wanted to achieve. And he did achieve it.

Except, of course, that Scott's Scotland in this form strikes the modern Scot as faintly preposterous (as indeed it struck some of his contemporaries). Embarrassment, a feeling that this is a man we do not really want to know about, has contributed to the reaction against him and helped to demote him from his former eminence as a supreme master of literature who was both popular and profound.

Walter Scott and Robert Burns* were once equals in Scottish affections, but Burns has overtaken Scott. Burns is more the paragon of what modern Scots would like to be, and is revered on that account. The fact that his cult, as Hugh MacDiarmid* observed, can also turn Scots into the most repulsive caricatures of themselves, sunk in alcoholic and provincial complacency, seems to make no difference. Burns would now be taken on almost every hand as a better Scot than Scott. So perhaps it is worth reminding ourselves of the ways in which Scott was superior to Burns.

Scott invented a genre, the historical novel, which proved to be of vast range and power, which influenced many other literatures and which, as the Marxist critic Georg Lukacs pointed out, helped to add a faculty to humanity, the faculty of looking at ourselves in historical terms. In that respect, Scott belongs with the giants of western civilization. It is worth remembering, too, that these highest accomplishments were blended with an eye for individual quirks of character matching that of William Shakespeare or Charles Dickens. And he did all this, or at least a great deal of it, with the matter of Scotland. What fuelled Scott's genius was his universal sympathy, his ability to enter into and recreate in his art all that Scotland was and had been, Cavalier or Covenanter, Jacobite or Hanoverian, nobleman or peasant, countryman or burgher, patriot or traitor, good or evil, success or failure, together with all the English, European and any other influences that had borne on them.

His personal preference in this rich tapestry seemed often to lie with wishy-washy moderation, as in his mediocre heroes. But consciously or not, he made the extremes more interesting, which is itself very Scottish. The fact remains that Scott could take the whole of Scotland and give it back to us enriched in ample measure. That is why he was a great writer, a great human being and a great Scotsman.

FRANCIS JEFFREY (1773–1850)

As a struggling young advocate, Francis Jeffrey had a modest flat, on the third floor of 18 Buccleuch Place, a house on the south side of Edinburgh which still stands. One day in March 1802 three friends came round, two fellow advocates, Henry Brougham and Francis Horner, and a clergyman, the Rev. Sydney Smith, all of them underemployed, to drink tea and talk. During their conversation, Smith suggested they should set up a magazine to cover political and literary events. This was the origin of the *Edinburgh Review*, which would become the most famous journal not only in Scotland, but in the rest of Britain, Europe and America too, and maintain Edinburgh's cultural reputation far into the nineteenth century.

None of the young gentlemen had any money so they turned to Archibald Constable, imperious publisher of Walter Scott* and other literary lions. He agreed to bear the cost of the launch so long as they produced the four initial monthly numbers for nothing. The first, in 750 copies, appeared in October 1802 and sold out. By the third, they were printing 2,500, and at its peak the circulation would be ten times that. Constable now agreed to pay them handsome fees. He kept the *Review* going and sustained its quality long after the circle of founders dispersed: Jeffrey would edit it for twenty-nine years, but the rest went to London, Smith to be the most renowned wit of his day, Horner to die young though not without making a name as a brilliant economist, Brougham to become Lord Chancellor of England. Replacements were readily found, among them Henry Cockburn, who said the *Review* 'drew authors from dens where they would otherwise have starved, and made Edinburgh a literary mart, famous with strangers, and the pride of its own citizens'.

The true importance of the *Review* was that it popularized the teachings of the Scottish Enlightenment and helped to transform them into Victorian orthodoxies. Jeffrey, Brougham and Horner had as students at Edinburgh sat at the feet of Professor Dugald Stewart, who was himself a pupil of Adam Smith.* But they did not regard *The Wealth of Nations* as carved upon a tablet of stone. They wrote about a Britain which had now acquired an industrial economy and a global empire, in a commercial system where commodities from the periphery fed manufactures at the centre. The account of free trade they developed was modest compared to the conceptions prevailing later in the century. But Jeffrey maintained the broad-minded outlook of the Scottish Enlightenment, balking at the logical rigour and crude accountancy of the emerging utilitarian school in England.

In politics the *Review* was liberal, much concerned with the lessons of the French Revolution and the avoidance of violent upheaval in Britain. To Jeffrey the overthrow of the old order in France seemed an expression of genuine grievances with no other outlet, so that savage repression would be the worst thinkable response to similar problems elsewhere. Britain had gone to war against Napoleon, who disrupted trade with Europe, causing unemployment and unrest in the industrial areas. Jeffrey was about the only man of any standing to argue that economic distress should be met by political reform so as to give a voice to the as yet voteless masses. With this line he and the *Review* won a remarkable authority in the prelude to the Reform Act of 1832, which finally did grant a wider franchise in Britain and in effect proved him right. He had already been elected an MP himself and as Lord Advocate piloted the Scottish Act through. He finished his career as a judge.

With hindsight his literary judgement looks less sure — though it was good for the *Review*, his criticisms often being ferocious to the point of sensational. One angry poet, Thomas Moore, challenged him to a duel. But his dismissal of Walter Scott and William Wordsworth made him appear unable to appreciate what was best and most enduring in the literature of his time. He had no sympathy with, or even understanding of, the Romantic movement. In literary matters he remained a man of the eighteenth century, who believed there were standards of correctness any good writer had to observe, following rules and using artificial language. As Thomas Carlyle* pointed out, Jeffrey's blend of artistic timidity and liberal politics added up in the end to a stifling bourgeois respectability.

His most lasting achievement lies in his development of journalism. Cockburn said the *Review* burst upon a public that seemed to be waiting on something of the kind. Till it came along, news of major events, even of the excitements of war, had been conveyed through boring reprints of official documents and dispatches in a press often subsidized by the government, whereas Jeffrey gave more graphic and objective accounts. Again, about the only way for the general reader to get to know about the latest books had been through publishers' puffs, which were no more reliable then than later, but by contrast the *Review* offered independent criticism. Altogether, this new type of periodical marked the emergence of a middle-class public opinion that was culturally and politically aware, served now by an organ which could articulate and promote its interests. We see its continuing legacy in the higher journalism even of our own time, clever, probing and irreverent.

THOMAS CARLYLE (1795–1881)

The decline in Scottish culture from the great days of the Enlightenment can conveniently be reckoned to have set in from 1828, when Thomas Carlyle was rejected by St Andrews University for the chair of moral philosophy. We do not know quite why, except that Carlyle was clearly an upstart; the chair went to a former Moderator of the General Assembly of the Church of Scotland.

We may also guess what kind of faults the selectors saw in him, for instance his tendency to carry literary values into more academic disciplines: in his histories, we are in a kind of world that could have been created by Walter Scott* rather than by David Hume* or William Robertson,* a world where the characters are humans in triumph and disaster, in laughter and in tears, not mere authors of state papers for the instruction of posterity. It is unlikely that Jeffrey's rule-bound limits would ever have constrained Carlyle, to judge from his often grotesque but always vivid and above all innovative style, which constantly strained at the leash of linguistic convention. We are more than compensated by the fact that, as George Eliot said, 'there is hardly a superior or active mind of this generation that had not been modified by Carlyle's writings; there has hardly been an English book written for the last ten or twelve years that would not have been different if Carlyle had not lived'.

The fact is rather that, rejected in Scotland, Carlyle moved to seek fame and fortune in London. There he remained, more or less, for the rest of his long life. He was the first Scot of superlative abilities since the Enlightenment began to have found Scotland too narrow, and to have decided that only the great metropolis in the south would do for him. If Scotland did not want Carlyle, then that, we have to assume with hindsight, said more about Scotland than it said about him. Scotland was on the intellectual, and moral, retreat.

He had come to Edinburgh in 1809, walking from his humble home at Ecclefechan in Dumfriesshire to study at the university. He wanted to be a minister in his own austerely pious sect, the Burghers.

Life in the big city broke this piety, or at least the conviction that salvation had to come through a particular church – though according to his biographer, J.A. Froude, God remained to him a pledge of some ultimate justice in the universe, 'an awful reality to which the fate of nations, the fate of each individual man, bore perpetual witness'. What remained unbroken was his moral sense, which also helped to make the late Scottish Enlightenment unbearable to him in its increasing provincial complacency and shallow unoriginality.

The space in his mind which might have been occupied by God or Enlightenment was in the first instance filled by the new Romantic sensibility of his age, with its faith in the individual and search after the heights and depths to be found in him (even, occasionally, in her). Since most people are fairly mediocre, however, this meant a cult of the hero, which issued in Carlyle's famous work of the 1840s, *Heroes and Hero-Worship*. The Romanticism fostered besides an obsessive interest in German literature. As a young journalist and translator, which was how he first made his living, he was already conducting a lively correspondence with Goethe in Weimar. Teutonic moral earnestness impressed him: he felt the spiritual conflicts of the age were being played out in Germany, no longer in a superficial Scotland.

Different as they were, Scotland and Germany did have one or two striking features in common. Both were stateless nations. In neither was there much continuity between politics and culture (as is so obvious, for example, in Victorian England). In both countries the universities were primarily bearers of the culture, not finishing schools for the ruling class. That must have made it all the more galling for Carlyle, who felt he had so much to give, to be spurned by an academic establishment. In Germany this cultural role would gradually transform the universities into focuses for nationalism and everything that nationalism then entailed, from a quest after the meaning of history to a concern with the ever more burning social questions of an industrializing era. But the Scottish universities would turn their backs on all that. After the Disruption of the Church of Scotland in 1843, which split the whole of Scottish society, the universities were to be consumed by sectarian bitterness and to abandon their role as bearers of the culture. One possible corrective was to Germanize them in ethos and structure. After being elected Rector at Edinburgh in 1866, Carlyle did something towards this, though the project was in the end to be defeated.

Meanwhile in London he was writing a sequence of sensational books: *Sartor Resartus*, part autobiography and part satire; *The French Revolution*, depicted as a passionate moral drama; *Past and Present*, published amid the social crisis of the 1840s when it seemed even England might succumb to revolution and offering the vision of an organic society as the alternative to a soulless and divisive utilitarianism. But it contained the paradox of a critique of individualism from the point of view of an even more exalted individualism, and Carlyle never quite managed to convey to readers the moral and spiritual distinctions which to his mind resolved the paradox. By the time he got round to presenting Oliver Cromwell and, still worse, Frederick the Great of Prussia as moral heroes for the modern world, he was losing his public.

ROBERT LOUIS STEVENSON (1850–94)

The remains of Robert Louis Stevenson lie in a tomb of white stone at the top of Mount Vaea on Western Samoa in the South Pacific. The situation is some hundreds of feet above Vailima, the house Stevenson built for himself, by far the biggest and grandest in the island; it served till a few years ago as the residence of the head of state. After Stevenson's death the furnishings were taken by his widow, Fanny, to their previous home at Monterey, California, where they can still be seen today. Vailima, now under the care of a foundation, has been refurbished to give the feel of a late Victorian interior. In one corner there is even a hearth where, on the couple of days in the year when it was just about cool enough, Stevenson would light a fire and sit, four degrees from the equator, gazing at the coals and thinking of home, 'that cold old huddle of great hills', as he called it in a letter. Scotland could have been easy to forget here on the opposite side of the globe, and his choice of refuge might well give an impression of wanting to get as far away as possible. Yet he seemed doomed to carry his native country with him.

This degree of fidelity is not enough for modern Scots. The escapism meets with disapproval. James Bridie, not exactly a hunk himself, damned Stevenson as forever 'trembling on the brink of life', and scorn for a figure so unwilling to take his medicine still pervades compatriots' attitudes. That he declined to follow in his family's tradition of building lighthouses was fair enough, since not everyone wishes to spend their days rowing round jagged rocks in high seas. But he also refused the perfectly respectable alternative of the law, the resort of every bourgeois Scotsman with nothing better to do, and instead devoted himself to composing children's books, of all things. This is not thought in Scotland to be a useful occupation, and it will be vain to point out that he wrote other works as well.

Most Scots are amazed to hear that, in Europe and America, Stevenson is regarded as a proto-modern master, a highly self-conscious artist, who was among the first to have set about disintegration of his characters, rather than the integration prescribed by literary convention up to his time. It is a truism that the greatest Scots go unsung in their own country. If Stevenson is a great Scot, this is certainly true of him. Some explanation is needed of what drove him from Scotland and what bound him to Scotland, together with what it is in both impulses that causes the Scots' blindness to his genius.

A basic fact is that he was an invalid all his life, a sickly child who grew into a skeletal man and died young of a stroke. The weakling first sublimated his condition in the pose of aesthete, with velvet jackets, chain-smoking and visits to scented ladies of the night, disciplined by nothing more than the production, admittedly steady, of light prose. This character gradually transmuted into the adventurer, who firmed up his whimsy with acute but still charming observation of strange and winning ways, as in *Travels with a Donkey*, the narrative of a holiday in the French Cevennes. The greater depth proved, perhaps unexpectedly, to be the key to greater freedom, to throwing off shackles which seemed in retrospect almost to have imposed caprice on him. He would find a yet fuller freedom in America, then in the boundless spaces of the Pacific.

More surprising still was that maturity came with the first of the children's stories, *Treasure Island*. This masterpiece of the genre is hardly diminished in appeal over a century later, precisely because there is nothing aesthetic about it. The opening still chills boys' hearts, which then thrill as they learn to overcome childish terrors. Stevenson moved on as a writer in finding a less fastidious voice, though not one that limited him further, as the subsequent *Kidnapped* showed. Its hero, David Balfour, remains locked in a world resting on moderation in all things, security of class and property, justice of authority and assurance of reward for virtue, none cast in doubt by any degree of exposure to the world of the anti-hero, Alan Breck (who, of course, is much more interesting than David), with its treachery and violence, fierce loyalties and casual aggression. The universal in the normal, tried and tempered, wins through.

The most famous finished work, *Dr Jekyll and Mr Hyde*, has attained mythic status as an exposure of the split personality of modern man. Yet it is hard not to rate higher the unfinished *Weir of Hermiston*, at which Stevenson was working the day death struck him down at Vailima. Because it is unfinished we cannot tell where the split personality working itself into the young hero, Archie Weir, would have carried him. He represents in immature abstraction an idealistic morality while his father, Lord Hermiston, underneath his roughness, crudity and brutishness actually exhibits a deeper humanity, which adheres to standards rather than merely responds to impulses. Stevenson fled Scotland, which can certainly be a hard parent, but he was always coming back, persuaded by the experience of the world that there was a great deal to Scotland after all; had he lived, perhaps he would one day have got home in person. Scots have lost the certainties about themselves and the world they still had in his time, and they would be better for understanding him now.

SIR ARTHUR CONAN DOYLE (1859–1930)

'Steel true, blade straight' is the terse epitaph on the grave at Minstead, Hampshire of this physician, turned man of letters, turned spiritualist. But it is as a writer that he is best remembered, and especially as the creator of the legendary detective Sherlock Holmes. Doyle was born at Picardy Place in Edinburgh (a pub nearby now bears his name), the son of a Government clerk of Irish ancestry, who earned enough to send the boy to Stoneyhurst College, a Jesuit private school in England.

He went on to study medicine at Edinburgh University; one of his contemporaries there was J.M. Barrie,* with whom he co-wrote the light opera *Jane Annie* over a decade later. He financed his medical studies by working as a doctor's assistant and supplemented his income by writing short stories. Before his final year, he worked for seven months as ship's doctor on a whaling ship in the Arctic. On graduating he went to sea as a doctor on an ocean liner before setting up in practice in Portsmouth in 1882.

One of the outstanding teachers he encountered in Edinburgh was Dr Joseph Bell (1837–1911), upon whom he based the character of Sherlock Holmes, down to the aquiline profile and sharp mind. Bell was famed for the trick of being able to diagnose patients before they even told him their symptoms, and R.L. Stevenson* was quick to note the similarity when he read his first Holmes mystery, *A Study in Scarlet* published in 1887. 'Can this be my old friend Joe Bell?' he wrote to Doyle, who readily acknowledged the debt in a letter to Bell himself in 1892. The detective's surname comes from the American writer Oliver Wendell Holmes, whom Doyle admired.

Detective fiction was not Doyle's first passion and his interest in history led him to write historical novels. But it was the serialization of the Holmes stories in the *Strand* magazine in the early nineties which caught the public imagination. There is hardly anyone who has not become familiar with Holmes from the catalogue of books, films and television portrayals, but Doyle felt his character was eclipsing his other works and finished him off in *The Final Problem* during a battle with Professor Moriarty at the Reichenbach Falls in December 1893. Public demand forced an ingenious storyline which resurrected him a year later.

Doyle went off to become a war correspondent in South Africa during the Boer War (1899–1901) and this yielded two books on the history of the war. He was knighted in 1902, and rewarded the insistent public with another Holmes novel (*The Hound of the Baskervilles*) the same year. Later Holmes tried to interest his public in another hero, Professor Challenger, who enabled him to explore new backdrops, but he was forced to keep satisfying the demand for more tales of Holmes. Doyle employed the device of telling the story through a companion, utilized in the original detective story, Edgar Allan Poe's *Murders in the Rue Morgue* (1841), and by countless detective writers since. Sherlock Holmes's faithful amanuensis was Dr John Watson, a medical practitioner, who was based on Doyle's friend Dr James Watson, president of the Portsmouth Literary Society.

As a doctor Doyle himself practised as an oculist, but few at that time were aware of his occultist tendencies. From 1887, when he participated in experiments in thought transference with a friend to see if they could transmit diagrams, he began to interest himself in psychic research. He attended spiritualist séances and joined the Society for Psychical Research (SPR), which had attracted many well-known scientists to its ranks. Some were sceptical about the phenomena produced by spiritualist mediums. Doyle was less so, and was often accused of credulity. (In one famous case, he accepted as genuine a series of photographs, subsequently shown to have been faked, which featured two sisters handling tiny flying fairies). One of the most famous mediums in London during the late nineteenth century was the Edinburgh-born Daniel Douglas Home (1833–86), who produced many stunning phenomena and who throughout his career was never exposed as a fraud. Doyle had several sittings with Home and from these and other experiences over a period of thirty years gradually became a believer in spiritualism.

His public commitment to spiritualism came with the tragic death of his son Kingsley from pneumonia during the First World War. Shortly afterwards, Doyle attended a séance with a Welsh medium and avowed not only that he heard his son's voice but that facts were disclosed which could not have been known to the medium. At another séance he saw his mother and nephew 'As plainly as I ever saw them in life!' Doyle became more than simply an investigator. He was an evangelist for spiritualism. It led to a break with the SPR when Doyle defended the integrity of a medium they had questioned. Sir Oliver Lodge FRS, an eminent scientist who had a similar interest in psychic phenomena, said of him: 'His methods are not mine, he regarded himself as a missionary, a trustee of a great truth ... occasionally I think he lacked the wisdom of the serpent but the goodness of his motives must be manifest to all.'

Doyle's later years were occupied chiefly with books and campaigns supporting spiritualism, which was attracting frenzied interest in the years following the war. He travelled all over the world to further the cause, and became honorary president of the International Spiritualist Congress in Paris in 1925. There was a concession to the Holmes fan club in *The Casebook of Sherlock Holmes* in 1927.

There exists a recording of him just before his death in 1930 declaring, in his strong Scots accent, 'People ask what you get from spiritualism? Well, the first thing you get is that it removes all fear of death. Secondly it bridges death for those dear ones whom we may love.' But Doyle's life story did not end with his death. Various mediums claimed contact with him beyond the grave, many on flimsy grounds, but a year after he died the celebrated medium Eileen Garrett convinced many that she had made contact. Definitive proof might have been provided had any of these mediums been able to reveal the contents of the sealed packet which Doyle had left behind in order to provide evidence of survival, the contents of which were known only to him. No one was able to do so before the expiry date and this 'final problem' remained unsolved.

SIR JAMES M. BARRIE (1860–1937)

'Life is a long lesson in humility,' says one of Barrie's characters, the Little Minister. It was true of his own life in which, despite the fame he enjoyed in later years, he experienced many failures and much personal sadness. Barrie might be called Scotland's Lewis Carroll: both men had an ability to mesmerize children with their stories, but the relationships they developed with the children of other families would today be found odd and even unhealthy.

Barrie was strange to look at. Five feet tall as an adult, his head was large in proportion to the rest of his body. His father was a hand-loom weaver in Kirriemuir, and he was the youngest in a family of nine. His mother Margaret enjoyed telling her children stories about the characters of rural Angus. She doted on David, his elder brother, and never recovered from his death at the age of fourteen in an accident. It is hard not to avoid the conclusion that Peter, the boy who never grew old, is an echo of David. The name of the little girl befriended by Peter Pan derives from the attempts of the six-year-old daughter of one of his associates at Edinburgh University to greet him as 'My Friendly'. Little Margaret could not pronounce the words properly and they came out as Wendy.

Graduating in English literature in 1882, Barrie found work as a leader writer with the *Nottingham Journal*. Soon he was freelancing for London papers, sending stories in which he dressed up the antics of one of the more extreme Presbyterian sects in Scotland, the Auld Lichts. This encouraged him to set off for London in 1885 and after four productive years he established a reputation for himself as a witty and whimsical writer. *Auld Licht Tales* found their way into book form, as did *A Window at Thrums*, featuring many of his mother's tales and provoking the reaction in Kirriemuir that 'wee Jimmy Barrie' was mocking them. R.L. Stevenson* remarked that *The Little Minister*, which was serialized at this time, was the work of a genius.

Barrie wrote several plays, which flopped, but was successful with *Ibsen's Ghost*, a dialogue between characters from Ibsen's plays, and

Walker, London, about a con-man, which ran for over 500 performances. He married Mary Ansell, an actress in the latter play, but the marriage was a disaster and ended ten years later when Mary began an affair with another man. Barrie had done little to claim her affections, spending most of his spare time with the Davies children who lived near them in their apartment overlooking Kensington Gardens. The eldest boy, George, was the apple of Barrie's eye and his younger brothers, Peter, John, Michael and Nico, were eagerly 'adopted' by Barrie as they appeared. So much so that their parents, Arthur and Sylvia Llewellyn Davies, at one point moved house in order to escape Barrie's influence.

Barrie's career as a playwright had taken off in the USA, where a talented producer, Charles Frohman, put on his plays. In 1904 Frohman came to London to produce a new work which had already been performed in embryonic form by Barrie and the five Davies boys in the park where he took them for walks. This was *Peter Pan*, which met with an ecstatic reception when it opened on 27 December 1904 at the Duke of York's Theatre, London. Barrie gave the royalties in perpetuity to the children's hospital in Great Ormond Street, and gave the credit for the creation of Peter to the five little Davies boys: 'I made Peter by rubbing the five of you violently together, as savages with two sticks produce a flame. I am sometimes asked who and what Peter is, but that is all he is, the spark I got from all of you.'

Friendly relations had been restored with their parents, and when Arthur Llewellyn Davies suffered a long, eventually fatal illness, Barrie was generous with help. When Sylvia died soon after, he was heartbroken, having obviously had deep feelings for her. He adopted the five boys as his own but suffered further agony when George was killed in 1915 in the First World War. A few months later Frohman was drowned when the *Lusitania* was torpedoed, and his last words, recorded by a survivor, were Peter Pan's immortal line: 'To die will be an awfully big adventure.' There were other deaths which affected him deeply. Captain Robert Scott, the ill-fated polar explorer, had named his son Peter after Barrie's character. In 1913 he wrote one of his last letters to Barrie as he waited to die at the South Pole, asking him to look after his widow and declaring 'I never met a man in my life whom I admired and loved more than you.' In another tragedy, Michael Davies drowned with a friend (possibly in a suicide pact) in 1921.

The shadow of this grief did not help the manic depression which Barrie endured throughout his life. Nevertheless he continued to produce witty material, albeit in much reduced quantity. When he suffered writer's cramp he shifted hands, always claiming he produced different stuff according to the hand used. He invented an alter ego, McConnachie, who was his invisible conscience and companion. His love of cricket was expressed in the team, mischievously called the Allahakbarries, for which he played along with Conan Doyle.* Knighted in 1913 and made chancellor of Edinburgh University in 1930, he received many honours before he died at the age of seventy-seven, never having grown old in spirit.

While Barrie and Conan Doyle remained writers all their lives, the other great talent of this period had by the end of his life transformed himself into a statesman.

JOHN BUCHAN, LORD TWEEDSMUIR (1875–1940)

Scotland's most prolific author of the twentieth century, John Buchan, arouses some suspicion in his own country today. He was of impeccable native credentials, the son of a minister of the Free Church brought up in Fife, the Borders and Glasgow, where he went to school and university. But he took the high road to England and acted afterwards as if he was a member of the English establishment: classics at Oxford, apprenticeship in the colonies, aristocratic marriage, service to the state, stint in Parliament, imperial office and a peerage. This, in the eyes of many modern Scots, brands him as having sold out. Yet in one great particular he understood (which may mean he loved) his nation more profoundly than those who stayed behind.

That emerged not in his public life, where he was a Tory who lauded tradition and distrusted experiment, sympathizing with Scots who became Nationalists but preferring Union and Empire. It emerged rather in his writing, which through his many other avocations he continued with hardly believable fluency: novels, poetry, history, biography, journalism, criticism, propaganda, fifty-five books in all. He was a serious scholar, though mainly remembered by the tales he wrote for amusement and labelled 'shockers'. At least one, *The Thirty-Nine Steps*, has achieved lasting fame. Like the others, it moves fast, surprises endlessly and voyages into the unknown, yet with a sure eye for nature, landscape and human types. These works are intricately plotted, if a little too reliant on flukes. Their durability lies deeper, though. Buchan appeals to readers because he reminds them of the darkness in the world and in themselves. Connoisseurs of Buchan tend to prefer as his best novel another one, *Witch Wood*, set in the Scotland of the seventeenth century with a tense dissection of the grimmest Calvinism.

This might have matched the mood of Scots who during the twentieth century never had a great deal to be proud of, seeing the bright promise of the previous era dissipated in political subordination, economic depression and cultural decay. The turning point came with the First World War. Before it everything appeared to be going so well and after it everything went wrong, not to go right again till the approach of the millennium. The literature written by Buchan marks this change, if intuitively rather than explicitly, better than any other contemporary cultural product. Where others felt confused and demoralized by what was happening, he saw clearly that, amid changes to the whole world, there was one deep change peculiar to Scotland. It was a change in her ethos: grand old ideals, mixing romantic nationalism with imperial aspiration, dissolved.

At that turning point we hear an alteration in the tone of his literary voice. Up to the war the heroes of his stories, often placed in an imperial setting, had been essentially aristocratic, if sprung in several cases from the Anglo-Scottish *haute bourgeoisie*. They were the sort of men the author had met, and become one of, while serving in South

Africa. While looking like amateurs, they knew their business backwards and conducted it with superb skill, whether building a commercial combine or ruling a conquered territory. With them Buchan
helped to create a major image of imperial Britain, of a noble ideal
elevating the workaday virtues of a nation of shopkeepers. For Scots
the ideal was more austere: personal mettle, trained mind and technical mastery stood to be proven in the crucible of the fallen world,
issuing in a stoical devotion, a sort of secular Covenanting.

The war had asked that kind of stoical devotion from Scots
soldiers, who freely gave it. Yet it went for little, or at least victory
exacted such a price of it as to cast doubt on its moral value. In
Buchan's later works his favourites from the earlier ones — Richard
Hannay, Sandy Arbuthnot and Edward Leithen — still figure, but
now afflicted by malaise. The vitality is displayed by new characters,
representing Scottishness in more authentic, not to say humane
form: Dickson McCunn, a Glaswegian grocer, and the Gorbals
Diehards inseparable from him. None appeared in the previous
novels, nor would they have really been conceivable there. In place
of nobility we see bourgeois values and proletarian worth. Surely
Buchan's moral odyssey represented something wider in the nation's
experience. It still led to no certain destination. Scots of all stations in
life expected rather that peace would bring back the old Scotland,
but Buchan knew by instinct that could not be so.

He was a man of uncommonly sound instinct. In everything he
wrote there is a strength stemming from certainty of personal belief.
It makes him understand a certain view of the world and express that
understanding through his characters. Yet he is not self-satisfied.
Thanks to his Calvinism, he accepts the inevitability of sin in a corrupt and destructive human nature. Alienated from God and history,
man is a slave to his own pride. There are good people and, just
about, they may win in the end, but usually after they have been
humbled and have suffered retribution. They win not because they
are good but because they prove themselves in their life and works.
So human existence is a trial. The degree of civilization we achieve is
always under threat from dark forces outside us and inside us. Every

act is a moral choice, and a warding off of temptation. One day, per-haps, Scotland will see through Buchan's superficial faults, such as they were, to the mettle of the man beneath.

Turning to the modern period of Scots literature, we meet a complex and contradictory character who was once asked about the signifi-cance of his entry in *Who's Who*, which listed 'anglophobia' among his interests. Was this fear of the English or simply distaste for them? 'Certainly not fear,' he replied. 'And it's something stronger than distaste. I would call it hatred.'

HUGH MACDIARMID (1892–1978)

Hugh MacDiarmid was the greatest Scottish poet of the twentieth century, not least because he set out to make the country's literature once again national, growing out of Scotland's past, relevant to the present, determining the future. The national literatures created in Norway or Ireland served him for models, but he stressed that Scotland's must have a higher vocation – to reflect the huge contri-bution made by an authentic Scottish form of civilization ever since the Enlightenment (at least) to the civilization of the whole world. As a guru, the closest parallel to MacDiarmid is Thomas Carlyle* a hun-dred years before, who had to leave Scotland as a young man for London. It was to MacDiarmid's credit, and to Scotland's, that he stayed, finding supporters and readers.

Even so, his challenge has not yet revived an authentic Scottish civilization. He met more failure than success in every non-poetic field he ventured into, in language, culture and politics. He neither overcame popular apathy in the face of his efforts, nor shook a single one of the many detested members of the Scottish establishment from their perches.

Yet MacDiarmid could boast of two accomplishments. He did make his countrymen, or at least enough of them, conscious of what qualities their civilization had once possessed. He summed these up in a term borrowed from a critic, the 'Caledonian antisyzygy'. It means the national taste for dualism, opposites and extremes, together with disputation between them, originally owed to Calvinism and whetted in the intellectual crucible of the eighteenth century. MacDiarmid believed this to be utterly different from the spirit of English civilization, with its muddy compromises and limp consensus – which was why the Scots had to be an independent people again. In proclaiming the antisyzygy he did do something to enliven the mute, cowed, leaden state of the country, depressed by its misfortunes between the wars. Even so, he found it hard to diffuse beyond his own work the acuity which had once marked the national intellect.

A second achievement was greater. Since the Union, Scottish nationhood had one way or another gone down and down, now slower, now faster, sometimes against the Scots' will, sometimes with their acquiescence or even encouragement, sometimes to their complete indifference. Before MacDiarmid, nobody conceived that this decline ever would or could be reversed. But he imagined, thought, wrote and said how Scottish nationhood might come up again. By fits and starts, and seldom as far or fast as he wished, up it has come, all the same.

That said, MacDiarmid remained primarily a poet. His prose can be graceless, no doubt reflecting the fact that for twenty years, on each side of service in the First World War, he made his living as a local journalist. His politics were self-indulgent, often designed just to shock. After almost embracing Fascism, he won more notoriety by getting expelled from the Nationalist Party for his Communism, then from the Communist Party for his Nationalism. None of this made much difference to his poetry, which had deeper concerns. Probably he placed too much faith in his own processes of thought, which tended to view uncritically the successive ideologies he swallowed whole. Yet they were grist to the mill of his poetry: if ideology has not often been seen, at least among English-speakers, as fit matter for poems, that goes to show MacDiarmid's ambition and originality.

He wrote his first, rather conventional poems in English. But in 1925 he published a collection in Scots, *Sangschaw*. It had lines like 'I' the how-dumb-deid o' the cauld hairst nicht, the warl' like an eemis stane wags i' the lift', understood by few Scottish readers, let alone others. This was Synthetic Scots, a language nobody spoke, fashioned from literary sources, learned articles and dictionaries. A brother poet, Edwin Muir, argued that it 'may turn out to be a fact of great importance for Scottish letters. For if a Scottish literary language is possible then a Scottish literature is possible too.' MacDiarmid defended his use of a 'vast unutilized mass of lapsed observation made by minds whose attitudes to experience and whose speculative and imaginary tendencies were quite different from any possible to Englishmen and anglicized Scots today' — as different as Dostoyevsky or Proust were. His great achievement in it, *A Drunk Man Looks at the Thistle*, tries to envisage Scotland's place in the civilized world, indeed in the cosmos.

Dazzling as these feats were, MacDiarmid put them behind him in the 1930s, spent in self-imposed exile on Whalsay, Shetland. In place of a clogged and cerebral Scots, he turned to a sparer English, as in the *First Hymn to Lenin*, concentrating on the outward expression rather than the inner significance of thought. He shifted by degrees to what he called Synthetic English, for intellectual, didactic or polemical verse assimilating a mass of scientific terms. Many admirers found this an aberration, but MacDiarmid showed no sense of going astray. It is interesting to speculate that, with each of these synthetic languages, he may have considered himself to be doing much the same thing for their respective mother tongues. He added little to his work after 1945 but by then he had secured a reputation as one of the world's most challenging writers; though one who always started from Scotland, and so put his country on the cultural map again.

In the creative arts Scots have always excelled in literature rather than in art, music or acting. It is not immediately evident why this should be so. There were and are actors and comedians, composers and musicians, painters and designers who are the exception to the rule, but it remains a rule. Scots write rather than sing or dance or paint.

Perhaps it arises from the traditional emphasis put on reading and writing skills in Scottish schools. Some would argue that this emphasis is changing not simply because the schools have changed their approach to teaching, but because of television and the internet. Nevertheless, the fact remains that during the twentieth century Scotland has continued to produce writers whose work has been not only of interest to the wider world but immensely popular. Some works have gained an even greater impact by being filmed or televised, such as A.J. Cronin's *Dr Finlay's Casebook*, or Muriel Spark's *The Prime of Miss Jean Brodie*. One captured the sedate world of a rural town, and the other the starchy quality of bourgeois Edinburgh. Another prolific author, Compton Mackenzie, is now best known for his hilarious saga *Whisky Galore*, and Neil Munro, the novelist and journalist, for his *Para Handy* stories, both celebrating the pawky humour of the Western Isles. Kenneth Grahame's *Wind in the Willows* (turned into the play *Toad of Toad Hall*) has more of J.M. Barrie about it, while Lewis Grassic Gibbon's tales of the Mearns in *A Scots Quair* are of a much darker hue.

There is no common formula they exploit, no common culture they share. Cronin's Tannochbrae is as different from Gibbon's Kinraddie as Glasgow is from Edinburgh. Yet they share the quality of being able to be both quintessentially Scots and universal in their appeal. More recently two internationally known Scots authors with journalistic roots have written escapist books: George Macdonald Fraser's *Flashman* tales and Alastair Maclean's thrillers. They in turn are of yet another genre, while the Scots vet Alf Wight who lived in Yorkshire and wrote under the name of James Herriot seems to have more in common with Cronin and Mackenzie.

In each generation it seems Scotland still has the capacity to produce several new writers whose talents are acclaimed outside Scotland, plus a superstar with international appeal. Currently among the first category are Allan Massie, A.L. Kennedy and James

Kelman. The latest superstar is J.K. Rowling, the authoress whose boy wizard Harry Potter seems destined to eclipse even R.L. Stevenson and J.M. Barrie in popular appeal. Perhaps the secret lies in having two initials before your surname.

6

Pioneers, Prophets and Patriots

There is no such job description as pioneer. No professional body which awards credentials to explorers. Likewise the term missionary is an inadequate word to describe people whose talents were as mixed as their motives and whose contribution to the development of far-flung areas of the world went far further than registering converts for Christianity. The people who are called pioneers, explorers and missionaries were often all three. Some were interested in making a fortune from foreign conquests. But many of them were doctors and scientists, driven by curiosity for undiscovered worlds as well as compassion for their fellow creatures. Their stories are as varied as the lands in which they found themselves and whose histories they altered by their presence.

JAMES RAMSAY (1733–96)

In 1784 Zachary Macaulay, one of twelve children of the minister of Inveraray in Argyll, was sent at the age of sixteen to seek his fortune in Jamaica. He disliked his bookkeeper's job on a plantation, but especially the fact that 'by my situation I was exposed not only to the sight but also the practice of severities on others, the very recollection of which makes my blood run cold'. Little more than a boy, he feared that protest would make him look 'foolish, childish and ridiculous', or worse, ungrateful to his parents, patrons and employers.

Macaulay consoled himself by setting down the facts to a friendly minister at home, writing that he would hardly recognize the young fellow he once knew, 'were you to view me in a field of canes, amidst perhaps a hundred of the sable race, cursing and bawling, while the noise of the whip resounding on their shoulders, and the cries of the poor wretches, would make you imagine some unlucky accident had carried you to the doleful shades'. He came back after eight years but in 1793 left again to be Governor of Sierra Leone, a colony in West Africa just formed by a society of abolitionists as a refuge for liberated slaves. Afterwards he spent the rest of his life in the struggle in Britain to end slavery and the slave trade which was eventually successful. He was also the father of Lord Macaulay.

But during his time in Jamaica the overwhelming impression he had given was of helplessness in the face of horrors. This was not uncommon. While enlightened men, including many Scots, had no doubt that slavery was wrong, it seemed impossible to defeat the vested interests sustaining it. The West Indies generated vast wealth from sugar, wealth well represented in Parliament by the owners of plantations able to purchase seats there. Attacks on them seemed almost counter-productive, since only with their assent might any improvement at all in the slaves' condition be made. But in 1784, while Macaulay could only protest in private letters, one Scot did start to speak out.

James Ramsay came of a Jacobite family in Aberdeenshire, though, being only a child at the time of the 1745 rebellion, he grew up accepting that the Union was here to stay. For those Jacobites who, like the Ramsays, belonged to the Episcopalian Church and suffered under the penal laws imposed on it, a career in the Empire was a way out. James studied at Aberdeen University and started working as a naval surgeon. This did not satisfy him, and at length he decided to take orders in the Church of England – not an automatic ticket to preferment for men like him from a suspect background, who were often fobbed off with colonial charges. So, in 1762, Ramsay found himself on the Caribbean island of St Kitts, where he would stay for nearly twenty years.

Life on the island appalled him, yet he found his true vocation there. Nobody cared any more for the slaves' spiritual welfare than for their physical welfare, and most of them probably practised voodoo. Ramsay wanted to convert them to Christianity, but found them living in a state so debased, and working under conditions so exhausting, that he could scarcely get them to listen to him. Naturally he was an owner himself of domestic slaves in his household, since no white man could be seen to lift a finger. These slaves were usually intelligent and responsible, enjoying relatively high status among their own kind, but the planters refused to regard them as different from the rest. When Ramsay treated them decently, the white community ostracized him. He was not deterred from evangelizing among the slaves and trying to improve their material welfare as best he could. But he had to admit, after two decades at it, that he had not got far.

The key lay not in the West Indies but in Britain, a liberal society with a conscience that could be pricked. Indeed, while Ramsay was away, slavery had been declared illegal in Scotland. A domestic slave called Joseph Knight had been brought to Perthshire where, wishing to marry, he applied to the sheriff to oblige his master to pay him a living wage. The case went to the Court of Session which, with Henry Dundas* pleading in Knight's favour, declared that any slave setting foot on Scottish soil by that fact became free.

So the political climate had begun to change, and Ramsay was able to exploit the shift on his return in 1781. Few others who had been in the West Indies had an interest in telling the public what went on there, so his revelations proved novel and sensational. In 1784 he published an *Essay on the Treatment and Conversion of African Slaves in the British Sugar Colonies* which described the blacks' brutalized lives, the monotony of their work and the suffering they endured under the lash. Ramsay appealed for them to be recognized as human beings capable of reformation, indeed salvation. This was just the start of the fierce campaign he conducted in the press, in pamphlets, lectures and general public controversy. He met bitter, even ruthless opposition: his character was attacked, he was threatened with violence and challenged to duels. But with courage and determination he carried on. The Scottish philosophy he had imbibed long ago at Aberdeen helped him. He argued from the concept of sympathy as the basis of a just and moral society, employing in particular a line from Adam Smith* that servitude was not just wrong itself but also inefficient, since slaves would never work as well as free men who had a personal stake in their labour.

JAMES BRUCE OF KINNAIRD (1730–94)

By 1500, thanks to the pioneering Portuguese, the coasts of Africa were more or less known in the West, but even three centuries later the interior had hardly been penetrated by Europeans, whether in pursuit of trade or of war or of Christian missions. Stories abounded of fabulous beasts and still more fabulous wealth, but no outsider really knew what lay beyond the deserts and jungles or up the great rivers. There was only one way to find out, and it fell to a Scot to inaugurate the classical era of African discovery which, after another century, unlocked the secrets.

This was James Bruce of Kinnaird. Bruce was a man of the Enlightenment, who sought neither trade nor war nor the glory of God but the extension of knowledge, and who thus became the first of the great scientific explorers. Born into the landed gentry of Stirlingshire, he was educated at Edinburgh University and discovered in himself a prodigious linguistic ability. As a student he mastered the major ancient and modern languages of Europe, as well as Hebrew and Arabic, to which he later added tongues of the Near East – Chaldean, Syriac, Ge'ez, Amharic, Tigrinya and Ethiopic.

He first put his talent to mundane use as a wine merchant in the Iberian peninsula, for his family had no money and he had to earn a living somehow. An old school-friend living in London eventually got him the appointment of consul in Algiers on account of his knowledge of Arabic, then unusual. He had to spend much of his time trying to ransom British sailors captured by Barbary pirates, with no great success. But it was from here that he launched himself into the African interior.

What he most wanted was to solve the mystery, dating from ancient times, of the source of the River Nile. European knowledge had not advanced since the history written 2,000 years before by the Greek, Herodotus, who speculated how a river flowing out of the Sahara could flood so enormously every season, and recorded a story that it rose from four fountains on a single mountain in the middle of Africa.

It was impossible to sail up the Nile, because of the annual flood, a sequence of cataracts and other hazards. When Bruce moved to Egypt, he began to prepare for a journey which would take him down the coast of the Red Sea to a point where he could strike inland for the mountains of Abyssinia. In 1768 he set off. It would be, of course, a perilous journey. This was a turbulent quarter of the globe disputed by the Ottoman Sultan and the Emperor of Ethiopia, not to speak of other kings, chieftains and governors.

Along the way Bruce survived battles and bloodbaths, witnessed massacres and mutilations, braved robbers and lions. But at last he found the source of the Blue Nile in a line of bubbling springs, and at that moment his thoughts flew home: 'I remembered,' he later wrote, 'the magnificent scene in my own native country where the Tweed, Clyde and Annan rise in the one hill.' He followed the river to its confluence with the White Nile, and so descended to regain Cairo in 1773, the first to accomplish that journey. In his success, however, lay his failure. This was the wrong Nile: the White divides from the Blue near Khartoum but it is the White that is longer, stretching down to what is now known as Lake Victoria in the heart of the continent.

At home Bruce had been given up for dead and his reports of the unknown met only scepticism when he got back, not least from that scourge of Scots, Samuel Johnson. Bruce was never to receive any official recognition. In understandable high dudgeon he retired to Kinnaird. From this period, the last twenty years of his life, he gained an unenviable and undeserved reputation for being disagreeable and dishonest. True, he had a short temper, which the baseless attacks on his good name made shorter, and he did not avoid the temptation to embellish his experiences in the published account of his journey. But the main accusation against him, that he had never even been to Abyssinia, was outrageous, though not to be finally set to rest till half a century after his death — not much use to him.

Bruce was all the same a luminary of the social scene in enlightened Edinburgh. One of John Kay's portraits poses him, a huge figure of six foot four, against the tiny Peter Williamson,* who had returned after surviving kidnap by American Indians. Not only exotic but also charming when he wished, the handsome Bruce was adored by women everywhere from the harems of Algiers to the salons of Paris, not to mention the Ethiopian court. He could ride like an Arab, shoot partridge from the saddle at a gallop, and he faced every danger with cool composure.

In retrospect he appears a giant of exploration, inspiring others and inaugurating modern scholarship on the ancient empire of Abyssinia. David Livingstone would write in 1868:

> *Old Nile played the theorists a pretty prank by having his springs 500 miles south of them all! I call mine a contribution, because it is just 100 years since Bruce, a greater traveller than any of us, visited Abyssinia, and having discovered the sources of the Blue Nile, he thought he had solved the ancient problem. It hardly detracts from his achievements that the ultimate solution of the problem eluded him.*

MUNGO PARK (1771–1806)

What James Bruce of Kinnaird did for East Africa, Mungo Park did for West Africa. In opening up the interior for the first time, his task was if anything even more arduous. Bruce had faced, in going from the Red Sea to the mountains of Ethiopia, extremes of heat and cold as well as danger from man and beast. In addition to all these Park ran the risk of pestilence, for no part of the world was reckoned more unhealthy than West Africa. Europeans who ventured there, mainly to slaving outposts, counted themselves lucky to survive more than two seasons. But by the end of the eighteenth century there were people trying to put relations between the two continents on a level higher than the brutal exploitation represented by the slave trade. In London an African Association established in 1788 devoted itself to scientific study of unknown regions, largely under the inspiration of Bruce's travels. It was this body that first sponsored Park.

Park was a cottar's son from the banks of the River Yarrow in Selkirkshire. Foulshiels, the tiny house where he was born, still stands, adorned with a plaque to him, but it is now a ruin. He went to the local high school and was apprenticed to a doctor in Selkirk called Thomas Anderson, whose daughter he would later marry. At the age of seventeen, fairly late by Scottish standards, he went to Edinburgh University to study medicine. Then he became a naval surgeon, a common destiny for poor students.

As such he voyaged about a bit, and this had the beneficial effect of arousing his interest in exploration. Returning at length to London, he offered his services to the African Association. It had turned its attention to another major geographical puzzle, the River Niger. Here was a second huge flow like the Nile's, this one issuing in the Atlantic Ocean at the Gulf of Guinea apparently from a course which stretched straight down from the north. But in the north was desert. So where did all the water come from? A great river also figured in reports of Timbuktu, a trading city deep inland and further to the west, from which no European had yet returned alive; its name would become in English a metaphor for exotic inaccessibility. But that river was said to flow north-east, thus into the desert. How were these factual fragments to be reconciled? Park got the job of doing so. It says much for the impression of resource and resolve he must have given that so much confidence could be placed in a young and relatively untried man. After months of careful preparation he set out.

His journey was to last two years, from 1795 to 1797. From the African coast he penetrated to the upper reaches of the Niger and worked with the utmost diligence, often in the most trying conditions, at the systematic mapping of its course. Discovery was Park's personal priority, but he did not close his eyes to economic opportunities. It is a measure of the difference between him and Bruce. The latter was a gentleman from a Scotland where agriculture still dominated, Park a self-made man from a Scotland discovering the potential of intercontinental trade: 'I had a passionate desire to examine into the productions of a country so little known, and to become experimentally acquainted with the modes of life and character of the natives.' The Niger, however, was 2,000 miles long and a single expedition could only do so much.

After Park's return he sat down to write his *Travels in the Interior Districts of Africa*, published in 1798. In its real and sensitive interest in native life, it still merits its reputation as a classic of travellers' literature. Again there is a contrast with Bruce, so vain and boastful in print as to arouse suspicion of his reliability. Park, on the other hand, is modest and self-effacing, anxious only to inform. Thomas Carlyle* was to call him 'one of the most unpretending and at the same time valuable specimens of humanity'.

With these adventures behind him, Park found it hard to settle down with his wife in the obscurity of his chosen position as a doctor in Selkirk. After a few years, he jumped at the chance of going back to Africa when offered the leadership of an expedition to be financed by the British Government, and so not lacking for feasible support. The aim was to settle once and for all the scientific dispute over the direction of the Niger's flow by the simple expedient of following its course down to the ocean from where Park had left off last time. The

Government's prime purpose was economic, and now Park too harboured a more definite hope that 'I should succeed in rendering the geography of Africa more familiar to my countrymen, and in opening to their ambition and industry new sources of wealth, and new channels of commerce'.

Starting again from the upper stretches of the river, he sailed all the way down it till, on the eve of reaching the delta, he lost his life when tribesmen attacked his boat at Bousa. But he had established that the course described an immense arc, from the rainy mountains on the western coast along the fringe of the Sahara and so to the sea. This achievement was secure despite Park's death, and he left an honourable reputation behind him. Unlike many explorers he was not neurotic, not driven by inner demons. A brave yet amiable man, he did not seem eager for fame, still less for wealth, being quietly content that the world should benefit from his labours.

Park's most notable successor, and the man most associated with nineteenth-century mission in Africa, is probably better described as an explorer than a missionary, although he was both.

DAVID LIVINGSTONE (1819–73)

The funeral of David Livingstone at Westminster Abbey in April 1874, after his embalmed corpse had been carried by faithful bearers out of the heart of Africa, struck a note of intense patriotic emotion not heard since Admiral Horatio Nelson was brought back from Trafalgar. It had been a long road from Livingstone's birthplace in a humble tenement at Blantyre in Lanarkshire, or indeed from Cape Town where he first landed on the dark continent in 1841. That it would end in canonization as a Christian, imperial hero, he would never then have believed – with good reason, for it was a false picture.

He had remained a sincere evangelical Christian, a dissenter in Scotland and a Congregationalist in England, where he went to be trained as a missionary. But this perceptive youth had hardly arrived in Africa when he realized evangelism was not getting far with the inhabitants. The early missionaries seem to have seen themselves like St Paul in the Acts of the Apostles: they expected just to arrive in an exotic spot and announce the good news for instant conversions to take place. It puzzled them that this never happened.

Livingstone's outlook would be marked by an intense love of Africa and the Africans, remembered by them to this day. It meant, though, that he was never much use as a missionary. In his whole career he made just a single conversion. He preferred the excitement of exploration, to fill in the map of an Africa still largely blank to Europeans. His greatest good work along the way was to seek to suppress the slave trade, the curse of the continent.

That first phase of his career lasted sixteen years. He then took a long furlough in Britain. He toured lecturing to huge audiences, promoting his book, *Missionary Travels*, and collecting funds for his return. He got a promise of £5,000 from the Government to carry 'commerce and Christianity' into the heart of darkness. Livingstone had decided Christianity was not by itself enough to cure Africa's ills. If it was to be accepted by native societies, they had to change in other ways too. Commerce was the key. It would give Africans better means to enrich and advance themselves than making war and capturing slaves. A general transformation of their lives would take place, which conversion would crown. So Livingstone believed that Africa needed, beside the missionaries, white men to come in for practical purposes, to give a lead in social and economic improvement. They would not rule the Africans but live alongside them, with no racialism — on the contrary, he welcomed the prospect of 'a fusion or mixture of the black and white races on this continent'.

With the money raised in Britain, he wanted to try some such scheme. He had identified the River Zambezi as 'God's highway into Central Africa'. Its huge basin seemed to offer every prospect of healthy areas for missions, markets, agriculture and settlements. He bought a steamboat to ascend the river from its mouth but was shattered when he found it to be unnavigable, blocked upstream by a fearsome gorge. He still refused to give in, and diverted into the tributary River Shire. At its source he did discover highlands bordering

Lake Nyasa which he seized on as promised land. This region was to become the modern Malawi, where the influence of Scottish churches has been so strong. But the churches were not yet ready to follow Livingstone's lead, so he had to turn to the Universities' Mission to Central Africa, young, muscular Christians from Oxford and Cambridge. Nine of them set out with him as guide in 1861, but they had not reckoned with his eternal yearning to make off into the bush alone. He did so as soon as he discovered a suitable base for them near Lake Nyasa.

He made one last trip home to recuperate in 1864–5. Then he launched himself into a final effort. Its missionary content being nominal, this created the real riddle about an always opaque character. His treatment of his wife when they first arrived in Africa had been callous even by the chauvinist standards of the time. Now, forgetting the lands of Nyasa, he spent the decade till his death in an obsessive search for the source of the Nile. Perhaps it was a stubborn Scot's defiance of fate. It revealed an old man daring beyond all reason, ruthless in disregard of others' interests or reputations, driven by an apparently selfish ambition to open up Africa and to be the first in every region. With a life's work crowned by this, his later canonization was again more than might have been expected.

Of course, the canonization ensured, and was meant to ensure, that his work continued beyond the grave, if now in ways defined by his disciples. Soon missionaries were back by Lake Nyasa, to start a sustained Scottish evangelism which goes on even now. By 1900 the British did rule Central Africa. But just as Livingstone had a different outlook from missionaries before him, so he did not envisage the imperialism that followed. He had never mentioned British rule and perhaps did not imagine it could come about. Certainly he would have disapproved of later colonial policies which displaced tribal structures and seized African lands for whites all the way from the Cape to Kenya.

In African history he was an odd man out, and our modern views of him have been distorted through the prism of the high imperialism dividing his era from ours. High imperialism created his legend, yet he acted on the beliefs of a pre-imperialist age. He proposed for imperialism a shape it never took, one without a chasm between white rulers and black subjects.

In that he remained very Scottish, a poor boy who grew up into the young man, awkward and by his own admission rather simple, working his way through college, assimilating his nation's moral and intellectual heritage in popular, practical form — a world away from the ethos of the English public schools that shaped high imperialism. Livingstone's Scottishness also helps us to understand his elevation of commerce rather than government into the great force for civilization — this on the part of a man who never made or sold anything.

Livingstone's exploits were to inspire many, including a successful missionary who started life as a mill girl in Dundee. Called 'Great Mother' by the Nigerians, when she arrived in Africa she faced such practices such as human sacrifice.

MARY SLESSOR (1848–1915)

Mary Slessor exported to Africa the warm heart and sharp tongue of Scottish proletarian matriarchy. She took them with her from the tenements of Dundee, where she was brought up the daughter of a ne'er-do-well cobbler drinking himself to death. Her first experience of the world came with the grinding, unhealthy toil of twelve-hour days in the weaving mills. But she made the most of the few consolations available: she bettered herself through reading at night and devoted her spare time to the Secession Church, an austere evangelical sect. It had an interest in foreign missions, especially one at Calabar, on the sluggish estuary of the Cross River in what is now eastern Nigeria. Moved like many Scots by news of David Livingstone's* death in 1873, she offered herself as a missionary and was accepted to go out there. Three years later, after a few months' training in Edinburgh, this strapping, plain, bony lass, who had never even crossed the Tweed, found herself amid steaming, tropical swamps four degrees above the Equator, where she would stay till she died in harness nearly forty years later. Her career showed, though, how Livingstone's earlier form of mission was turned towards ends he would never have dreamed of, to become an adjunct of imperialism. Missionaries had been stationed at Calabar, an old slaving port, for three decades before Mary Slessor arrived there. They had put a stop to slavery, human sacrifice and similar savage practices. But to do this they had to win the co-operation of the tribal chiefs, and in return were obliged to acquiesce in other aspects of native culture, such as polygamy, which while less horrible still had a heathen origin. All the same, this special relationship at Calabar was gradually civilizing the town and tribes round it.

With a resurgence of missions in the 1870s came missionaries impatient of such slow but steady advance, appalled at survivals of paganism and determined to stamp them out, if necessary by calling on imperialist force. Mary Slessor was one of this new generation, though by no means the most impetuous. While she never stood for any nonsense, by and large she used her talents successfully to breathe life into the mission's methods. She attained new heights of ingenuity in running its educational efforts on a shoestring, and applying its stretched resources to the backward hinterland. This work would give her a status in Scottish evangelical literature second only to Livingstone's. Still, she was not a pioneer like him. She took her place in an enterprise already established, with considerable achievements in education of the people, and her contribution would have been impossible without a foundation long laid.

The legends propagated in the literature nevertheless depict a woman penetrating the heart of darkness. Her biographer, William Livingstone, introduces her in bloodcurdling vein: 'The first sight she saw on entering her new sphere was a human skull hung on a pole at the entrance to the town.' But, certainly at Calabar, the stark opposition between her Christian rectitude and the heathen darkness around existed only in the literature. It pandered to popular taste for exotic tales of heroism, especially about a woman, and swelled the flow of funds. It also obscured the special relationship at Calabar, in terms belittling alike the missionaries' accomplishments and the indigenous peoples' needs. This African society thriving on a symbiosis of Scottish democracy and negro aspiration had still to be defined as savage.

Mary Slessor herself grew disillusioned. Perhaps she could not feel content till she came face to face with barbarism. She got permission to leave for a place, and amid a tribe, called Okoyong, well up-country, in surroundings that were more primitive and not so far evangelized. Even here she found that the great obstacle to Christian truth and progress lay not in human sacrifice or cannibalism but (just as among Dundonians) in alcohol. It was consumed by old and young, at noon and at night, and by her own account most of Okoyong went to bed drunk. She had to start education from scratch, but made it widely available by training teenage teachers to pass on the rudiments of learning. She prided herself on the numbers of makeshift schools she founded.

The legends also misrepresented the reasons for her status in the interior. A British consul came to Calabar in 1878 to set a seal on progress by signing a treaty under which the chiefs undertook to desist for ever from their bad old ways. From there it took but a step for them to defer to external power. They put up little resistance to the occupation of Calabar in 1889, when Britain proclaimed a Niger Coast Protectorate. It became necessary to appoint a deputy consul to Okoyong, and Mary Slessor was the obvious person. The missionary passed over into the colonial official, though she fulfilled both roles with deepening sympathy for Africans now beset by bewildering changes. They flocked to find out from her how they might conform to their new masters' demands. She was at her best presiding for hours in the native court, knitting her way through palavers to stop litigants getting excited.

She did worry at the diversion from her true purpose: 'Where is the time and strength for comprehensive and consecutive work of a more directly evangelistic and teaching type? – specially when the latter is manned year by year by the magnificent total of one individual.' In the end she integrated her missionary endeavour with imperial expansion, but on the whole Scotland approved of this.

Many of the best known stories of great explorers, pioneers and missionaries are associated with Africa, or as in a previous chapter, with North America. But there are many other parts of the British Empire explored and developed by Scots pioneers whose stories cannot fit into this book. **James Andrew Broun-Lindsay, Marquis of Dalhousie** (1812–60) was not an explorer but can certainly be classed as a pioneer. He carried out the peaceful annexation of the Punjab, systematically introduced railways, roads, and irrigation as Governor-General of India and opened the Ganges Canal.

Then there are the explorers who opened up Australia, and whose names live after them in the names of towns and rivers. Mount Stuart in that country is named after **John McDougall Stuart** (1815–66), the first man to cross Australia from north to south. The city of Brisbane is named after **Sir Thomas McDougall Brisbane** (1773–1860), Governor-General of the Australian state of New South Wales, who was born in Largs in Ayrshire. Brisbane was both a soldier and an astronomer who set up an observatory and catalogued more than 7,000 stars.

Another name associated with Australia is **Sir Roderick Impey Murchison** (1792–1871), after whom the Murchison River is named and who predicted the discovery of gold there. But this geographer and geologist, who was born in Tarradale, Scotland, spread his influence to a number of continents. The Murchison Falls in Uganda are also named after him and between 1840 and 1845 he led a survey of the Russian Empire. He was a founder of the Geological Society in London and defined the Silurian geological period, from 435 to 408 million years ago, when land plants first appeared. Along with Sedgwick he was also involved in classifying the Devonian period, from 408 to 360 million years ago, which produced extensive marine sediments and fossils.

There is not a corner of the globe where, it seems, a Scot has not cast some shadow. In Antarctica the Ross Sea, Ross Island, Ross Ice Shelf and Ross Dependency are all named after one man – **Sir James Clark Ross** (1800–62), who claimed Antarctica for Queen Victoria in 1841. He named the twin volcanoes of Antarctica, Erebus and Terror after his two ships. The tradition of polar expeditions was carried on by **William Spiers Bruce** (1867–1921), an oceanographer who studied medicine at Edinburgh University and went to the Antarctic in 1892. He was the leader of the Scottish expedition which in 1902 discovered Coats Land. In 1912 he advised Captain Scott before his attempt to reach the South Pole that his supply dumps were too far apart, advice which proved all too accurate. The race to the magnetic South had already been won in 1909 by Shackleton's expedition, which included **Alastair Forbes-Mackay** (1878–1914), a Scots Navy surgeon.

Our next story illustrating the pioneering spirit of the Scots is set in an even more unlikely place to find Scottish influence.

THOMAS BLAKE GLOVER (1838–1911)

Glover's former home is a tourist attraction which attracts nearly two million visitors annually, yet most Scots have never heard of him. The riddle is solved when it is revealed that most Japanese, revere him as a national hero. The house in question is the centrepiece of Glover Garden in Nagasaki, where Glover is regarded as one of the founding fathers of modern Japan.

Few would have guessed at such a bizarre outcome to the life of the child born at 15 Commerce Street, Fraserburgh, a bleak fishing village in the north-east of Scotland. Glover's mother was a 'quine' from Fordyce, a village in nearby Banffshire, and his father an English naval officer who became chief coastguard at Fraserburgh. In 1851 the family moved to Bridge of Don, just north of Aberdeen, and on leaving school there, Glover found that, like his father, he had the sea in his bones. He travelled the world working for a trading company, and found a ready market for ships and weapons in the Japan of the 1860s, an unstable and violent country ruled by a Shogun in place of the traditional Emperor.

In 1863, Glover settled in Nagasaki and moved into a western-style house built for him; it is now the oldest remaining building of its type in the city. He became involved in local politics and was instrumental in helping the samurai topple the Shogun and restore the Emperor to his throne. He married a Japanese woman called Tsura who was the daughter of a samurai; she wore butterfly emblems on her clothes, leading some to speculate that she may have been the inspiration for the name of Puccini's heroine.

But Glover was no Pinkerton. He stayed in Japan and prospered, commissioning three warships for the Japanese navy from Aberdeen shipyards and eventually establishing his own shipbuilding company which grew into the giant Mitsubishi corporation. Although he helped re-establish a traditional system of rule in Japan, Glover was also a modernizer and promoted a system which enabled many young Japanese women to be educated abroad. He was responsible for bringing many of the benefits of the Industrial Revolution to Japan, introducing the first railway locomotive and opening the country's first mechanized coal mine. As reward for his efforts he became the first non-Japanese to be presented with the Order of the Rising Sun, one of Japan's highest honours.

If it was somewhat unlikely to find a Scot at the centre of affairs in Japan, this could not be said of India. The man chosen to illustrate the story of how Scots influenced the great sub-continent is in fact the great-great-grandfather of the author.

ALEXANDER DUFF (1806–78)

Alexander Duff was one of the first two missionaries sent overseas by the Church of Scotland, and he remained the dominant figure in Scottish missionary work till David Livingstone* arrived on the scene. Born in Perthshire, Duff attended St Andrews University, where he became a brilliant pupil of Thomas Chalmers, the greatest Presbyterian thinker of the age. Duff absorbed his combination of evangelical religion, scientific confidence and social conservatism.

These he took with him to Calcutta in 1830. In Bengal, already under British rule for seventy years, a cultural revival was under way in reaction to western ideas, not least to those imported by enlightened Scots. Leading Bengalis wanted to use the ideas to promote social progress, yet without giving up their own culture. Duff held an uncompromising view on this, believing that they must forsake Hinduism and embrace Christianity; the one would hold them back while the other would carry them forward. He maintained a dim view of India's civilization though he stayed in the country more than thirty years, rejecting opportunities at home, even the succession on Chalmers's death to his final academic post, the chair of theology at New College, Edinburgh, the most honorific position the Free Church of Scotland could offer. Duff did come back to raise funds in 1851, and for that year was made Moderator of the General Assembly, the first missionary to be thus distinguished. After he left India for good in 1864, he continued to exert an indirect influence as convener of the Free Church's Foreign Missions Committee. He was the world's greatest authority on missionary education right till his death.

His major contribution to the complex situation in Bengal was to introduce there the Scottish educational tradition. Shortly after landing he founded a school, which still exists under the name of the Scottish Church College. A great demand for western learning had arisen from the wealthy Indians of this thriving commercial city, and he had a full roll of their children in no time. This was a little surprising, since he made clear his intention to turn the boys into Christians. He knew they came to him for useful knowledge, but to his mind that made no difference: he followed Chalmers in holding that all truth formed a unity, that philosophy and science confirmed the Bible, that divine revelation did not conflict with modern consciousness and that the laws of nature had been laid down by God, so that studying them could only confirm the faith.

His success in luring able pupils was due in no small measure to the fact that he gave instruction in English, while other missionaries used Bengali. Significantly, he himself had been brought up to speak Gaelic, still the vernacular in his part of Perthshire. English there had long been the medium of Protestantism and social advance, so he could readily associate it with the culture he meant to impart to his pupils. He compared them to the young Highlanders who completed their education at the English-speaking universities of Scotland. His pioneer days in Calcutta coincided with the climax of a debate over education in India between orientalists and anglicists, that is to say, between those who wanted public funds used for sponsoring classical eastern learning and those who wanted them spent only on teaching European literature and science. It brought total victory for the anglicists, enshrined in a decree of 1835 from the Governor-General, Lord William Bentinck. Duff's institution became all the more a magnet to the ambitious youngsters of Calcutta.

Yet the teaching of western culture in English did not bring the flood of conversions to Christianity he hoped for. On the contrary, progress on what he regarded as his main task remained slow. Not till 1848 could a Bengali congregation, mainly of wealthy intellectuals, be formed. One member, Lal Behari Day, atypical in that he went to the length of becoming an ordained minister, also won literary prominence as editor of periodicals and novelist of peasant life. This was just what Duff wanted: the replacement through education of the old Indian elite by a new one ready to reform the country. Most, however, showed little interest in taking the next step and acting as a channel to the masses for Christianity and westernization. What they did instead was demand rights from their British masters, and by the end of the nineteenth century a politicized Indian intelligentsia formed the core of a nationalist movement.

The mission of Duff and the Scots who followed him thus had an effect, but not exactly the one they hoped. They carried to India an integrated philosophy owing much to the Scottish educational tradition. They not only preached the gospel and set an example of piety and virtue. They sought also and above all to make positive use of education as a weapon against heathenism, inculcating godliness and a sense of human equality together − which can be taken as an expression of Scottish values. While they got the secular side of this across, they remained quite unsuccessful on the religious side, since conversions numbered only 3,000 in the whole of India by the end of the century. Education was easily imparted, but Duff was somewhat naïvely put out to find that Indians could not be brought to share his contempt for their culture, which included their religion.

Duff was a Free Church missionary. The schism which tore apart the Kirk in the nineteenth century was exported to the mission fields around the empire, resulting in bitter rivalries. Long after the actual split in 1843, a spirit of intolerance hovered around church affairs, and when the Free Church produced one of the finest Old Testament scholars in the world, he was to become the victim of it.

WILLIAM ROBERTSON SMITH (1846–94)

William Robertson Smith, the last man in Scotland to be tried for heresy, was a son of the manse from Keig in Aberdeenshire. He went to the Free Church of Scotland's theological seminary, New College, Edinburgh, where his accomplishments as a student were prodigious. He won the chair of Hebrew and Old Testament at the corresponding institution in Aberdeen at the age of twenty-three. Already he was earning international repute as a pioneer of comparative religion, in particular as an authority on scripture through precise understanding of the text with its background in the beliefs and practices of ancient peoples in the Middle East. He was to set an example to all scholars of how to see past civilizations from within and understand them as totalities. It was, however, already too much for some of his clerical brothers that he returned from tours of German and Dutch universities to apply to sacred texts the latest in the higher criticism practised there. To their horror he went on to prove that the Old Testament, far from having been directly dictated by God, was transmitted through the hands of numerous human editors.

The Free Church, the most evangelical of the Scottish Presbyterian sects, had many members who believed in the inerrancy of scripture. They resolved to stifle Smith's influence. They drew up charges of heresy against him, on which they tried him before the courts of the church in a series of actions from 1878 to 1880. His small stature and sprightly demeanour belied his lion-hearted courage, and his integrity would not let him recant. Moreover, he had the better of the altercations. His foes might have preferred to burn him at the stake, but the General Assembly, always managed with care, struck a balance: it admonished yet, in a half-hearted way, absolved him. The price he paid was a promise not to publish any more questionable work unless he cleared it with his superiors.

But one article slipped through the net, having been delayed in the press. It argued that Abraham, Judah and David had contracted marriages incestuous within the degrees of Leviticus, indicating the survival in Israel of a pre-Judaic system of matrilineal kinship. It also showed that many persons and place-names in Old Testament genealogies represented animal totems, evidence that God's chosen people had worshipped them. That sealed Smith's fate. His prosecution was forced by a Highland clique of fanatical Calvinists. If anything, these people aroused distaste among Scots at large; all the same, in 1881 Smith was deposed from his chair.

History has vindicated him against his accusers, and the affair cast Scotland in a poor light. He himself had no future there. He moved to Cambridge University, where he continued to produce highly distinguished work. One way in which he afterwards earned his living was as editor of the ninth edition of *Encyclopaedia Britannica*, 'the scholar's encyclopaedia', so called because it featured essays by a wide range of eminent international authorities. He died in 1894, aged just forty-eight, and had his body sent home for burial at Keig.

Smith's basic ideas are contained in *The Prophets of Israel* (1882) and *The Religion of the Semites* (1889). He started off by analysing the many types of sacrifice mentioned in ancient records. In its highest form, at turning points of the year or at times of danger, members of the group killed their totemic animal, otherwise taboo to them, and devoured it as their brother-god. It is easy to see how others in the Free Church feared this might appear in a different light to those of weak or questioning faith or of none. Why should such people regard the culmination Smith found in Christ as symbolism qualitatively separate from its primitive forms? Why should they not conclude that when Christians took communion they were acting out a modern survival of totemic bloodletting? Why should they not see Christianity as another product of primeval confusion and error? A trial for heresy did not get rid of such disturbing questions.

Smith's work won a more than religious significance by the way he set aside the Presbyterian, indeed Protestant, assumption that the vital relation was the one between an individual and God. Instead he implied that the group was the basic unit of religion. In a primitive tribe, for example, members were linked by blood but included within it their deities and the totemic animals from which they thought they were descended. They accepted a religious duty of performing rites needed to uphold the order of things in their world, that is, to preserve the group and affirm their identity as its members. Among Semites the main rite was a sacrifice.

Smith traced the idea of sacrifice back through the Old Testament to yet earlier sources, then traced forward the sanctification of this savage bloodletting as God revealed his purposes to man. To him the whole gave proof of a divine plan. What the Semites really worshipped, he believed, was their order of things, their own society idealized and deified. They gave it religious sanction because it seemed to their primitive minds natural and inevitable, and therefore divinely ordained. Thus the source of symbolic behaviour lay in the group. Beliefs had a social origin. This idea made a huge impact on other disciplines such as sociology and psychology and influences our views of humanity to this day.

The folly of dissipating energy between three competing denominations with similar creeds and forms of worship was eventually to impact on the three Presbyterian churches in Scotland. In 1900 two of them united to form the United Free Church, the great part of which re-entered the national Church of Scotland in 1929. The ecumenical spirit which prevailed in Scotland during this generation was to bear fruit in the World Missionary Conference in 1910, which is generally recognized as the birth of the modern ecumenical movement and which eventually gave rise to the World Council of Churches. It owed its genesis and management to two Scotsmen.

JOHN NICOL FARQUHAR (1861–1928)

John Nicol Farquhar carried comparative religion, the science founded by William Robertson Smith,* into study of the oriental faiths. He was no armchair scholar but a missionary himself, and missionaries were among those who felt they had most to fear from Smith's challenge. Alexander Duff,* for example, saw in them a threat to his life's work: while he had never doubted the superiority of his own culture, Smith set it in its place alongside other cultures.

There was immediate relevance to missions in his demonstration that, among primitive religions, the rite took the place of the creed, almost in inverse proportion to the importance bestowed on each by Protestantism, and by the Free Church of Scotland especially. That meant missionaries deceived themselves if they looked, as they did by instinct, for the creed of the people among whom they went. Missionaries found no creed, because there was none to be found. So they fell back on a second best, myths of the gods. It foxed Duff how any sane person could believe such a jumble of rubbish. Hence, he concluded, nothing existed among such people worthy of the name of religion. Nobody unversed in comparative method could have appreciated that myths were a secondary development, and that the significant acts of a religious community lay in its rites.

By the time Farquhar came to do his mature work, he had absorbed the lessons of comparative religion. He was a clever Aberdonian who went on from school and university in his native city to Oxford, then out in 1891 as a professor to the college run in Calcutta by the London Missionary Society. He soon found its focus on conversion too narrow, and resigned to pursue broader purposes in the Young Men's Christian Association. He gave his spare time to scholarship, as a liberal critic of the Bible and of the Hindu scriptures. In *Christianity in India* (1908) he was already repudiating the practice of Duff, arguing that missions should concentrate not on the western education of an elite but on the vernacular education of the poor if they were ever to found Christian communities in the sub-continent. In *Crown of Hinduism* (1913) he developed an argument that the many rites of Hinduism could not in the end fulfil the needs which the individual Hindu felt on a different level — the level which, for example, was fulfilled in a Christian society by following the commandments of Jesus. Hinduism need not be rejected, but should be seen as a step on the way to a higher religion. Christian society represented the 'evolutionary goal' for every other one.

Farquhar brought his ideas out in another way as the leading figure at the first World Missionary Conference in 1910. Protestants from all churches and continents, including a few non-whites, met to plan a universal strategy which today is recognized as the blueprint of the ecumenical movement. It paid homage to Scotland's Christian efforts that Edinburgh should have been chosen as the venue. The 1,200 delegates reached agreement on various practical points: that the advance of Islam presented the greatest threat in Africa; that they must remedy their relative neglect of China; and that they should co-ordinate their efforts in an International Missionary Council.

Intellectually the conference was less coherent. European delegates tended to advocate tolerance of indigenous traditions and the erection of native churches which would preserve and develop the culture of converted communities. English and North American missionaries tended to link their evangelical or humanitarian work with the introduction of legitimate commerce and western ways advancing in step with imperial power. Scottish experience encompassed both outlooks. Scots came from a small country overshadowed by a big one, with an ethos that instilled sympathy for native peoples. It was perhaps a consequent need to prove themselves and vindicate national pride that drove them to tackle the toughest challenges on the furthest missionary frontiers. But missionary heroism, even unto martyrdom, made them ambitious to transform indigenous societies too. Sometimes it had also made them ready, where such societies proved intractable, to call on the resources available to Scotland as a constituent of the world's greatest empire.

The missionary movement in general felt baffled by now at its meagre progress in conversion. That was why Farquhar's presentation to the conference on the concept he called fulfilment made such a deep intellectual impression. He said that while every religion was human, only Christianity satisfied at once humanity's religious instincts and the critical spirit of the modern age. He wanted, however, to discard the concept of contrast between different faiths, and by skilful work on the floor of the conference got his own view on to the official record. A conclusion was reached that the accepted, orthodox missionary attitude, holding Christianity to be true and all other religions to be false, was no longer tenable. The missions' practical contact with these others, and on a different plane the elaboration of a science of comparative religion, showed that they all contained some kernel of truth.

J.H. OLDHAM (1874–1969)

J.H. Oldham is arguably better described as a pioneer than a prophet, but he ranks in the forefront of the ecumenical movement from the watershed conference held in Edinburgh in 1910, through the Life and Work movement in the inter-war years, to the setting up of the World Council of Churches (WCC) in 1948. Motivated after hearing D.L. Moody preach while a student at Oxford, he went on to take a divinity degree at New College, Edinburgh.

Aiming for a parish of his own, he found himself a 'stickit minister' and had to settle for a desk job with the Mission Council of the United Free Church in 1905, but when Scotland offered to host the influential missionary conference in 1910, Oldham found himself in at the birth of something much bigger, which was to develop into the ecumenical movement. He moved to England, where he acquired a circle of influential friends and acquired a reputation as a fixer.

He is reputed to have said: 'Find out where power lies and then take lunch at the Athenaeum.' His conversation circle, known as 'The Moot', included T.S. Eliot, John Baillie and Alec Vidler, a formidable team by any assessment.

In the thirties he was supportive of Bonhoeffer and his colleagues in the Confessing Church which refused to bow the knee to Hitler, but by trying also to accommodate the conformist church, at the key Oxford conference in 1937, Oldham and his colleagues did not realize how dire the situation had become. Although he formed a close friendship with John Moot (after whom the conversation circle was named), an American whom he met at Oxford, there were often tensions between these two founders of ecumenism on the direction the ecumenical movement ought to take.

Oldham's work in the inter-war years was mostly directed towards Africa and as a backroom person, but he had charisma as a speaker. In 1921, he gave an address to the Student Christian Movement. W.A. Visser t'Hooft, the Dutchman who is generally credited with setting up the World Council of Churches after the Second World War, described it as one of the most influential moments of his life. Oldham eventually was honoured by the WCC, becoming an honorary president in 1961. He died in 1969 at the age of ninety-four.

His style may be seen as elitist or as cronyism by many WCC radicals today, but it is thanks to his quiet conciliation skills that many of the issues which are now the staple diet of ecumenical assemblies were first raised and put on the world's agenda.

As has been noted, there is no such job description as pioneer; many of the early explorers were missionaries and vice versa. The same might be said for our next three characters, none of whom can be neatly subsumed under one job description, but who all shared creative talent of one kind or another.

ROBERT CUNNINGHAME GRAHAM (1852–1936)

The fate of Scotland today probably lies in the outcome of the battle between the two biggest parties in the new Parliament in Edinburgh, Scottish Labour and the Scottish Nationalists. It is an intriguing thought that one man founded both, or can at least be numbered among the main founders of both. Even so, his name is best remembered not by political historians but by connoisseurs of the literature of travel. He was Robert Cunninghame Graham of Gartmore in Stirlingshire, a flamboyant figure known in his own day as 'Don Roberto' or 'the uncrowned King of Scots'. Indeed he was descended from Robert Bruce and had through the dormant earldom of Menteith a claim to the Crown of Scotland.

He spent his youth abroad, largely in the Hispanic world, as a rancher in Argentina, Mexico and Texas, then travelling round Spain and Morocco. His journeys gave him a fund of experience on which he drew in his writing for the rest of his life. They also gave him radical opinions. With the approach of middle age he returned home, where his first step was to go into politics. As a local laird with a declared sympathy for the oppressed proletariat, he seemed an ideal candidate in the constituency of North-West Lanarkshire, where Liberal bigwigs were worried about unrest among the miners. He was chosen candidate and elected in 1886.

In these years trade unions started to flex their muscles, though more often in London than in Scotland. Their main demand was for a statutory limitation of forty-eight hours on the working week to bring down unemployment. In the summer of 1887 they called a demonstration in Trafalgar Square, only to be banned by the Government. They went ahead all the same. As police tried to clear the square, scuffles broke out. Cunninghame Graham was there supporting the unions. By design or not, he got arrested and was sentenced to six weeks in jail. This made him a hero to the workers, 'the damned aristo who embraced the cause of the people' as Hugh MacDiarmid* later described him.

The next year, trade unionists in Scotland, led by Keir Hardie, decided to extend their organization into politics and set up a Scottish Labour Party. Hardie knew Cunninghame Graham and invited him to be the president. It was as the SLP's representative that he sat for the rest of the Parliament, though he stood down in 1892 'no longer able to endure the concentrated idiocy of the asylum for imbeciles at Westminster'. The SLP eventually merged into the Independent Labour Party, which in turn merged with the modern Labour Party in 1918. Cunninghame Graham stayed with it.

Scottish Home Rule formed part of the platform of the SLP, ILP and Labour. But Labour, covering the whole of Britain, was dominated by Englishmen. In the 1920s they backtracked on whatever promises for a Parliament the Scots thought them to have given. Patriots such as Cunninghame Graham felt so upset that they decided only a party specifically committed to Scotland's interests — a nationalist party, in other words — could be relied on to do what Scotland needed. A Scottish Home Rule Association had existed since 1886 as a pressure group trying to ensure that any political concessions to Ireland should be made to Scotland too. But now Ireland, or at least twenty-six counties of it, was an independent state in all but name, while Scotland had made no progress. The association determined to turn itself into a proper political party. With like-minded groups, it set up the National Party of Scotland in 1928, which in 1932, after further changes, became the Scottish National Party. Cunninghame Graham was president of both. He made a splendid figurehead, always ready with a witty comment or a rousing speech. But politics is mainly a matter of hard graft, and for this Cunninghame Graham had no taste.

What did call forth his most meticulous efforts was his writing, and it is only sensible to conclude that this was where his true passion lay. His extravagant and eccentric appearance, with perhaps a cloak, a sombrero and a long, pointed beard, surprisingly found little counterpart in his prose, which is rather the product of minute attention to detail and nuance. It is not the most obvious technique for the exotic scenes in which he specializes, but at his hands they grow out of a corner of a townscape, or a strange character, or an unfamiliar custom. He was skilled at evoking traditional cultures losing their vitality, the cultures of the Argentinian pampas or the Arab souk, or indeed of the old Scotland passing away before the misty eyes of himself and his compatriots. It was understandable how a romantic like Cunninghame Graham felt ever more ill at ease in the humdrum and dispirited Scotland between the wars, losing what had once distinguished it as a nation. But, always looking backwards, he did not appear to grasp what essence was keeping it alive: hence, perhaps, the light weight of his literature and the inconsequential nature of his politics.

PATRICK GEDDES (1854–1932)

Patrick Geddes, botanist, town planner, social reformer and economic theorist, was the sort of polymath Scotland has always been wont to produce. In a small country it was as ever hard to find use for his multiple talents, and he ended up wasting some of them, partly by his own fault. He was born at Ballater, Aberdeenshire, and first worked in a bank. Before he was twenty he went to carry out researches in London under T.H. Huxley, the eminent biologist. He learned much from his mentor, but disliked the English capital so much that he determined to free Scotland 'from the intellectual thraldom of London'. After a long trip to Mexico, the first of many to exotic places, he returned to Scotland. But he could not find a job for eight years, till in 1888 he became professor of botany at University College, Dundee, then part of St Andrews University. There he stayed in person, though not in spirit, for the rest of his working days.

He had early in his life come to a mature view of the world: that in modern times there is too great a tendency to separate spheres of experience. It would be better to retain some image of the whole, because without it the separate spheres made little sense. The view sprang from the traditional generalist philosophy of Scottish education, but that was now in decay under the pressure of anglicizing reforms in the universities. Geddes's efforts to sustain it intellectually did not always turn out a success: his attempt to stop economics getting too specialized, for example, rested on ideas that were little short of dotty.

He put his abilities to better use when he descended from the ivory tower. He became active in a group called the Social Union in Edinburgh, which was concerned with the condition of the Old Town, stretching from the Castle to the Palace of Holyroodhouse and rapidly becoming a slum as bourgeois suburbs spread out from it.

The aim was to save the historic centre from dereliction and its people from destitution. Here was an object lesson in Geddes's theories. Edinburgh had once been a whole city. Now it was split, and in the most visible fashion, by the valley between the Old and New Towns. Geddes set up home himself in James Court, just off the High Street, and sought to attract the middle class around him by erecting the picturesque Ramsay Gardens just below the Castle. He transformed the disused Observatory on Castle Hill into the Outlook Tower, where a camera obscura mounted to scan the complete townscape showed the links of land, work and people. His vision was not quickly realized, but today the Old Town is again a desirable residential area.

Geddes carried this socio-biological vision into the Empire, notably to India, where he drew attention to the effects of colonialism on the built environment. Three of the four great cities – Calcutta, Bombay and Madras – were British foundations and creations. Each imposed an alien pattern on indigenous life, setting an example which cast a long shadow over public planning. Two official aims seemed bizarre to Geddes: in the villages to fill in the tanks, a rendezvous for daily work and play, because they bred mosquitoes; and in the towns to drive needlessly wide roads through poor quarters, displacing the people along with their evolved social patterns. Such crassness arose from western assumptions. On the plains round Madras, by contrast, Geddes found an Indian urban form in the great temple-cities of Dravidian culture, expressions of a way of life imbued with religion and history. He believed he could demonstrate how, in a union of robust Scots intellect and earthy Tamil spirituality, renewal could come by interaction of the world's marginalized cultures.

So he sought to revive Indian urban forms. He drew up reports on fifty cities, showing how to improve them without violence to their inherited structures, and in another series worked out ideas to sustain the villages. He befriended Indian intellectuals, Chandra Bose, Rabindranath Tagore and above all Mahatma Gandhi, who told him: 'You could not be more pained than I am over our base imitation of the West.' Geddes felt anxious that Delhi, the fourth great city of the sub-continent and from 1911 again its capital, should not ape the others. He broadcast his dismay at Sir Edwin Lutyens's grandiose plans for New Delhi, in which he saw the unseemly symbol of a Raj nearer its end than a new beginning. Lutyens lost his temper at the impudence, but the domes and vistas of his New Delhi would anyway arise in due course, and posterity has approved his taste.

Geddes was a paradoxical figure, an educator with books on an arresting array of topics to his name, yet hardly taken seriously by academic peers, relying rather for his reputation on faithful disciples and on the benefits he brought to ordinary people whose interests counted for little among the great and good. He is more famous in our day than in his own, appealing to a taste for some coherent view of the world we live in and for means of restoring harmony with a nature we have ravaged. But he had an offputting way of advancing his case (he was, by all accounts, one of the great bores of all time) and he remained, perhaps necessarily, vague about detail. He became a guru for succeeding generations of sociologists and planners, though they seem often to have created the kind of urban disaster he deplored. He was the inspiration for a humanist ideal of civic existence, but there is still room for argument about just what he inspired.

CHARLES RENNIE MACKINTOSH (1868–1928)

The magnificent Musée d'Orsay in Paris, consecrated to the art of the nineteenth century, contains a room dealing with the beginnings of the modern movement in architecture. Over its portals it bears the inscription 'Chicago-Glasgow-Vienna'. Though the French are a chauvinist race, they see nothing untoward in this. To them culture, while it may originate in other lands, consummates itself when it reaches France and there takes its place in the universal civilization. The French can be as grateful for these gifts from afar as their donors can be proud of the recognition thus accorded to them. We may smile a little at the patronizing attitude which underlies such generosity, while reflecting that little recognition of any kind has come from a complacent London for the achievements of Glasgow as a metropolis of art 100 years ago.

But then Charles Rennie Mackintosh, the focus of this attention, was a prophet without honour even in his native city till recently. Glasgow has been physically recast since his time, when it was a compact but monotonous conurbation, its million citizens housed in street upon street of four-storey tenements spreading from a centre of dignified but modest public buildings, with the exception of the grandiose City Chambers and the spectacular University built on a hill to the west. The most striking feature otherwise was the miles of cranes along the River Clyde.

Mackintosh designed his works to fit into this townscape yet to transform it artistically. A small but fine example is the church at Queen's Cross in Maryhill Road, a blend of Gothic and Art Nouveau made for a narrow, hemmed-in site. Though preserved in its elegance, it looks embarrassed now its old surroundings have been replaced by erections too low, too mean and too cheap. And that really sums up modern Glasgow, except that the buildings are more often too high than too low. As a result of its helter-skelter expansion during the Industrial Revolution, the city Mackintosh knew had the worst slums in Europe, fetid dens of poverty and disease. After 1918, when the municipal authorities took over the task of housing the population, they gave Glasgow the worst architecture in Europe. Mackintosh, who might have brought a civilizing imagination to it, was by then in exile. Unable to win commissions at home, he had taken to drink and gone to England, which was no more receptive to his talents then than it is today, and to France, where he stopped designing anything and painted floral watercolours, exquisite but clearly reining in the once awesome ambition of the artist who wrote: 'All great and living architecture has been the direct expression of the needs and beliefs of man at the time of its creation.'

He was born the son of a superintendent of police and grew up in Glasgow's heyday, marked by three great international exhibitions in 1888, 1901 and 1912. In the middle of that span he married Margot

Macdonald, herself a designer of great talent, whose sister Frances married the painter Herbert McNair. Their city had seen the integrity of Scottish art re-established with a new lease of life, in place of the academicism to which the classical school of Ramsay, Raeburn and Wilkie had descended. The Glasgow Boys — Guthrie, Walton, Melville, Macgregor, Hornel and others — generated enormous excitement with exhibitions in Munich from 1890. Into their midst stepped Mackintosh in 1899 with his masterpiece in his own genre, the Glasgow School of Art. At this stage he was far from the lonely pioneer he later seemed to himself, but a precocious genius in a scene of rich and wonderful creativity.

Today the School of Art is hailed as the first important monument in the modern movement in Europe, yet it is also Glaswegian in its synthesis of craftsmanship and technology, as well as Scottish in its fusion of national style and modern theory. The same is true of his other works in or near Glasgow, the Martyrs' and Scotland Street Schools, the Willow Tearoom, Windyhill at Kilmacolm and Hill House at Helensburgh, together with the interior of his own home preserved at the Hunterian Art Gallery.

This oeuvre is all the same a meagre legacy: no municipal palaces, no museum or gallery, no concert-hall or stadium, no offices or factories, just a single church. In the nick of time for his centenary, newly appreciative Glaswegians realized Mackintosh's plans for a house that was never built and a further example of his work came through a time-warp into Bellahouston Park, where it is named House for an Art Lover .

The sad fact is that Mackintosh had no lasting professional success, despite the international reputation he won through his part in the Viennese Sezession of 1900. Back home, these things did not count. He found admirable clients like Miss Cranston, who let him and his wife design everything in her tearooms down to the cutlery, but that seemed a waste of his talents when in London or Paris, in New York or Berlin, he might have had the chance to create the great architectural structures characteristic of the era. Mackintosh became at length unable to work and in 1913 he left his native city for good.

The critic Nikolaus Pevsner wrote of his houses: 'Their combination of windows, chimney stacks and oriels is of a subtle irregularity, at first appearing arbitrary, but then revealing itself as most sensitively placed and scaled — very much what Le Corbusier did in his later works — but without the brutality.' The brutality is just what disfigures the Glasgow of our own day, and we can only mourn the city we never had through neglect of the greatest Scottish architect of the nineteenth or twentieth centuries.

Military heroes are a different breed of men from the explorers and pioneers, the missionaries and creative talents we have met so far. But in the greatest — and Scotland has had more than her share of these — we often find the same spirit of adventure and indomitable courage as pioneers. For that reason we close this section with four very different stories of military men.

SIR HECTOR MACDONALD (1853–1903)

On 25 March 1903, Major-General Sir Hector Macdonald shot himself in Room 105 of the Hotel Regina in the Rue de Rivoli, Paris. On 30 March he was buried at dawn in the Dean Cemetery, Edinburgh, where so many of Victorian Scotland's most famous sons lay. Later during the day a swelling stream of people came to the graveside. By nightfall 30,000 had paid their respects. Macdonald went to his death in shame, yet that scarcely diminished the honour in which he was held. Scots often make a point of unifying opposites, but even by their standards this was an extreme example.

There were several reasons why Scots saw a hero in Macdonald. He was a Highlander, and in the nineteenth century the Highlander had by a bizarre reversal come to represent to the world the best in Scotland. In earlier times he had been taken by the Scots themselves (by Lowland Scots, that is) as representing the worst; now he was supposed to be carrying forward into a civilized era what had been his noble virtues even amid his earlier barbarism. Macdonald was also a son of the people, born on a humble croft, who had risen to high military rank and so satisfied the Scots' belief in democracy and egalitarianism. Finally, he had won fame fighting for the British Empire, demonstrating for all to see what a huge role Scots played in its expansion, and so justifying to them the fateful step their fore-fathers had taken by entering into Union with England in 1707.

Macdonald was what Scots call 'a bonnie fechter'. As a youth he joined up with the Gordon Highlanders, and in that regiment he won a commission for his courage in battle and qualities of leadership. He fought on the frontiers of the Empire in India, Sudan and South Africa. Under fire he was always cool and brave. His troops loved him and he found a special rapport with native auxiliaries from the martial races often compared with the Scots. At the Battle of Omdurman, under the command of General Kitchener, his imper-turbable demeanour made him the real victor in the eyes of many observers. One recalled that a 'non-combatant general officer who witnessed the scene declared that one might see 500 battles and never such able handling of men in the presence of the enemy'. Macdonald went on to take command of the Highland Brigade in the Boer War, after it had been crushed at the Battle of Magersfontein, and restored it as an offensive force. He was wounded in that war, and the end of it saw him receive a knighthood. Other honours were showered on Fighting Mac, as Scotland now called him.

Early in 1902, after a period of leave during which he toured Australia and New Zealand and served as aide-de-camp to King Edward VII, he was appointed military commander in Ceylon. He had nothing special to do on this tranquil tropical isle, but distin-guished generals such as he often proved hard to employ when the Empire was at peace. He could expect to remain there only so long as no wars demanded his presence elsewhere, but in fact his career was now to come to an abrupt and distressing halt.

Out of the blue the Colonial Office in London received a message from the Governor of Ceylon, Sir Joseph West Ridgeway, saying of Macdonald: 'His immediate departure is essential to save grave public scandal which I cannot explain by telegraph.' The nature of the accusation against him has never been spelled out, and now never can be because the relevant official records were at some point destroyed. The trouble concerned an encounter between Macdonald and some schoolboys on a train, but the circumstantial evidence points to something that would by today's standards be regarded as fairly innocuous. Whatever it was, Ridgeway felt he had to hush it up. He advised Macdonald to go on extended leave, return to Britain and confer with his superiors at the War Office, then either obtain a command elsewhere or retire into private life.

Macdonald followed this advice. Once in London, he had an interview with the commander-in-chief, Lord Roberts, who said he could not stay in the Army unless he cleared his name. He should therefore return to Ceylon and face a court martial. 'He protests his innocence,' Roberts wrote to Kitchener, 'but if he is innocent, why on earth did he not insist on having the matter cleared up?' Again, Macdonald followed the advice given to him and set out for the east, passing through Paris. While staying at the Hotel Regina, he learned that his story had been splashed by the *New York Herald*. He went up to his room and shot himself.

Nobody wanted an imperial hero involved in this sort of scandal. The conspiracy of silence allowed wild stories to circulate. The strangest was that Macdonald had faked his suicide and gone off to join the German army, assuming the character of the officer who became Field-Marshal August von Mackensen, a commander during the First World War. Others suspected Macdonald to be the victim of a peculiarly British kind of plot, in which a snobbish expatriate community in the colonies wanted rid of a rough-hewn Scot because of his social inferiority. Whatever the reason, the tragedy of Macdonald seems to have been an unnecessary one.

DOUGLAS HAIG, EARL HAIG OF BEMERSYDE
(1861–1928)

After any great ordeal, it may take a while for people to realize just what has happened to them. In 1918 the Scots, like the British in general, felt victorious. They knew of their appalling sacrifices but, with their enemies crushed, they were assured the sacrifices had not been in vain. Douglas Haig, a Scotsman and commander-in-chief of the British army, was a hero. Only later did a debate start about the human cost of the First World War, and it brought revulsion against the methods which had won that terrible victory, against Haig's methods above all. This was besides a risky period for the United Kingdom. Twenty-six counties of Ireland seceded from it. Nationalism stirred in Scotland, even in Wales. It was not a time to dwell on inequity among the four nations.

When statistics for the war came to be compiled, the bland procedure was adopted of estimating Scottish casualties according to rough shares of population, that is, dividing the British total by ten. Scots have always been suspicious of this. Every parish in the country set up its memorial to the fallen, and the number of names listed on them often seems unbelievable by comparison with the small size of the local communities. But nobody took an alternative count till recently. Now we know that the total of Scots who joined up between 1914 and 1918 was 558,000. Of these 147,000 died, more than a quarter of the recruits, one in ten of all males aged fifteen to forty-nine and over three per cent of the entire Scottish population. This was at least double the average British death rate. In fact no other nation in the war lost so many of its sons as Scotland except Serbia and Turkey, which had been invaded and beaten. Yet Scotland fought this tragic, wasteful struggle to the end in high patriotic spirit with no disaffection from the British state and hardly a thought of protest even against the boneheaded generals. By common consent, Haig was the most boneheaded of all.

He stands forever indicted of the two most bloody battles in British history, the Somme in the summer of 1916 and Passchendaele in the autumn of 1917; to which may be added, in the particular case of Scotland, Arras in the spring of 1917 where, of 120 battalions deployed, forty-four were Scottish — more men than the entire British army at Waterloo, and seven times the number under Robert Bruce at Bannockburn. One reason for the extreme casualties among Scots lay in the fact that Haig believed them to be the best soldiers, as they believed themselves to be, and always turned to them in the most difficult and dangerous conditions. Each of those three battles of the First World War followed the same pattern, with a huge barrage of artillery less effective than expected, followed up by attacks on the ground continuing long after any chance of a decisive breakthrough.

Haig persisted in this costly offensive pattern, despite its lack of success, right up till he finally broke the Germans on the Hindenburg Line in 1918. By that time the British Cabinet itself, now with serious worries whether it would be humanly possible to carry on fighting, expressed doubt about letting its commander-in-chief try yet again with his threadbare strategy. That Haig remained undaunted says much for his moral courage, or perhaps for his mulish obstinacy, which at last paid off when it could have brought definitive disgrace. It has all the same remained unforgivable to many, and created an image of Haig and his fellow generals as aloof, inept and heartless, neither knowing nor caring what ordeals they put their brave men through. Despite the generally held view that Haig was a charmless and inarticulate character, this verdict does him less than justice.

There are a few things to be said in his favour, and historians have begun to say them. Faced by a moral and physical challenge with no precedent in the history of warfare, Haig's nerve and confidence in ultimate victory never failed. His private writings reveal a deeply religious man, even seeing himself as an instrument of providence, a view in which he was encouraged by the minister he consulted as, in effect, his spiritual director, the Reverend George Duncan, who went on to become Principal of St Mary's College in St Andrews. Hence his ability to endure when everyone else despaired. In any event, the war ended as Haig always thought it would, in the total victory of a British army advancing at speed along its entire front.

Detractors of Haig credit the breakthrough in 1918 either to the arrival of the Americans (though most came later), to the success of the French (who in fact had been bled white) or to the economic and political collapse of Germany (which actually followed from defeat in the field). The revisionists stress rather that now Haig was able at last to embark on the war of movement he had always wanted, and he conducted it brilliantly. Nobody, on either side, had been at the outset in a position to predict what sort of conflict the war would be. Probably nobody could have understood how great a superiority defensive weapons had by this stage attained over offensive weapons, and generals of all armies certainly took time to grasp it. If the Germans did so earliest, this was because their strategy of a war on two fronts required of them no more than to hold firm in the West while they tried to destroy the Russians in the East. The only counter available to the western powers was to attempt the breakthrough, and attempt it again and again till it succeeded, after which a German collapse would quickly follow. The cost beggared belief, yet that was just what happened in the end.

SIR HUGH (LORD) DOWDING (1882–1970)

For a few days in 1940, Goering hurled the Luftwaffe incessantly against the south-east of England, to soften it up for the inevitable invasion which would follow. That the invasion never came was principally because the Royal Air Force, despite the handicap of inferior numbers, was able to win the battle for air supremacy.

Churchill immortalized the Hurricane and Spitfire pilots – some of them still teenagers – in a famous phrase after the battle: 'Never in the field of human conflict has so much been owed by so many to so few.' 'The few' were indeed one of the main causes of victory, but two Scotsmen played a critical role in their success. The first was Robert Watson Watt,* the boffin from Brechin. But the man who encouraged him, fought for the building programme for Spitfires to replace the old biplanes still in use in the thirties, and took charge of

Fighter Command during this vital period, was another Scotsman —
Air Chief Marshal Sir Hugh Dowding.

Dowding's role in the Battle of Britain was crucial, in preparation
before it and strategy during it. Yet despite the victory, within three
months a group of colleagues conspired to oust him from his post,
leading to the serious neglect of his importance in the years after the
war. Dowding's father taught at Fettes College, and went to establish
a boys' prep school in Moffat where he was born in 1882. After
education at Winchester on a scholarship he joined the Army and
signed up for flying lessons on credit, which he gambled would be
refunded if the Royal Flying Corps accepted him. They did, and
when his father demanded he stop 'this ridiculous flying' the RFC
replied they could not accept his resignation, since the 1914 war had
just begun.

'Stuffy' Dowding soon rose through the ranks to command his
own squadron and by the end of the war in 1918 was a brigadier-
general. His nickname derives from his complaint to a senior officer
that inexperienced pilots were being sent up to meet the enemy
without adequate training. 'Don't be so stuffy, Dowding,' came the
reply. When he became commanding officer of 16 Squadron in 1915
his own pilots called him 'the Starched Shirt' because of his reserve
and aloofness, and one of them in his memoirs suggests that
Dowding created a gloomy atmosphere by his presence. However, he
concedes that Dowding was also 'efficient, strict and calm'.

During war service he encountered three men whose lives were
later to affect his own: Keith Park, the fighter ace, who became a
close friend; Trafford Leigh-Mallory, who was anything but a friend
of Park's; and William Sholto-Douglas, another ace pilot, whom
Dowding was ordered to put on trial by court martial. Dowding
refused since he believed him innocent, but in a twist of fate, it was
Sholto-Douglas who was to play a leading part in Dowding's downfall in 1940. All four men remained in the RAF and Dowding rose to
be commander-in-chief of Fighter Command. Ironically, he was due
to retire when the Second World War began in 1939, thrusting him
once more into the forefront of the action.

Dowding was dour, diffident and dogmatic, but he knew more than anyone about aerial warfare. When Churchill ordered more Hurricanes to be sent to France in the days before the withdrawal at Dunkirk, he refused, since it would have left home defences vulnerable. He built up night fighters and resisted the demands that 'Big Wings' be made part of Fighter Command strategy. These were founded on the idea of safety in numbers and involved bringing together planes from as many airfields as possible to fly missions together. Advocates of the strategy, such as fighter ace Douglas Bader, claimed they gave greater firepower while Dowding argued they were cumbersome to assemble and manoeuvre, and left no reserve defences. When he chose to give Park command of the front-line sector in the south-east of England and left Leigh-Mallory with the Midlands, the smouldering feud between the two men began to heat up.

Despite his regard for his pilots (whom he called 'my Fighter Boys' and whom others referred to as 'Dowding's Chicks'), he never visited airfields, so rendering himself open to the charge of callousness; after the war he defended himself on the grounds that it was his concern and admiration which led him not to interfere. Given his uncharismatic presence, it may have been better that his efficiency and calm remained at a distance.

Nevertheless his admiration for his pilots was reciprocated. They were sickened to learn on 25 November 1940 that Dowding had been ordered in a short telephone call to leave his desk. He yielded with a curt 'Good morning' to Sholto-Douglas, who had supplanted him in a coup in which Leigh-Mallory and Bader played a part, and in the face of whose machinations Churchill had acquiesced. The exhausted Dowding departed to organize support in the USA before retiring from the RAF in 1942.

After that, Dowding was more communicative with his 'Chicks', but in an extraordinary way – by means of a spiritualist medium with whom he was friendly. Belatedly ennobled as Lord Dowding of Bentley Priory before his death in 1970, he was proclaimed at his memorial service an 'Architect of Deliverance'. A generation later we can see the truth of that description, perhaps more clearly than was possible in 1940.

The three military figures above were all leading figures in different theatres of war: Macdonald in Empire, Haig as commander-in-chief of the British Army in the First World War, Dowding in the Battle of Britain in the Second. Our final figure founded the Special Air Service (SAS), famed in more recent years for its counter-terrorism operations.

SIR DAVID STIRLING (1915–90)

The operations of the SAS are cloak-and-dagger affairs, and the dagger often draws blood. Its recruits are special volunteers, drawn from within a wide variety of specialities, experts in survival techniques who often fight using unorthodox methods. Their role in counter-terrorism has sometimes been controversial but in dozens of cases they have rescued hostages when other means have been exhausted, such as in the siege at the Iranian Embassy in London in 1980. Their record in hunting down IRA terrorists has led them occasionally into the area of 'black operations', and they operate in unique secrecy and confidentiality. But as far as most British people are concerned, they live up to their motto, 'Who Dares, Wins'.

Those who think the phrase has vague echoes of the arms of Scotland, 'Who dare meddle with me', will not be surprised that the SAS was founded by a Scot. David Stirling, born in 1915 the son of a laird, was the embodiment of the motto in every inch of his six feet five. He was set to climb Everest when war came in 1939; instead he joined a Special Commando Unit, then frowned upon as mavericks by a high command which liked to do things strictly by the book. Wounded during a drop in North Africa when his parachute snagged on the aircraft, he crafted a plan for the unit which became known as L-Detachment, Special Air Service Brigade, and tricked his way into the office of commander-in-chief General Auchinleck, normally inaccessible to one with the lowly rank of subaltern. But Auchinleck approved his plan. Stirling joined forces with Australian Jock Lewes, inventor of the oil and thermite 'Lewes' bomb which weighed only a pound — enough of them could easily be carried by a few men to blow up a squadron of planes on the ground.

Working behind enemy lines as the Long Range Desert Group, they were so successful that Hitler issued the infamous *Kommandobefehl* (Commando order) that, contrary to the Geneva Convention, they should be killed on capture, an order which Rommel, the Afrika Korps commander, to his credit ignored. Stirling was captured and taken to Colditz Castle prisoner-of-war camp, where he spent the rest of the war while his brother Bill battled on, commanding 2 SAS as it operated within France in preparation for D-Day.

Many who shared Stirling's buccaneering spirit found it difficult to adapt to peacetime, but with the SAS disbanded, he had new mountains to climb. He moved to Rhodesia and began there the Capricorn Society, a movement whose aim was to create a united states of Africa on the basis of racial equality; but it failed to make ground against the winds of change which were creating independent states in Africa.

Stirling became a successful TV mogul for a while, establishing independent stations that aimed educational programmes at rural Africa and the Middle East.

But in 1963 he saw the need in the Far East for a revived SAS-style force. The regiment, reborn under 'Mad Mike' Calvert, carried out operations in Malaya, Oman and Borneo. Drawn into the efforts to resist the annexation of Yemen by President Nasser of Egypt, he eventually set up a private army called Watchguard International, designed to perform in countries where, for diplomatic reasons, the SAS could not operate. But with public opinion turning against such mercenaries and the idea of white men fighting black Africans, Stirling was viewed more as a colonial white elephant than a hero. He in turn, convinced that Britain was being torn apart by the trade union militancy of the seventies, became involved in the ill-fated

Great Britain League, which would have restored order by means of a kind of a private army. Some of his supporters in that venture were the larger-than-life characters who with him frequented the gambling club run by John Aspinall in Mayfair, such as James Goldsmith, Tiny Rowland, Jim Slater and Lord Lucan.

Yet despite the neo-fascist image that Stirling acquired latterly, he was a proponent of devolution and a Bill of Rights, an avid environmentalist who fought actively against the poaching of rhinos. A curious mixture of gambler and visionary, his character caught precisely the spirit of 'Who Dares, Wins'; he was a Knight of the Round Table who could not fit the square categories the world offered. He was knighted towards the end of his life and died with the consolations of the Roman Catholic Church in 1990.

Medicine

'Whence Came These Arrayed in White?'

A sick patient in the early eighteenth century could deliver himself up to the tender mercies either of surgeon-barbers, who with knife or saw might at best make quick work of tumours and amputations, or else of physicians who were usually quacks, prescribing placebos for diseases of which they knew nothing. In 1746 it was said of the doctors in Dundee that 'they dangled gold-headed canes and looked wise; and according to the strength or weakness of their natural constitution, the patients survived or died'. Even so, genuine progress in the healing arts was going on, much of it pioneered by Scots to whose practical and humanitarian bent the work appealed. Scottish doctors grew familiar in many parts of the globe, as will be seen from the portraits here presented of those at the court of the Tsars, and through them this progress became one of Scotland's great gifts to the modern world.

Earlier than in most countries medicine had been fully accepted as an academic discipline at the Scottish universities, following on the example of the Dutch universities. In both these Calvinist nations the authority of ancient medical texts was abandoned in favour of scientific investigation into the workings and the disorders of the human body. Edinburgh turned itself into the leading centre of medical education in Britain, and into one of the best in Europe. Big hospitals, the infirmaries, were founded in Scottish cities, where techniques of surgery could be developed. The rival colleges of physicians and surgeons in Edinburgh and Glasgow today have museums to exhibit artefacts of their early days, such as bleeding bowls or vacuum devices to raise blisters. Perhaps to our eye they belong rather in a chamber of horrors, but it is reassuring that Scottish medical progress has continued up to the present day. It is a history to be proud of.

JOHN ARBUTHNOT (1667–1735)

The designation 'physician and satirist' is not a common one but Arbuthnot was just that. He was born in Aberdeenshire in a village with which he shared his name (Arbuthnott), and educated at Aberdeen, Oxford, and St Andrews. His claim to eminence as a doctor can be seen in his appointment as physician in ordinary to Queen Anne in 1704, and his publications which stress the value of diet in combating disease.

But he is much better known as a political satirist. He created the character John Bull, clad in Union Jack waistcoat, who appeared in 1727, a caricature of the typical Englishman, in a collection entitled *The History of John Bull*. The third pamphlet in the series introduces John's mother (the Church of England) and her sister Peg (the Church of Scotland) who has a love affair with Jack (Presbyterianism). Arbuthnot's work, which included other masterpieces such as *The Art of Political Lying*, was as popular as that of his near-contemporary Jonathan Swift, one an Irish divine, the other a Scottish doctor. But Arbuthnot was linked with another great satirist of the time, Alexander Pope, with whom he co-wrote most of *The Memoirs of Martinus Scriblerus*, a work which pokes fun at pedantry and pomposity in officialdom.

WILLIAM SMELLIE (1697–1763)

Smellie,[1] born in Lesmahagow, may be regarded as the founder of midwifery, for he removed many of the horrors with which childbirth was surrounded. He was the first to describe accurately the passage of the baby through the birth canal during delivery.

In his first nineteen years in practice in Lanark he became increasingly frustrated at the habit of midwives of calling a doctor at the last minute, generally when a disaster had occurred.

He was determined to gain more knowledge in his subject and after a trip to Paris, settled in London in 1740 for another nineteen years. There he meticulously recorded the details of every case he attended. His *Treatise on the Theory and Practice of Midwifery* became the standard work in the field, used in conjunction with 'A Set of Anatomical Tables of the Practice of Midwifery', which he also produced in 1754. These were accompanied by superb illustrations by Jan Van Rymsdyke, a court painter of the time, engraved by a Mr Grignion; of the latter's work Smellie wrote: 'delicacy and elegance however has not been so much consulted as to have them done in a strong and distinct manner, with this view chiefly that from the cheapness of the work it may be rendered of more general use'. This does scant justice to the quality of the work, which sold at 46s.

Although Smellie advocated natural childbirth, he realized that sometimes it was necessary to assist a baby's entry into the world. The forceps then in use appalled him, as did the habit of many of his colleagues of applying them wherever a grip could be obtained. He devised a shorter, lighter instrument and invented a device for interlocking the blades in a simple way, modifying the blades to follow the curve of the pelvis. His first forceps were made from wood, so patients would not be alarmed at the sound of the metal scraping

---

1 He was not the William Smellie (1740–95) who published the first edition of the *Encyclopaedia Britannica* in 1768 and the Edinburgh edition of the poems of Robert Burns in 1787.

together, but these were eventually discarded in favour of metal ones.

Smellie's work helped to systematize and civilize midwifery. His detailed records faithfully and honestly record even his own mistakes, rendering them of even greater use to those who came after him. Eventually in 1759, after developing a 'bronchial affection', he retired to Lanark where he died in 1763.

JAMES LIND (1716–94)

Lind's claim to fame was that he developed the cure for scurvy, the notorious disease which, springing from vitamin deficiency, in the mid-eighteenth century ravaged the sailors of the Royal Navy. It was said by one senior naval officer at the time, Sir Richard Hawkin, that he had known of the deaths of some 10,000 men from the condition during his career.

Born in Scotland and trained as a surgeon in Edinburgh, Lind obtained a post as a naval surgeon, seeing service in the West Indies, the Mediterranean and the English Channel.

On longer voyages he saw at first hand the effects of scurvy. Sometimes a squadron might lose up to a third of its men from the disease, which arose from a lack of fresh fruit and vegetables. His book, *A Treatise on the Scurvy*, describes in detail how he discovered his cure during a voyage aboard HMS *Salisbury* in May 1747. Taking twelve patients with the typical symptoms of putrid gums, skin lesions and lassitude, he divided them into six pairs, each of which was fed a different diet. It was the misfortune of one pair to be fed a diet of vinegar, and of another to be required to drink a half pint of sea water, 'by way of gentle physic' as Lind puts it. But the fifth pair were given a daily diet of two oranges and one lemon, with the result that one of them was soon able to return to duty and the other fit enough to nurse the remaining ten.

Modern scientific method would be sceptical of such a small statistical sample, and the Admiralty were slow to adopt Lind's findings.

But before it became official policy to feed lemon and lime juice to sailors, word of mouth had spread the wisdom of his prescription; Captain James Cook employed it during his famous voyage of discovery in HMS *Endeavour* in 1768–71. Its adoption eventually led to the eradication of the disease from the Royal Navy and can be cited as one of the factors in the growth of British sea power during the nineteenth century. With lower levels of scurvy than their French enemies during the Napoleonic wars, the British sailors were in better shape for the sea battles, earning the nickname of 'limeys' because of their diet of citrus juice.

ALEXANDER MONRO I (1697–1767)

Monro senior was the founder of the Edinburgh medical school. Like so many Scots of the time, he had travelled to increase his knowledge, first to London and then to Leiden where he was a student of one of the most influential medical men of the century, Dr Hermann Boerhaave. Of the eleven presidents of the Royal College of Physicians of Edinburgh between 1727 and 1772, no less than eight had been students of Boerhaave.

On return to Edinburgh in 1719, Monro organized a series of lectures on anatomy and surgery, the first of their kind in the city. He helped set up a hospital (now the Royal Infirmary) and held a portfolio of posts ranging from a directorship of the Bank of Scotland to a fellowship of the Royal College of Surgeons in Paris. His *Treatise on Osteology*, published in 1726, underwent eight different editions in his lifetime and was translated into most European languages. It reads strangely now, relegating the female skeleton to an appendix and attributing differences between the sexes to 'a weak lax constitution' in females, whose wider pelvis caused them when running to 'shuffle more from one side to the other than men'.

In the same year, 1726, the introduction of inoculation against smallpox into Scotland by Aberdeen surgeon Charles Maitland led Monro to mount an investigation into its efficacy, the results of which he sent to the Faculty of Medicine in Paris. He describes the practice whereby parents encouraged their children to play with mild sufferers from smallpox (and even share a bed with them), and the way in which the inoculations were made, thread which had been passed through 'pocky matter' being bandaged to a scratch on the arm of the patient. His own contribution was to undertake a detailed analysis of death rates from the disease in what must have been one of the earliest postal surveys. He found that inoculation was effective and that extraneous infection was introduced fairly rarely. Such studies significantly increased public confidence in the procedure.

Monro, a Jacobite, became less influential following the defeat of the rebellion in 1746, but his works were collected and published in 1781 by his son of the same name, who followed him as professor of medicine, anatomy and surgery at Edinburgh and as president of the College of Physicians. Of especial interest is his treatment of his own Achilles tendon which, he reports, snapped 'as if I had suddenly broken a nut under my heel'. Monro devised a splint which ensured that his toe was extended like a ballet dancer's for five months, then wore high-heeled shoes for two years to complete the cure.

Scottish medicine is packed with family dynasties like the Monros. Later, in Glasgow, there were the Cowans and the Glaisters.* But first we meet a quartet of illustrious medics linked by family ties who exercised influence in both Glasgow and London.

JAMES DOUGLAS (1675–1742), WILLIAM HUNTER (1718–83), JOHN HUNTER (1728 –93) AND MATTHEW BAILLIE (1761–1823)

James Douglas is best known among doctors as being, in 1730, the first to describe accurately the recto-uterine peritoneal fold, known as the 'pouch of Douglas'. He came from Badds, West Calder, where his father was a landowner, third child of a family of twelve. After graduating from Edinburgh in 1692, he went on to Utrecht and Rheims for postgraduate study before settling in London in 1700, the vanguard of a Scottish medical and scientific invasion in the years to come.

Douglas produced papers and lectured to the Royal Society, of which he was a member. His paper of 1707 showed the comparative dissections of the muscles of a man and a quadruped. As befitted an eighteenth-century man of science, Douglas had wide interests. He wrote about the speech of Londoners, and collected the works of the Roman poet Horace as well as anatomical specimens.

His elder brother and two younger ones also became Fellows of the Royal Society, but he was prevented from taking up membership of the Royal College of Physicians in London because he was a graduate neither of Oxford nor Cambridge. He later became an honorary Fellow and was made physician to Queen Caroline, wife of George II, in 1727.

Douglas's second wife was the aunt of John Wilkes the politician. Their youngest child, William George, was tutored by a young Scots doctor who had come to London, named **William Hunter**. Born in East Kilbride, Hunter had studied theology in Glasgow at the age of fourteen, when he came under the influence of William Cullen, then in medical practice near to the boy's home at Hamilton. After three years of study and travel, Hunter arrived in London to take lodgings first with William Smellie,* then with Douglas, who also had a practice in obstetrics.

Hunter's links with the family became closer after two personal tragedies hit the Douglases. Their son, whom he tutored, died holding Hunter's hand in 1742, and in 1744, just before his engagement to their daughter Jane Martha was made public, she also died. He reacted strangely, as if jilted, remaining bitter and estranged from women for the rest of his life. He plunged himself into his work in obstetrics, and between 1751 (when he first received permission to dissect the corpses of pregnant women) and 1774 assembled 400 specimens, from which thirty-four were selected for his magnum opus, *The Anatomy of the Gravid Uterus*. The book was produced in elephant folio size so that the drawings (by Jan Van Rymsdyke) could be life-sized. The printer, John Baskerville, was said to be an atheist; Hunter added to this accusation imputations that Baskerville was 'ignorant and illiterate', although he said he could forgive him his trespasses because he was an excellent printer.

Despite the sourness in his soul, Hunter's career prospered and he became physician extraordinary to Queen Charlotte, delivering the future King George IV. He acquired from James Douglas the habit of assembling collections, not only of medical specimens but of coins and paintings which are now housed in the splendid surroundings of the Hunterian Museum at Glasgow University.

John Hunter attained similar eminence in London when he arrived to join William, his elder brother. He shared also William's passion for collections. Despite renown as a anatomist, surgeon and teacher, and although he became royal surgeon extraordinary to George III in 1776, and surgeon-general of the Army in 1789, his museum of natural history became his chief interest. His home at 28 Leicester Square became too small for the collection and he built a separate building to house it in the garden, then moved to Earls Court so that it could have even more space.

Although John Hunter gained a reputation for his operations on aneurysms, he also made studies in venereal disease, gunshot wounds and inflammation. At one point his apprentice was Edward Jenner, later famous for his work on smallpox. Hunter also produced, in 1778, a pioneering work, *The Natural History of Human Teeth*, which is regarded as having first established a scientific basis for dentistry. In a bizarre experiment he once combined his surgical and dental knowledge to transplant a human tooth into a hen's coxcomb.

The last member of this formidable quartet was **Matthew Baillie**, whose mother, Dorothea, was the sister of William and John Hunter. Baillie's father, a minister in Shotts at the time of Matthew's birth in 1761, became professor of divinity at Glasgow University in 1775, the year after Matthew began there as a student. With both his uncles riding high in the medical establishment in London, Matthew was sent to stay with William Hunter while he studied at Balliol College in Oxford. Uncle William tutored him in medical science in the vacations, setting him on his way to a distinguished medical career which saw him become physician extraordinary to George III in 1810. His book, *The Morbid Anatomy*, went through eleven editions between 1793 and 1833.

Through this work Baillie made a significant contribution to medicine by being the first to give a clear outline of alcohol-induced cirrhosis of the liver. In the second edition he described 'rheumatism of the heart' (rheumatic fever) and was the first to distinguish common renal cysts from a rarer form, parasitic hydatids, caused by a tapeworm. The immense popularity of the book led to such demands upon his services as a consultant that it diverted him from carrying out further research into morbid anatomy. The effect of sixteen-hour working days led to the eventual breakdown of his own health and his death at the age of sixty-two.

JAMES BRAID (1795–1860)

Not to be confused with the golfer from Fife who was five times winner of the Open Golf Championship, Dr James Braid, who was also born in Fife, studied medicine at Edinburgh and went on to become a surgeon in Manchester, but he was also one of the giants in the history of hypnosis.

Braid's interest in Mesmerism began in November 1841 as a result of watching a demonstration by Lafontaine (1803–92), who practised hypnosis in much the same manner as stage hypnotists do today; to him it was a gimmick, a trick to dazzle an audience. Braid, a man of quite different character from the showy, extrovert Lafontaine, was nevertheless intrigued and quietly began to experiment in hypnotic induction for himself.

It soon became obvious to him that hypnotism did not depend on some kind of special power possessed by the hypnotists, nor on the theories of 'animal magnetism' advanced by the Mesmerists. Braid began to demonstrate and lecture on hypnosis, insisting that the claims being made for it should be discussed in a rational, scientific manner. He ran into trouble on two fronts: first from the Mesmerists, who resented the undermining of their 'magic' powers, second from the sceptics, who were convinced that the whole thing was a trick and that Braid was doubly dishonest in claiming it as a medical tool.

He collected his studies together into a book under the title of *Neurypnology: or the rationale of nervous sleep considered in relation with animal magnetism.*

Fortunately he decided that easier terminology was required, and coined the word 'hypnotism' and its derivatives.

He developed also a simple and extremely effective method of hypnotic induction. This involved requiring the subject to focus on a small bright object held close to and above the eyes, thus inducing eye strain. The effect could be enhanced by moving a finger close to the eyes, with the result that the eyelid would close. Braid regarded the hypnotic state as something which could either depress or enhance the activity of the nervous system, but refused to develop a detailed theory of how it operated. Although this was scientifically wise, it meant that he gathered no 'school' around him and the centre of hypnosis moved to France after his death.

SCOTS DOCTORS IN THE SERVICE OF THE TSAR

For over a century Scottish doctors played an influential role at the court of the Tsars. The association began with **Robert Erskine** of Alva, who trained as an apothecary in Edinburgh before going to study medicine at Utrecht and Paris. He arrived in Russia in 1704; within two years he had become chief physician to the Tsar and was put in charge of the country's medical services. Erskine created a physic garden at St Petersburg to supply him with medicinal herbs and encouraged other Scots to follow him to Russia.

He also created the nucleus of the library of the Russian Academy of Sciences with his own collection of books and those of **Archibald Pitcairne** (1652–1713), a colourful character and a polymath. The son of an Edinburgh merchant, Pitcairne had gone to Paris to study law, switched to medicine and graduated from Rheims in 1671. When he defended William Harvey's theories about the circulation of the blood, Leiden University invited him to take the chair of physic, but his wife disliked life in Leiden and so he returned to Edinburgh.

There he was often involved in quarrels over politics and religion fuelled by his appetite for claret. By the time of his death at the age of sixty-one he had amassed a huge and eclectic library, enriched by friendships with James Gregory, the astronomer, and Isaac Newton.

Erskine died in 1718, soon after Pitcairne. The next Scots doctor at the court of the Tsar was **James Mounsey** (1694–1788) from Lochmaben, who arrived to take charge of St Petersburg Naval Hospital in 1736. One of his early successes was to save from amputation the leg of General James Keith, a Scot then serving in the Russian Army. Becoming in due course first royal physician to Empress Elizabeth, he remained in the post for six years until she succumbed to alcohol excess in 1761. Promoted by her son, Tsar Peter, to head the medical faculty of the Russian Empire, the cautious Mounsey returned to Scotland when Peter was murdered in 1762, bringing with him seeds of a species of medicinal rhubarb which he introduced to Britain.

Tsar Peter's wife, Catherine (the Great), had succeeded him and sought his advice on another Scottish doctor to attend the court. Mounsey recommended a Dumfriesshire physician, **John Rogerson**, (d. 1823) who arrived in Russia in 1766. Ten years later he became Catherine's personal physician and a counsellor of state. He was also a close confidant and for twenty years, until her death in 1796, accompanied her on most of her travels.

Catherine had a huge sexual appetite; one of Rogerson's duties was to screen her numerous lovers for venereal or other diseases. As a precaution, two of the Empress's ladies-in-waiting were then invited to have sexual intercourse with them, becoming known throughout the courts of Europe as 'les éprouveuses'. On Catherine's death, Rogerson retained his position and was promoted to privy councillor by Tsar Paul. He continued under Tsar Alexander, finally returning to Scotland in 1816.

Before he left he had recruited two other notable Scots doctors. **James Wylie** (1768–1854), an Edinburgh graduate, had come to the court in 1790 as a surgeon in ordinary to Tsar Paul. He joined

Rogerson at the Tsar's post mortem in 1801 after his murder by drunken officers, the pair recording the official cause of death as 'apoplexy'.

Wylie continued as a royal physician and surgeon under Tsar Alexander I until 1825, then served under his successor, Nicholas I, until his own death in 1854 at the age of eighty-six. He had proved to be an energetic and skilled surgeon and saw service in the Napoleonic wars, during which he successfully amputated the leg of the Russian commander, General Moreau. He founded a medical academy in Moscow and St Petersburg, and encouraged the training of military surgeons and a programme of hospital building. He left his fortune to the Russian nation; part of it was used to build a large hospital in St Petersburg. Ironically, it was Wylie who was responsible for ending the practice of recruiting foreign doctors for the Russian armed forces.

Rogerson also brought to Russia, **Allan Burns** (1781–1813), whose elder brother, John, was professor of surgery at Glasgow Royal Infirmary. Burns was recruited to take charge of a new hospital to be established in St Petersburg. However, he did not stay long in Russia, since brother John needed support back in Glasgow against charges of bodysnatching to provide specimens for his anatomy classes. Allan went on to become a lecturer in anatomy and surgery and in 1809 produced the first cardiological textbook in the English language, *Observations on Some of the Most Frequent and Important Diseases of the Heart*. Its value is mostly historical, yet amid its vivid descriptions, Burns made two interesting suggestions on resuscitation which placed him well ahead of his time: namely that death should not be assumed until unequivocal signs of it appear, and that inflation of the lungs and passing of an electric shock through the chest should also be tried. Had he not died at the early age of thirty-four, such resuscitation techniques might have gained wider currency; perhaps 150 years would not have passed before they were put into clinical practice.

SIR JAMES SIMPSON (1811–70)

Without benefactors and sponsors, many of the most famous Scots scientists would not have escaped their humble origins and made the moves which brought them success. This seventh son of a baker in the town of Bathgate would never have done so, had not his brothers, recognizing his scholastic abilities, clubbed together to raise the funds for him to go to university in Edinburgh at the age of fourteen. Two other Bathgate boys were studying medicine and after joining them at the lectures of Dr Knox (recipient of many of the cadavers of the infamous bodysnatchers Burke and Hare), Simpson changed to medicine at the age of sixteen.

It took a strong stomach to enter an operating theatre in the earlier part of the nineteenth century. Long before antiseptics, infections were common and consequently so were amputations. Without anaesthesia, patients were fully conscious during operations and very often had to be held down, screaming in pain and terror while the surgeon did his work. If that didn't finish them, trauma often did. Simpson nearly quit medicine when he was confronted with such scenes, but was eventually to be instrumental in banishing them from operating theatres for ever when he developed the most effective anaesthesia yet known.

After graduating in 1832 he began as a general practitioner and through his sympathetic manner soon built up a good practice. When the chair of midwifery at Edinburgh became vacant in 1839 he was appointed. The high rate of infant mortality in that era, along with the tendency to think of women's medical problems as unimportant, made midwifery the Cinderella of subjects. Simpson soon changed that. His lectures were packed and even doctors in practice returned to register for them. Since they paid to do this, he swiftly became prosperous, and his list of patients from the upper classes made him one of the most fashionable doctors in Britain.

Fame did not go to his head. Soon after he received a letter appointing him a physician to Queen Victoria, he wrote to his eldest brother in Bathgate, 'Flattery from the Queen is perhaps not common flattery, but I am far less interested in it than having delivered a woman this week without pain while inhaling sulphuric ether. I can think of naught else.'

Simpson's search for the holy grail of anaesthesia led to some hilarious moments. Experimenting with hypnosis, he once found a ready volunteer in a young woman sitting next to him at a dinner party, whom he forbade to open her mouth until he gave permission. Unfortunately he was then called from the room for a long absence, to find upon his return an angry scribbled note from the speechless victim.

Not all subjects were so susceptible to the effects of hypnosis and Simpson turned to chemical forms of anaesthesia. Nitrous oxide gas had already been used in dentistry, as had ether. Simpson and his friends would use themselves as guinea pigs in experiments to find the most effective substance.

Late on the evening of 4 November 1847, a group of them returned to his home in Queen Street, Edinburgh (which, by a strange irony, was used over a century later as a church centre for substance abusers) and began to test various cocktails of chemicals, with little success. Then, from underneath a pile of papers, Simpson unearthed a sample of 'perchloride of formlye' (chloroform) sent to him by a chemist in Liverpool. It produced great gaiety and loquacity among the assembled company until with a crash they began to fall like bowling pins. Upon waking, Simpson's first thought was that this was much better than ether; and so indeed it proved to be.

The first child born while her mother was anaesthetized was soon supplied by a medical colleague (and christened Anaesthesia). A soldier, one of the first surgical cases, was so enthralled by the experience that upon waking he seized the sponge soaked with chloroform and began to inhale again as if he did not want to stop. Chloroform was a huge success. By 1895 the firm of Duncan and Flockhart were producing three-quarters of a million doses per week.

Not all were so admiring of Simpson's discovery. He was taken aback to be criticized by religious fundamentalists who saw anaesthesia as interference with nature, since pain in childbirth was divine law. Others suggested that chloroform itself might have led to deaths on the operating table. Simpson defended himself against both objections with biblical quotes and mortality statistics, but it was only when Queen Victoria was anaesthetized by chloroform in giving birth to Prince Leopold that opposition disappeared and its employment when performing surgery became standard.

There was sadness in his life. The deaths of his four children led him to write of his knighthood, 'I felt this baronetcy such a bauble in health and now when sick and heartsore, what a bauble it is.' Probably what made him such a good physician was that he was an emotional man. Devoted to his mother, who died when he was a child, and his only sister, who brought him up, it is said that he could not see a woman sewing a child's clothing without tears coming to his eyes. He endowed a prize at his old school for needlework, reckoning there were enough prizes for academic endeavour. Despite tempting offers and the honours heaped upon him, Simpson stayed in Edinburgh, near to his beloved Bathgate. When he died in 1870, his wife declined a place for his body in Westminster Abbey in London, knowing he would have preferred to remain in Scotland.

SIR WILLIAM MACEWEN (1848–1924), SIR GEORGE BEATSON (1848–1933), JOHN MACINTYRE (1859–1928)

Sir William Macewen has often been called the greatest innovative surgeon to have emerged from the Glasgow School of Medicine. In 1877, at the age of twenty-nine, he was appointed surgeon to three wards of the Royal Infirmary and during his fifteen years there he performed much of his pioneering surgery in the fields of rickets, inguinal hernia and brain surgery. The living conditions and poor diet of many Glasgow families at the time led to rickets being endemic, and Macewen devoted considerable energy to finding ways of correcting the limb deformities produced by the disease. He developed his own instruments, such as the 'osteotome' which he used alongside a chisel for bone operations. His work *Osteotomy* was acclaimed by surgeons around the world and translated into numerous languages, and his techniques adopted as standard.

Between 1875 and 1880 Macewen performed 835 osteotomy operations with only eight cases of septic reaction. This was in part by courtesy of the antiseptic methods of Joseph Lister (1827–1912), the Essex-born surgeon who taught Macewen at Glasgow in the 1860s and whose technique of employing an antiseptic spray of carbolic had greatly improved surgical success rates. But Macewen achieved such amazing results because he went one better by introducing aseptic methods. He insisted on utilizing stainless steel instruments, discarding any with bone handles; before use he boiled them in a fish kettle, bought by the nurses after the hospital authorities had refused to supply one. He insisted too that his theatre team should 'scrub up' and put on white surgical gowns, much to the derision of colleagues such as Dr Henry Clark, who on one occasion greeted the appearance of Macewen's team in a ward with a text from the book of Revelation: 'Who are these that are arrayed in white raiment and whence come they?'

The contempt was mutual. Macewen, with his walrus moustache, cut a fearsome figure; he was wont to refer to **Sir George Beatson**, his surgical colleague at the Western Infirmary, to which he moved in 1892, as 'that ambulance man'.

Beatson had been house surgeon to Lister in Edinburgh and became a pioneer of surgery for breast cancer, having discovered through his work the hormone dependency of some breast cancers. But he was also closely involved with the establishment of the St Andrews Ambulance Association and was knighted for his efforts in providing medical staff for the front during the First World War.

Another leading figure in medicine in Glasgow at this time was **Dr John Macintyre**, who had been an apprentice electrician and a student of Kelvin* before qualifying in medicine. When Roentgen discovered X-rays in November 1895 he sent his paper to Kelvin, who passed it to Macintyre. Remarkably, Macintyre had a clinical X-ray department up and running in March 1896, only four months after 'new light'— as it was then called — had been discovered.

Macintyre enjoyed an international reputation in his own right as an otolaryngologist; many of the greatest operatic singers and actors of the period offered their vocal cords for his examination at his consulting rooms in 179 Bath Street. Paderewski, Dame Nellie Melba, Luisa Tetrazzini and Sir Henry Irving were among his visitors, as well as Thomas Edison, who shared Macintyre's passion for recording the voices of his famous guests on wax cyclinders. Alas, this priceless archive, which was stored in Macintyre's attic, did not survive for posterity due to an uncommonly hot Glasgow summer during which the wax melted.

JOHN GLAISTER I (1856–1932) AND II (1892–1971)

Glasgow—Edinburgh rivalry is as keen in matters medical as in any other. If there were to be a Glasgow equivalent to Dr Joseph Bell, the model for Sherlock Holmes, it would be have to be John Glaister senior, doyen of forensic medicine. The two John Glaisters, father and son, between them occupied the regius chair of forensic medicine at Glasgow University for over sixty years between 1899 and 1962.

Glaister senior was a formidable figure and wore his silk top hat and frock coat long after these were regarded as old-fashioned. He was rarely without a cheroot; in his autobiography, *Final Diagnosis*, John Glaister junior relates how the spittle generated by the cheroot was used to telling effect in examinations by his father. A spittoon was always kept handy by the professor. 'The legend was that if the first blob of juice hit the spittoon, the student had passed. If it missed, well, he could always try again later!'

The first edition of Glaister's *Medical Jurisprudence* was published in 1902, and was welcomed not simply as a textbook but as a book of reference for practitioners. 'Young' John, as he was known to the family, at first wanted to become an actor but this profession was quickly vetoed by his father. On graduating from Glasgow in 1916 he served with the Royal Army Medical Corps in the Middle East and went on to become professor of forensic medicine in Cairo, from where he moved to succeed his father in 1932. He never lost his theatrical flair; his lectures occasionally resembled a cabaret in which he would play the role of an outraged lady interrogating the local GP (also played by him) to find out if her housemaid was pregnant.

The more serious side of his work was as an expert witness in murder trials, a task for which his thespian talents were well suited. His most famous case was that of Dr Buck Ruxton, a GP who had murdered his wife and maid, then removed all traces of possible identification from the corpses. Glaister and Professor J.C. Brash from Edinburgh reconstructed the skulls of the victims, thereby ensuring a conviction. He also updated versions of his father's classic work, which reached its twelfth edition by the time he himself retired.

SUFFRAGETTE SISTERS: ELSIE INGLIS AND MARIE STOPES

It is obvious from the previous pages that the pre-eminent Scottish physicians and surgeons of the Victorian and Edwardian period had one thing in common — they were all men. At the beginning of the twentieth century women still did not have the right to graduate from universities, nor to vote. First one barrier fell, and then, through the suffragette movement, the other. Two feisty Scots women who played a role in the battle for women's votes deserve their place also in the pantheon of medical achievement.

ELSIE INGLIS (1864–1917)

Scotland's answer to Florence Nightingale, at the time of her death Elsie Inglis was a heroine. When she fell ill in Russia in 1917, during her efforts to support Serbian soldiers, she was invalided out but lived long enough to die on British soil; her body lay in state at St Giles in Edinburgh and her sister received a letter of condolence from the Queen. She was more than an angel of mercy. This feisty lady fought many battles for women's rights, although she did not live to see the fruits of victory. During the twentieth century her name lived on through the maternity hospital named after her in Edinburgh, but that closed in 1988. Although there is still a ward of the Western General Infirmary which bears her name, Inglis is largely unknown today.

One of the first women to qualify in medicine in Scotland, Elsie Inglis was born in India of Scots parentage. When her father retired back to Edinburgh in 1878 to enjoy the prosperity he had acquired, Elsie set her sights on becoming a doctor. Since the medical schools did not admit women, she studied at an all-female college, the Edinburgh School of Medicine for Women. When its founder, Sophia Jex-Blake, dismissed two students for what struck Elsie as a trivial offence, her sense of injustice was roused. She persuaded her father and some wealthy friends to provide funds for her to set up her own school, the Edinburgh Medical College, where things were to be done differently.

Her own training was completed at the Glasgow Royal Infirmary and after qualifying as a doctor, she was appointed to a teaching post at the New Hospital for Women by its founder, Elizabeth Garrett Anderson. Active in the suffragette movement, she moved back to Scotland to establish a maternity hospital staffed entirely by women, and played a leading role in setting up the Scottish Women's Suffrage Federation.

When war broke out in 1914 she had the idea of sending to the front medical units staffed entirely by women. The British War Office and the Royal Army Medical Corps rebuffed her in the memorable phrase, 'My good lady, go home and sit still!' Undaunted, her suggestion was taken up by the Allied governments and she found herself in France three months after the start of the war. In 1915, she had a 200-bed hospital working in Royaumont Abbey. By April of that year she was in Serbia, isolated against Austria, Germany and Bulgaria. She took immediately to the Serbs ('a very charming people, very like the Irish in almost every way, but much better looking'). Engaged in fighting the typhus epidemic then raging, she was renowned for the aseptic techniques she employed when performing surgery. Elsie operated on men herself, which at that time was considered unusual.

When an Austrian offensive overran Serbia in the summer of 1915, she declined to leave her patients and was captured. Eventually, with the help of American diplomats, she was released, and was decorated with the country's highest honour, the Order of the White Eagle, by the Serbian crown prince in 1916. She then had the idea of establishing a hospital in Mesopotamia (now Iraq) but this was vetoed by the War Office. Instead she went to serve in Romania with the Serbian Division of the Russian army, remaining there until retreat into Russia and the discovery that she had cancer forced her to leave her post. One Russian official who saw her work at Costanza remarked, 'It is extraordinary how these women endure hardships; they refuse help and carry the wounded themselves. They work like navvies. No wonder England [sic] is a great country if the women are like that.'

Like many matriarchs of medicine, she expected others to be as tough as she in taking her treatment. One English nurse who came across Inglis's field hospital at Podgaysty described how tiny bags of salt were bandaged into open wounds to cauterize them, often producing excruciating pain for the patient. Inglis, seeing one soldier who was roaring in agony, remarked, 'Silly fellow! He doesn't know what is good for him.'

Her character and contribution was summed up by fellow Scot Arthur Balfour,* Foreign Secretary at the time of her death. 'Elsie Inglis was a wonderful compound of enthusiasm, strength of purpose, and kindliness. In the history of this World War, alike by what she did and by the heroism, driving power and simplicity by which she did it, Elsie Inglis has earned an everlasting place of honour.'

MARIE STOPES (1880—1958)

Readers of the *Guardian* newspaper in 1999 were sufficiently aware of her significance to vote her 'Woman of the Millennium', but Marie

Stopes is hardly a household name in Britain, and few Scots are even aware that she was one of their number. She suffered for being a woman ahead of her time, both in the causes she championed and the way she promoted them. Women's rights, contraception and sexual freedom were the issues she controversially espoused and the way she did so seems radical even today.

During her lifetime she became notorious for writing and speaking on family planning at a time when the churches, the medical establishment and society as a whole were opposed to it. She was a pioneer in proposing that women should be able to control their own fertility, and laid the foundations for many of the rights enjoyed by women today. Her talent for publicity was coupled with an ability to utter the telling phrase. In opposing chemical contraception, she said, 'Never put anything in your vagina you would not put in your mouth.' One of the stunts she perpetrated was to chain a book ridiculing Catholic birth control teaching to the font of Westminster Cathedral. Liable to lecture dinner-table companions on the joys of contraception, she was wont to produce a Dutch cap from her handbag to illustrate her views.

Her furnace of sexual revolution was stoked partly by her mother Charlotte, the daughter of the artist J.F. Carmichael, who had been the first woman in Scotland to obtain a university degree; although, forbidden as she was to attend lectures, her degree was designated a 'certificate'. She passed her passionate feminism to Marie. Her father, Henry Stopes, was a distinguished scientist. Marie vowed as a young girl that she would spend the first twenty years of her life in science, the next twenty in social projects and the final twenty years writing poetry. She duly did all three.

In 1901 she graduated with a double first in botany from University College, London. She went to Munich to complete a doctorate on fossilized plants which made her, on return to Britain, the youngest female doctor of science in the country. The marriage on which she embarked in 1911 was a disaster. Her husband, Reginald Gates, turned out to be impotent and she controversially petitioned for annulment in 1914 on the grounds that the marriage had never been consummated. Her eyes having been opened to many of the mysteries which then surrounded sexual mores, she began work on a book, *Married Love*, which a number of publishers rejected on the grounds that it was far too bold in its claim that women should strive to be the intellectual equal of their partners. When it appeared in 1918, 2,000 copies were sold in a fortnight and Marie was propelled into the public spotlight. She followed *Married Love* with a book advocating birth control, influenced by the ideas of the American campaigner Margaret Sanger, who argued that 'no woman can call herself free who doesn't have control over her own body'.

Married Love was banned in America as obscene, but Marie's support grew in Britain. In 1921 she founded the Society for Constructive Birth Control and with the help of a rich second husband, Humphrey Roe, established the UK's first family planning clinic in Holloway, London. She took to the road with her cause, in the first horse-drawn caravan in the world to offer birth control services.

By this time she was on collision course with both the Roman Catholic Church and the Church of England. She was doing everything she could to glamorize and publicize her cause, including suing a Catholic doctor who had libelled her in a book about birth control. She lost, then won on appeal, but lost again in the House of Lords. But the publicity did no harm to her aim of having 'a clinic in every country of the world'. She was well on her way to that aim in 1924 when her son Harry was born.

Alas her family life did not continue happily ever after. She and Humphrey became estranged and eventually drew up an agreement which permitted Marie to take lovers to satisfy her sexual appetite. A number of younger men obliged; her books of love poetry in 1928 and 1938 bear testimony to this period in her life. She continued to found clinics, and became involved in causes such as persuading the Inland Revenue to tax husbands and wives separately, and stopping education authorities from sacking women teachers who got married.

Stopes died from cancer in 1958, but her name lives on in the more than thirty countries where the organization bearing her name provides reproductive health services.

POSTSCRIPTS AND PENICILLIN

Scots medics continued to enjoy a high reputation throughout the twentieth century. The discovery that malaria is transmitted by mosquitoes was made by a Scotsman, **Sir Patrick Manson** (1844–1922). It was for his work on this hypothesis that Ronald Ross (1857–1932) won the Nobel Prize for Medicine in 1902. Manson himself founded the medical school in Hong Kong, and the London School of Tropical Medicine.

Over a century earlier another Scot, **George Cleghorn** (1716–94), an Army surgeon, had discovered quinine bark as a cure for malaria, a form of which was endemic in Britain at the time.

The treatment of diabetes was revolutionized by the discovery of insulin in 1921 and the Scots doctor involved in its discovery, **John J.R. Macleod** (1876–1935), shared a Nobel Prize with Frederick Banting in 1923. Macleod was a son of the manse, born near Dunkeld and educated at Aberdeen. From 1918 to 1928 he was professor of physiology at Toronto University, where his work on carbohydrate metabolism led to the discovery of insulin. He donated the proceeds from the patent to medical research. Macleod wrote eleven books and in later life went back to Aberdeen to a chair at the university and the Rowett Institute for Animal Nutrition.

Ian Donald (1910–87) made his contribution to medical science through the application of ultrasonics to obstetrics. The routine ultrasound scan which today gives pregnant women the first sight of their baby in the womb was pioneered by Donald, one of the most colourful characters in post-war Scottish medicine. Born in Moffat, educated at Fettes, he took a BA at Cape Town University before returning to study medicine in London. But it was not in a hospital or laboratory that he developed a passion for ultrasonics. Donald served in the RAF during the Second World War and was mentioned in dispatches for one incident in which he rescued airmen from a burning aircraft. In the RAF he learned about radar; he attempted to use ultrasonics on returning to his work in Glasgow, but was hampered by the primitive nature of the equipment. He was put in touch with Tom Brown, an electrical engineer with Kelvin & Hughes who was able to help him develop more effective equipment, and ultrasound rapidly asserted itself as a diagnostic tool.

Donald was a talented watercolourist but became better known for his opposition to the 1967 Abortion Act, which permitted terminations up to twenty-six weeks after conception. Three times on the receiving end of cardiac surgery, he wrote a telling account of his experience under the title 'On the Receiving End' in the *Lancet* in 1969. He contracted tuberculosis in 1984, dying three years later. Along with ultrasound, his legacy is the maternity hospital in Glasgow which opened in 1964; although it is called the Queen Mother's Hospital, its planning and design were greatly influenced by Donald. Important as discoveries such as ultrasound, insulin and a cure for malaria were, there is one medical breakthrough in the twentieth century which has captured the public imagination like no other. Since its discovery, there are few people who have never taken some form of penicillin.

SIR ALEXANDER FLEMING (1881–1955)

Despite the terror of surgery being diminished by Simpson's* chloroform, and the methods introduced by Lister and Macewen* for reducing infection in surgical wounds, well into the twentieth century the 'septic wards' of hospitals were packed with patients whose chances of survival were very slim. Septicaemia and pneumonia left doctors with very little prospect of a cure once an infection had gained a grip. The sea-change which enabled medicine to save so many lives was brought about by the discovery of antibiotics. The first and greatest of these was penicillin, discovered by the son of a tenant farmer in Ayrshire.

Alec, as he was known to his family and friends, gained his first education at the Loudon Hill school a mile from his farm, then in Darvel and Kilmarnock, which he left at fourteen to join his brothers in London where one (Tom) was a doctor. Tom persuaded Alec to use a modest legacy from their uncle to study medicine. In 1906 Fleming gained his medical qualification and joined the Department of Inoculation at St Mary's Hospital, where he had studied. His chief was Almoth Wright, a formidable character who quoted Shakespeare and was the model for Shaw's lead in *The Doctor's Dilemma*. Wright had carried out experiments with vaccines against typhoid fever and had gone to St Mary's after resigning in protest when the War Office refused to make immunization for soldiers compulsory.

Fleming completed a thesis on 'Acute Bacterial Infections'. Shortly afterwards he was to see at first hand the fatal consequences which they brought about when he accompanied Wright to France to establish a pathology laboratory during the First World War. After the war, Fleming returned to St Mary's and in 1921 was made assistant director of its laboratories.

Bacteriologists grow their cultures of bacteria in flat glass dishes about four inches across and one inch deep with a tight-fitting lid. At the bottom of the dish is a sterile jelly-like substance which contains sugars, proteins and mineral salts upon which the bacteria thrive. The usual method is to insert a small sample on the jelly and leave it to grow.

One day Fleming wiped his nose and out of curiosity smeared some of the nasal mucus on a culture dish. Some weeks later he noticed that no bacteria were growing around the area where the mucus had been. He concluded that there must be something in the mucus which dissolved the bacteria, and he named the mysterious substance 'lyzozyme'. He found it in all kinds of other bodily fluids and living organisms, but the paper in which he published his results was largely ignored. Unfortunately he lacked either the means or the knowledge to purify and separate lyzozyme.

In 1928 Fleming made his greatest discovery, and it came about by one of those chances with which scientific legend abounds. He was growing plates of staphylococci, the potent bacteria responsible for causing boils, abscesses and blood poisoning. Fleming, never the tidiest of workers, had left some of the plates lying around the laboratory without lids, with the result that mould spores had entered and grown in the dish. This greenish mould exuded a juice which prevented the staphylococci growing. Fleming called it penicillin (it was later classified as *Penicillium notatum*) and found it was effective against a whole range of bacteria.

Unskilled in chemistry as he unfortunately was, his numerous attempts to isolate the active ingredient were in vain. Almoth Wright gave no encouragement, declaring himself uninterested in 'antiseptics'. Thus it was that penicillin remained undeveloped for over a decade. In 1937 Dr Howard Florey, an Australian professor of pathology at Oxford University, and Dr Ernest Chain, a Jew seeking asylum from Nazi Germany, had taken up Fleming's work on lyzozyme. They came across his paper on penicillin and, with the aid of their team, managed to crystallize it as a brown powder. Tests on animals and humans produced amazing cures of severe septicaemia within days.

The tests took place in 1940 and 1941, during the worst days of the war for Britain, and resources to develop penicillin were not available. Florey turned to the USA, where big chemical companies were only too eager to produce the new antibiotic, especially when they realized that neither Fleming nor Florey had patented their discoveries and the pickings were theirs for the taking. But the trio of Fleming, Chain and Florey were not denied the honour of having discovered and developed the drug. All three were knighted and a flurry of research was started to find new strains of *Penicillium* which would be more productive. By means of X-rays, mutants were produced which were many more times powerful than Fleming's greenish mould. The chemical structure of penicillin was determined, making it possible to manufacture penicillins in the lab which were designed to deal with every known type of bacterium.

8

Prime Ministers

Scots Who Governed England (and an Empire Too)

Eight of the fifty-one British Prime Ministers since the eighteenth century have been Scotsmen. This is a number higher than would be expected from Scotland's share of the population of the United Kingdom, but has not necessarily been matched by political influence. Most of the eight were in No. 10 Downing Street only briefly, having done their best work somewhere else, and none can be reckoned among the great Prime Ministers. In fact, ever since 1707, Scots have taken rather uneasily to political life at Westminster in what is, in defiance of the legal theory, essentially the continuation of an English Parliament.

Scottish MPs have always carried an alien whiff about them, and seldom taken a prominent part in the proceedings. For more than a century, up to the re-establishment of a Parliament in Edinburgh in 1999, the House of Commons had special arrangements for legislation affecting Scotland. Scots MPs on the whole confined themselves to this type of business and few made notable contributions otherwise. In the short periods when they did, as at the beginning of the twentieth century and today, they tended to draw adverse comment from the English. It is striking that five of the eight Scottish Prime Ministers have been aristocrats, sitting in the House of Lords, with two from the world of business and only one man of the people. There is something in the Scotsman in the street also that sits ill with the ordered politics of Westminster, where rituals disguise the serious business of constant adjustment of interests; Scots are too impatient of dissembling, gentility and compromise alike. But scions of the upper class have usually been educated in England and fit in well enough even if, as we see from the record, they have been unable to dominate the parliamentary system.

JOHN STUART, EARL OF BUTE (1713–92)

Lord Bute was the first Scot to become Prime Minister of the United Kingdom after 1707, but he arrived at the top too soon. The Union had not yet brought Scotland and England close together enough for the English to accept a Scottish political leader. In fact they would not give him a chance at all. They thwarted him and pilloried him and made his life impossible. Though no great statesman, he was probably well up to the political average of his time and based his policies on a perfectly reasonable reading of the circumstances he faced. Yet he went down in history as a disaster, and there was not to be another Scottish Prime Minister for nearly a century.

He would have done better to stay at home on the Isle of Bute. He succeeded to his title in 1723 and was early on elected as a Scottish representative peer in the House of Lords. But he cared little for politics, preferring to pursue his interests in botany, agriculture and architecture on his own estate. Politics all the same intervened in this tranquil existence in the form of Jacobite rebellion. Several Stuart septs came out for their namesake Bonnie Prince Charlie, but the Stuarts of Bute were not one of them. On the contrary, the Earl strongly supported the Hanoverian succession, being related by marriage to the Dukes of Argyll, its mainstays in Scotland. Few Jacobites were to be found around the shores of the Firth of Clyde where Bute resided, but he was not the only loyal Scot to decide in the autumn of 1745 to take a holiday in London, just in case things should go horribly wrong at home. Nor did he hurry back when all was quiet again. This casual lethargy would determine the rest of his life.

One day in 1747 Bute went to the races at Egham in Surrey, which were also being attended by Frederick, Prince of Wales, son of King George II. It started raining, and the Prince's party retired to a tent to while away the time over a game of whist. They invited the Earl in: he sat at the same table as the Prince, and the two got along famously. Before long, Bute was appointed to Frederick's household. He became such a friend of the family by the time the Prince died prematurely in 1751, leaving as his heir the future King George III, that his widow asked the Earl, a high intellectual by royal standards, to act as the young man's tutor. George III succeeded to the throne in 1760, still only twenty-two years old. With little experience of life, he relied heavily on the man who had been the chief influence in his upbringing. It was the start of Bute's ill-fated political rise.

In 1761 the new king managed to have Bute brought as a secretary of state into the Government, which was dominated by two old political hands, the Duke of Newcastle and William Pitt the Elder. Bute now started machinating on his own account, and engineered the downfall of Pitt later that year. But Pitt was popular with the people. As Bute drove to the opening of Parliament he was insulted by the mob in the streets of London for being a Scot and a favourite at court. Undaunted, he went on to topple Newcastle too. On 26 May 1762, Bute himself became Prime Minister.

There was one major piece of business on hand, to end the war Britain and her allies had been fighting with France and other European powers since 1756. It had seen numerous feats of British arms, the conquest of Canada and destruction of French power in India, together with seizure of many strategic outposts round the world. France's last throw was to bring in Spain on her side, but British expeditionary forces at once sailed out and captured Manila, capital of the Philippine Islands, and Havana, capital of Cuba. The Royal Navy showed itself to be mistress of the oceans, establishing the maritime supremacy which would last for two centuries. Britain emerged from this struggle in triumph, for the first time clearly dominant over her continental rivals. But enough was surely enough: wars which go on too long can also go wrong. Bute had taken up secret contacts in Paris from the moment of his entry into the Cabinet, and now opened formal negotiations. He did some deals for the sake of a speedy conclusion, while holding on to the main gains. The French gave up Canada for good and agreed their presence in India should remain minimal. Bute's achievement was to choose the right moment for consolidating Britain's rank as a global power.

When the Treaty of Paris was signed the English, especially the mob in London, went mad. The minor concessions Bute had made were depicted as a total sell-out. His enemies accused him of accepting bribes from the French. Parliament was in uproar. John Wilkes, the radical agitator, wrote scurrilous articles in the press inciting English hatred of the Scots and accusing Bute of having slept first with the King's mother and then with the King himself. 'Few men have ever suffered more in the short space I have gone through of political warfare,' wrote the Prime Minister. On 9 April 1763, he resigned, after just ten months in power, and retired into private life. This episode persuaded David Hume* that there were barbarians living on the banks of the Thames, and that French absolutism might be more civilized than English liberty.

GEORGE GORDON, EARL OF ABERDEEN (1784–1860)

Lord Aberdeen was the next Scot to become Prime Minister of the United Kingdom and, though better qualified for the job, he did little better than the first, Lord Bute.* The careers of both ended in ignominy which, in Aberdeen's case, was much more unfair. He had spent almost his whole life in the highest circles of the British ruling class. An orphan at the age of eleven, he was taken under the wing of Henry Dundas,* political boss of Scotland and warlord against France. With patronage like that, Aberdeen became by 1813 ambassador to Austria, on a mission to form the vital coalition of European powers which within a couple of years would at last crush the Emperor Napoleon. The appointment required a hazardous journey across the war-torn Continent for which the Earl's sheltered upbringing had hardly prepared him. The Napoleonic wars brought special horror in the suffering of the wounded; though the firepower was modern, with heavy artillery and long-range rifles, medical care was primitive, without antisepsis or anaesthesia, and many men not killed outright died in slow agony after every battle. The sights and sounds Aberdeen witnessed gave him a permanent aversion to war.

Once home, he would have been happy to stay as a country gentleman on his estates, but various minor political posts led to his appointment as Foreign Secretary in 1828, again at an unusually early age, in the Tory Government of the Duke of Wellington. He faced a continuing crisis in Greece, which was attempting in savage struggle to throw off the rule of the Turks. Aberdeen, like most Scots, supported Greek independence, which was indeed to be gained shortly afterwards. But he had a big hand in formulating the more permanent British policy towards Turkey which would last till the outbreak of the First World War. In essence this amounted to managing the decline of the Ottoman Empire, supporting it against aggressors while not standing in the way of its subject peoples if they wished to break away; it stretched at the time from Algiers to Baghdad, and included most of the Balkans. But Aberdeen did not feel sorry to return to Scotland once the Tories were put out by the Whigs in 1831.

When he returned to the Foreign Office ten years later the problems still looked remarkably similar. France was urging Egypt to break from Ottoman rule, which Britain saw as a menace to her interests in the East. The quarrel grew so heated that at one point war had seemed near, but Aberdeen at once took steps to find a successful compromise. He was then the first Foreign Secretary to have to deal with the rising strength of the United States, in regions of the world remote from the great powers' usual concerns. Enmities between the two English-speaking nations dating from the revolutionary period were still not overcome, but he recognized that in the long run they would both gain from friendship. First he settled a small but stubborn dispute over the boundary between Maine and Quebec. Then he turned to the much more important question of the Pacific coast. Much of it had been opened up by Canadian fur-traders who used the Columbia River for transport, and in effect treated what are now the states of Oregon and Washington as British territory. But Americans also penetrated the area, and the time had come to draw boundaries. Long negotiation ended with division of the basin of the Columbia along the line which is still the border between Canada and the United States today.

In 1846 the Tory Party split over Sir Robert Peel's repeal of the Corn Laws and, after a long period of confusion, Aberdeen emerged as head of a coalition between Peelites and Whigs in 1852. Soon a fresh crisis erupted in the East, where Russia was pursuing the long-term ambition of an outlet to the Mediterranean Sea, interpreted in Britain as a threat to the route to India. The Russians presented themselves as protectors of the Christian peoples of the Ottoman Empire, and used this as the pretext for occupation of what is now Romania. The British and French felt alarmed that this might lead on to Russian seizure of Constantinople. They sent fleets to the Black Sea and, despite Aberdeen's desperate attempts to avoid it, war broke out in March 1854.

It became known as the Crimean War because the principal theatre of operations was Sebastopol, the main Russian naval base, besieged for nearly two years by allied troops landed on the peninsula of Crimea. It proved a grim and costly business, but what turned it into a decisive political issue was the reporting of it in the British press, aided by the new telegraphs. For the first time the public had immediate coverage of fighting, and the effect can be compared to that on Americans during the war in Vietnam over a century later. There was as yet no censorship: correspondents wandered round the battlefields at will. Much franker than their successors in the First and Second World Wars, they sent back reports which turned readers' stomachs. Then Florence Nightingale became a legend overnight as she was described tending wounded soldiers in appalling conditions. A scapegoat for the mismanagement and confusion (which were probably no worse than in previous wars) had to be found. It was Aberdeen. His Government collapsed early in 1855. It was a tragedy that a war he did not want felled a leader who had devoted his life to peace.

ARCHIBALD PRIMROSE, EARL OF ROSEBERY
(1847–1929)

When Lord Rosebery moved into No. 10 Downing Street in 1894 he seemed certain to make a success of the job. He had everything going for him: youth, riches, glamour, popularity, intelligence and ambition. True, the situation he faced was more difficult than he might have wished. He succeeded William Gladstone, who finally stepped down in exhaustion at the age of eighty-five, having definitively failed with the measure which obsessed his later years, a Home Rule Act for Ireland; it had just been defeated in the House of Lords after the narrowest of passages in the House of Commons, and so was abandoned. In pursuit of that aim Gladstone had sacrificed many others, he had split Liberalism in 1886 and seen almost its whole right wing secede into a Liberal Unionist party committed to keeping the four nations of the British Isles under a single Parliament at Westminster. But Rosebery was one figure on the right who had stayed loyal, and in him seemed to lie the best chance of a reunited Liberalism once he took over the reins of power. All these high hopes were to be dashed. Just eighteen months later Rosebery's Government collapsed in confusion, and the Conservatives easily won the ensuing election. He would never hold office again.

What went wrong? Much of the reason lay in Rosebery's character, and in the very image of golden boy he created from his first entry into politics. He was an aristocrat, from a family which had held the same lands of Dalmeny outside Edinburgh since the seventeenth century. His background gave him a certain wilfulness, an

arrogant lack of restraint and an unreadiness to listen, even (or especially) to older and wiser men. He did not have to work as hard as
others to get on in life, but he saw nothing wrong with that. On the
contrary, he expected the glittering prizes to come his way. Yet he was
a complex man with unsuspected sides. He seems, in a very Scottish
manner, also to have been suspicious of success, to have sensed that it
did not bring all a fulfilled human being should want. He devoted an
immense amount of a limited stock of energy — for he suffered terribly
from insomnia — to historical research and writing, which was of fine
quality and which in the second half of his life gave him more satisfac-
tion than anything else. He had no taste whatever for the seamy side of
politics, for wheeling and dealing, nor even for the normal parliamentary processes of compromise through constant, gradual adjustment
of interests. Scottish again was his impatience with lesser mortals
who could not share his firm principles and clear ideas. Altogether, he
was to be taken on his own terms or not at all; yet nobody could ever
be sure just what he wanted or which way he would move.

The man explains the career. He rose to early prominence as manager of the campaign in 1879 by which Gladstone became MP for
Midlothian and returned to politics after a period for reflection out
of Parliament. Rosebery badgered his leader to be made Scottish
Secretary, a post which did not yet exist. By the time it became available in 1886, he had already moved on to higher things in Cabinet.
Crisis over Home Rule supervened to put the Liberals out. When
they came back in 1892, Rosebery was Foreign Secretary and heir
apparent to Gladstone. He made no effort to consolidate support
from his colleagues. On the contrary, gambling on his own indispens-
ability, he demanded and got freedom to act with no interference
from them, or even from Gladstone himself. That did not augur well
for his premiership, which indeed turned out short and unhappy.
Before long he resigned the leadership of his party, yet spent several
years in bitter dispute with others over its future direction. Liberals
finally gave up on him, and left him in isolation.

It was a disappointing career of wasted potential. But some good
things can be said about it. One of Rosebery's motivations lay in a

heartfelt Scottish patriotism common in our day but unusual in his, especially in one of his social class, which had led Scotland's assimilation into a Greater Britain, assuming this to be both inevitable and beneficial. To him his nation was both an intellectual passion, most obvious in his concern for revival of Scottish historical scholarship, and a political cause: it was largely by his exertions that the Scottish Office, a special department of state for Scotland, came into existence.

His other main motivation lay in the Empire. As Foreign Secretary he actively promoted imperial expansion. He also worked for imperial federation, in which the dominions and colonies, at least the white ones, would set up some kind of unifying political structure capable of maintaining itself as a great power in the face of competition from upstart rivals such as the United States and Germany. This would solve the problem of Home Rule, too, because both Scotland and Ireland could be members of the federation. Connected with this was his desire to modernize Liberal philosophy. The tenets of laissez-faire, of complete personal, political and economic liberty, had scarcely been questioned in his party. But in Rosebery's view they had failed to uphold Britain's position in the world. It was necessary to set about deliberate social, industrial and educational reforms designed to serve national aims. In practice the Government would have to define the aims and push through the reforms. So Rosebery prefigured much of the political thinking of the twentieth century, but in a way that linked Scotland to a greater destiny. Like most men ahead of their time, he got no thanks.

ARTHUR BALFOUR, EARL BALFOUR (1848–1930)

Like his predecessor, Lord Rosebery,* Arthur Balfour inherited a crumbling Government. Unlike Rosebery, he was a Tory and, unlike him again, made the effort to find a basis for unity among his party's warring factions. His reward was the loss of his own seat in the greatest electoral debacle of the Conservative Party in the twentieth century, surpassing even that of John Major in 1997. Balfour left No.10

Downing Street with relief, but the most useful and distinguished part of his career was to come afterwards.

Though he sprang from the landed gentry of East Lothian, his sound Scots genes were mixed with those of the high English aristocracy: his father married a Cecil, from the family of the Marquises of Salisbury, who had been helping to run the state since the time of the Tudors. In their footsteps, Balfour had an education at Eton and Cambridge, a quick entry into Parliament and ministerial office before the age of forty. His first job was Scottish Secretary. He suppressed unrest by Highland crofters and passed on to a similar task in Ireland, where he was called Bloody Balfour. The current Marquis of Salisbury was Prime Minister, and soon treating his nephew Balfour as his heir apparent. He duly succeeded in 1903. He had not had to try too hard to get to the top, and once he was there showed no great enthusiasm, rather a gloomy scepticism.

This was the heyday of Empire, but it still seemed to its rulers a precarious construct, as indeed it was. The imperial federation proposed by Rosebery had supporters in both parties, though it was unclear how the project should proceed. A possible first step was formation of an economic bloc, much as the modern European Union started with a Common Market. The champion of this approach was the Colonial Secretary, Joseph Chamberlain, a former Liberal who had split with his party over Ireland in 1886. He told Balfour he wanted to launch a campaign for imperial preference. This would end free trade with all countries, a principle to which Britain had adhered with virtually religious fervour, and carry it on only with the dominions and colonies, while putting up tariffs against foreign goods. Balfour warily responded that this was not a policy on which the Government had been elected and, if Chamberlain wanted to campaign for it, he had better do so outside the Cabinet: in other words, resign. The merest hint of abandoning free trade, however, brought about the departure of several other ministers who did not think Balfour firm enough in supporting it. He tried to promote an alternative of fair trade, with retaliation against foreign tariffs, but only weakened further a Government doomed to defeat.

After losing, Balfour ruled out a return to the premiership by accepting an earldom. It was during this period out of office that he met the Zionist leader, Chaim Weizmann. He began to take a great interest in the plight of the persecuted Jews, especially in Russia, which according to his biographer and niece, Blanche Dugdale, arose directly from his Presbyterian religion and love of the Old Testament. During the First World War, when Balfour was brought back into an all-party coalition as Foreign Secretary, the allegiance of the Jews and the influence of Jewish finance became a matter of concern to the Government. The most anti-semitic power, Russia, was actually one of the Allies. The Germans made capital out of this with vague promises to the Jews of a refuge from the pogroms after the war, possibly in Palestine. The United States at this point remained neutral, and there was genuine fear that the Jews might impede American entry into the war on the Allied side. In these circumstances Weizmann pressed on Balfour the wisdom of making some formal statement in favour of Zionist aspirations for a return to the Holy Land, 2,000 years after the destruction of Solomon's Temple by the Emperor Titus. The result was the Balfour Declaration, which committed Britain to the establishment of a 'national home for the Jewish people', if in somewhat ambiguous terms. Even so, this can be seen as the origin of the concept of the state of Israel.

After the war, Balfour's world-weary realism proved ideal for redefining relationships between Britain and the dominions. Loyally as they had rallied round the mother country in a long and bloody struggle, several felt dismayed that a simple announcement by King George V in London had been enough to commit them to it. The Government of the United Kingdom conducted foreign relations on behalf of the whole Empire; even the Canadians, for example, lacked so much as a legation in Washington DC. Yet more or less complete internal self-government had now been granted to the white dominions and, with their growing maturity as nations, progress towards untrammelled independence could not be denied.

The Imperial Conference of 1926, where all their Prime Ministers met, commissioned the elder statesman Balfour to work out a formula expressing this evolution in terms which would also stress a desire to maintain close and warm connections among peoples united by blood, sentiment and tradition, yet scattered over the earth. Balfour decided he did not want an empty formula: the result was the renunciation by Britain of any right to rule or legislate for the dominions embodied in the Statute of Westminster (1931). The Commonwealth for which it furnished the basis rests on an identification of interests alone. Balfour had recognized that without it no legal powers would be effective, and with it no legal powers would be necessary.

SIR HENRY CAMPBELL-BANNERMAN (1836–1908)

The man who inflicted that crushing defeat of 1906 on Arthur Balfour's* Tories was a brother Scot, Sir Henry Campbell-Bannerman. A modest, jovial but shrewd Glaswegian, he made an improbable electoral wizard. Yet the Liberals, at least, never bettered his performance: this was their last great victory before terminal decline of the party set in. And generally he had a knack of confounding expectations.

Till his time, few born outside the traditional, largely aristocratic British ruling class ever managed to reach the top in politics. He blazed the trail for the commercial elite of Glasgow, which produced another Prime Minister and numerous lesser figures. His father, James Campbell, was a draper, a trade to which the city owes a great deal. In his case there was nothing humble about it, for he owned the largest mercantile warehouse in the world, Glasgow still being at the time an immense producer of textiles. He became Lord Provost, though among the few Tories in a solidly Liberal town council. His son changed allegiance and broadened his horizons, as well as inheriting more wealth (one legacy obliged him to add Bannerman to his own name, though he hated the double-barrelled result). In 1868 he was elected Liberal MP for the Stirling Burghs, which he would represent for forty years, and set off on a solid if unexciting ministerial career in various minor posts. In Lord Rosebery's* Cabinet of 1894–5 he was Secretary for War. There seemed little reason why he should get further, but the next few years would alter that.

In Rosebery's Olympian analysis, the driving forces among mankind for the future were going to be empires rather than mere nations. He thought the Liberal Party, which had dominated British politics from 1832 to 1886, was losing its grip because it could not or would not adapt to this movement of history: it was doomed unless it espoused his ideas. Such a glamorous figure found it easy to project these ideas into public debate and get them taken seriously. But there survived in his party a core of more stolid, down-to-earth types, well represented by Campbell-Bannerman, unimpressed with high-flown theory. There seemed to them nothing much wrong with the programme of personal, political and economic freedom Liberals had always championed, though of course it would have to change with the times. But in their view nothing had happened to justify discarding tried and trusted values in favour of others that remained as yet untested and speculative. Above all they believed the Liberals had to remain a party of the people, not a vehicle for an elite as Rosebery wished.

It was a desire at the grassroots for a return to Liberal basics that impelled Campbell-Bannerman into the leadership after the lengthy turmoil caused by Rosebery's petulant resignation. Little headway had been made in opposition to the Conservative Government, and the new man was scarcely settled into his job before the Boer War broke out between Britain and the Afrikaner republics of South Africa in 1899. Rosebery and his Liberal imperialists supported the war, while radical Liberals felt appalled at it. In Scotland especially, a stronghold of the party, there was much sympathy for the Boers — a small Calvinist people surviving against the odds in a remote region of the globe, asking nothing more than to live a life of their own but now attacked by a great power. Parallels with Scottish history seemed clear. Campbell-Bannerman tried with great difficulty to hold a balance in the party, and at times it seemed to be coming apart. Early victories in South Africa gave way to a phase of dirty guerrilla warfare which the British found hard to fight, except by herding innocent Afrikaner women and children into concentration camps where thousands died. Campbell-Bannerman now found the formula to rally the mass of Liberals and isolate Rosebery: he condemned not the war itself but the 'methods of barbarism' used to end it. And so he united his party for the electoral battle ahead.

He did not live long to enjoy the fruits of his smashing victory at the General Election of 1906, for he was already suffering from a weakened heart. He moved quickly to show what Liberals could do in South Africa, where the settlement was the major achievement of his two years in office. With surrender by the Boers to British sovereignty, he wanted to restore internal self-government as soon as possible. They were all the same adamant that this should not entail extension to their former republics of the more tolerant regime for blacks prevailing in the old British territories of South Africa – in Cape Colony, for example, members of all races could gain the vote if they passed a property qualification. Campbell-Bannerman had to choose whether to force racial equality on the Boers and risk another conflict, or let them remain masters in their own house, though oppressing non-whites. He chose the latter as the lesser of the evils. It meant institutionalizing racism, and missing the chance of building a multicultural society in the Union of South Africa formed as a dominion in 1910.

Campbell-Bannerman had little time, and his Government faced a heavy legislative programme. He marked the limits of Victorian radicalism, yielding to men with a feebler grasp of what made the Liberal Party work, and so less fitted to adapt it to the twentieth century. He was the last British Prime Minister to die in office, at No. 10 Downing Street in December 1908.

ANDREW BONAR LAW (1858–1923)

Bonar Law was a Scottish triumphalist even by the standards of a time, the imperial heyday, when the nation's self-esteem had never been higher. Unlike any other leader of it since Henry Dundas,* he owed nothing to England in background or education. In his blood ran the unyielding Presbyterianism uniting the West of Scotland and Ulster — capable also of export, for he had arrived in Glasgow as a child from New Brunswick, where his father, born at Portrush in Antrim, served as an emigrant minister. He qualified himself for public life as a member of the mercantile elite of his adopted city by trading his way to a fortune. In politics Bonar Law remained wedded to imperial commerce, unabashed about riches, egalitarian without being compassionate and tending to rigidity on certain matters of vital concern not always grasped away from the Clyde. That meant above all Ireland, for the Unionism he represented had sprung to life to defend the Irish Union when it came under threat from William Gladstone's scheme of Home Rule in 1886. This crisis detached from the hitherto dominant Scottish Liberal Party a large part of the Protestant working class in Glasgow and environs so as to unite its interest — mainly in keeping immigrant Irishmen out of good jobs — with the more conservative concerns of the bourgeoisie. This was a broad, populist force which tempered capitalism with welfare, and exerted a huge influence in Scotland till well on into the twentieth century.

Bonar Law, the sixth Scotsman to get to the top of British politics, was called by the English historian Lord Blake the 'unknown Prime Minister'. The key to knowing him lies in the renewed struggle against Irish Home Rule in 1913–14, when another Liberal Government tried to finish the dead Gladstone's business. Bonar Law, Tory leader at Westminster, rejoiced to champion his embattled kin in Ireland: there was 'no length of resistance to which Ulster can go in which I would not be prepared to support them'. Then and since, Englishmen have sought in vain to understand his austere view that, Ulster being right, Ulster had to fight. It was his almost treasonable conduct of opposition in the crisis that made him 'unknown' because it was so incomprehensible to them. They entertained expectations of a man refined by Westminster's parliamentarianism, not least that he should behave in an English manner. In some ways he did. He was a better unifier of his party than the silky Arthur Balfour:* while he had supported imperial preference ten years before and lost his first seat in Glasgow for his pains, he agreed that now was no time to argue about something so secondary as tariffs.

Yet Celtic obduracy and sectarianism formed a stronger part of his make-up, more chilling because it remained unwarmed by the Celtic fire the English could take account of, as in Lloyd George. Instead there was in Bonar Law an unsentimental calculation which put the interests of the Second City before those of the First: London lay at the edge of his world, Glasgow at the centre. He did not care a fig what people in London thought about Ireland, or their basic desire that the problem should just go away. He saw Ireland from Glasgow, especially its Presbyterian population in the North, forming one cultural and economic zone with the West of Scotland, washed by the wide Atlantic which represented at the same time opportunities for trade and a threat to security if ever Belfast or Londonderry should fall into the wrong hands. That gives a clue to the deeper motives of Scots, contrasted with Ulstermen, even in the solidarity of this new Irish crisis. To Scots it was the crisis not of a province but of an empire. Bonar Law regarded it as such and that fact would almost make him, in the strange way of a diehard, the man to clinch a compromise.

That never happened in 1914 because the outbreak of the First World War overtook the crisis in Ulster, and all merely political questions were brushed aside as the country girded its loins for the struggle against Germany. But it did happen after the war, during which the Easter Rising in Dublin had taken place, making it imperative for the Irish problem to be solved as soon as peace came. Circumstances had changed, but Bonar Law brought the same broad view to them. No man at this juncture did more to create the political entity of Northern Ireland, under a regime of Home Rule he had earlier rejected for the island as a whole, the difference now being that it would be set up separately in both parts. This monument to him survives into the new millennium.

Like other Scottish Prime Ministers of the United Kingdom, Bonar Law did his best work in lesser offices. He reached higher by a fluke. Lloyd George led the coalition which fought the second half of the Great War and won it. He carried on afterwards, though by 1922 most Tories were tired of being led by a slippery Liberal. As a fresh election approached, a meeting at the Carlton Club in London of the Conservative MPs decided to break with him, against the advice of their leaders. But Bonar Law supported the manoeuvre and in consequence found himself suddenly put in charge of the party, which also meant he shortly became Prime Minister. Within eight months he was diagnosed as suffering from cancer of the throat; he had been a heavy smoker all his adult life. He resigned at once and died soon afterwards.

JAMES RAMSAY MACDONALD (1866–1937)

In most western countries the men who headed the first socialist governments have won a special niche in history, not only for themselves but also as symbols of the rise of the proletariat and its admission to the inner sanctum of power after long pressure from outside. But in Britain and in Scotland this is not so. On the contrary, James Ramsay MacDonald remains a relatively minor figure in political history, while inside the Labour movement his memory is reviled. Even in his native Scotland he enjoys little esteem and will be considered, if at all, as a far lesser man than his mentor Keir Hardie, who is held in deep affection. By contrast MacDonald bears the stigma of a traitor to the working class, who sold out Labour during its first real chance of running the country. Seeing the turn the party then took, towards the statism, centralism and bureaucracy which kept it out of office for most of the twentieth century, one might have thought there was something to be said for him after all, and historians have indeed started to say it. He has even been seen as a forerunner of Tony Blair, though Labour is not yet ready to forgive him.

He rose not just from the ranks of the people but out of genuine deprivation, as the illegitimate son of a ploughboy and a serving girl in the north-east of Scotland. Life in such surroundings could have offered him little but, with the benefit of a Scottish education, he got away at the first possible opportunity to London, where the rest of his career was spent. He returned to Scotland only for speaking tours, holidays and then, briefly at the end of his public life, as MP for the Scottish Universities. He early moved in progressive political circles, but socialism in Britain took a form different from its counterparts in Europe, much less theoretical and revolutionary. Over here it was rooted in a pragmatic and gradualist tradition. MacDonald personified that: he had next to no understanding of economics or interest in dialectical reasoning, and certainly no intention of manning barricades or gunning down the bourgeoisie to transform society. His socialism was at bottom sentimental, inspired by the wretched condition of the poor in an advanced capitalist society. Even so, he stubbornly advanced their cause in the face of indifference or even derision, on cold street-corners and in draughty working men's clubs. These exertions quickly made him a fine orator, although he degenerated in later life into a windbag. Hugh MacDiarmid,* for example, could not abide his woolliness and would not even listen to him.

MacDonald first stood for Parliament in the 1890s though not till 1906, in the huge swing against the Tories of that year, was he elected MP for Leicester. He won national attention when he opposed Britain's declaration of war on Germany in 1914. This made him a hate-figure to the press and to public opinion generally. He stood by his principles and lost his seat in 1918. He had his reward on being re-elected four years later when Scots colleagues, those Clydesiders who had also mostly been pacifists during the war, made sure to elevate him to the leadership of the Labour Party, an action they afterwards rued.

Before long he was Prime Minister, the seventh Scot to reach the office. The Conservative majority of 1922 melted away at a further election the next year. It produced a three-way split in Parliament, but Labour emerged the larger of the non-Tory parties and Liberals agreed to support MacDonald as head of a minority Government. This unfamiliar experiment in British politics, not without value on that account, had no staying power and MacDonald resigned at the end of 1924.

In 1929 he came back in a stronger position, if still in a minority. The timing could hardly have been worse, for Britain and the rest of the world soon plunged into depression. Unemployment rose rapidly from one million to three million. The pound, again on the gold standard since 1926, came under severe pressure and in 1931 MacDonald proposed to his Cabinet drastic cuts in public spending in order to avert a devaluation. With one or two exceptions, his ministers refused to support him, any more than his backbenchers. MacDonald went to offer his resignation to King George V, who instead of accepting it urged him to form a National Government uniting all parties for this emergency. It was perhaps another chance for MacDonald to show himself right when everybody else was wrong, and he took up the royal commission. It meant he then had to go to the country at the head of a coalition largely Tory in composition.

His sweeping victory, the biggest of the twentieth century, came close to destroying the Labour Party. Economic policy over the following years turned Conservative while MacDonald, back in triumph for a third term, grandly concentrated on foreign policy, trying to secure disarmament in Europe and strengthen the League of Nations. He persevered for four years but, with failing powers, could not understand how the rise of Nazism in Germany ruled out permanent peace. On his retirement in 1935 he was the longest-serving of the Scottish Prime Ministers. Given the dismal competition, it would not be far-fetched to declare him the best: regardless of ideology he always did what he thought right and on the whole got the country, if not his party, to agree.

SIR ALEC DOUGLAS-HOME, LORD HOME OF THE HIRSEL (1903–95)

Lord Home was the eighth Scotsman to become Prime Minister of the United Kingdom, and he may well have been the last. It is not at all clear, now Scotland once more has a Parliament of her own, that the English will again submit to being ruled by the Scots.

The Earls of Home had been settled on the border between Scotland and England since the Middle Ages, but their money came from coalmines on a huge estate in Lanarkshire inherited through an heiress of the extinct Dukedom of Douglas. It was natural for Sir Alec, while still only heir to his title, to enter the House of Commons as Conservative MP for Lanark. Though at that stage he was best known as an amiable but somewhat diffident cricketer, political advancement came surprisingly fast, and it was a coup for him to be appointed in 1937 parliamentary secretary to the Prime Minister, Neville Chamberlain. He had Home constantly at his side as together they went off to the encounters with Adolf Hitler and Benito Mussolini culminating in the Munich Agreement of 1938, which was supposed to have brought 'peace in our time'.

Tory supporters of Munich usually branded themselves appeasers, and many in effect thus brought an end to their careers. But somehow Home escaped the stigma attached to the rest. Though hardly by his own fault, he did not have a good war either: a crippling illness kept him in bed for most of it. These were, by Tory standards, quite big handicaps to carry forward into the post-war era. Yet it was Sir Winston Churchill himself, returning to office in 1951, who gave Home his first ministerial post, at the Scottish Office. An upsurge of nationalism in Scotland had come with peacetime, and the Prime Minister always felt uneasy about the temper of the Scots: he had once been MP for Dundee, only to be thrown out after a bitter campaign in 1922 in which the issue of his habitual short way with social unrest figured largely. Now he urged Home to 'go up to Scotland and see if you can get rid of this embryonic Scottish nationalist thing'. Home manfully did so, at least for the time being, while impressing all with his own more realistic patriotism.

His success in Edinburgh led him straight into the Cabinet, at first in charge of Commonwealth Relations, just as Britain was dissolving the remainder of her Empire. In these years the main dividing line between left and right in the Conservative Party ran through Africa. The left wanted to hand power to black Africans as soon as possible, while the right wanted to maintain white rule as long as possible, directly from London or by local settlers where they existed. Home stood on the right, and often clashed with the Colonial Secretary, Iain Macleod, who belonged to the opposite camp. And it was Macleod that persuaded the Prime Minister, Harold Macmillan, to heed the 'winds of change' blowing through Africa which it would be impossible to resist for long. None of this, however, prevented Macmillan forming a high estimate of Home's abilities. In 1960 he made him Foreign Secretary, a job at which he excelled through a complex period of international relations, with episodes like the Cuban crisis offset by the first limits on nuclear weapons.

Even so, the next stage of Home's career came as a universal surprise, not least to himself. In October 1963 Macmillan fell ill and decided to resign. He had a deputy and heir apparent in R.A. Butler, another man of Munich, but that was not the sole reason why Macmillan hated him and resolved to stop him succeeding. But he had to find an alternative candidate, and there seemed to be nobody commanding the same experience and authority as Butler. Of those available, Home just about came closest, as a safe pair of hands whose abilities outweighed his invisibility to the electorate. There was also the problem of his being a member of the House of Lords, which Macmillan brushed aside. After much manoeuvring and back-stabbing behind the throne, Home was projected into No. 10 Downing Street, renouncing his peerage and fighting a Scottish by-election to re-enter the Commons. He faced an impossible task. The Tories had run out of steam after thirteen years in power. Home could only hope to stem the swing to Labour, which he did quite well, holding his challenger Harold Wilson to a tiny majority in the General Election of 1964.

He resigned the Tory leadership and loyally served under his successor, Edward Heath, for a second term as Foreign Secretary in 1970–4. He had the dignity of the old school, increasingly out of place in a politics growing more ruthless and vicious. Home's persona included a Scottish patriotism worn lightly in the manner of previous generations, and completely consistent with Britishness. He did urge his party to respond to another and stronger upsurge of nationalism.

But when the two sides of his identity were brought into conflict in the referendum of 1979, he urged Scots to vote down devolution. His authority helped to ensure it did not get through that time.

A Scottish parliament did not return to Edinburgh until 1999, but its presence poses the question of whether it will have an effect on the strong Scots influence within British politics. The initial signs are that it will not. During the eighteen-year Conservative administration which ended in 1997, there were several Scots in the Cabinet, and that has continued with the Labour Government which succeeded it. Ambitious Scots politicians still see Westminster as the place to be. And there might easily have been another name added to the tally of Scots Prime Ministers had not a heart attack claimed the life of Labour leader John Smith in 1995, when he looked set to win the next election.

9

The Scots Psyche

'I Kent his Faither'

When the world ends, Scotland will have an honoured place in the rituals, if only because someone will probably strike up a chorus of 'Auld Lang Syne', the international anthem which Scots have taught the world to sing. With words by Robert Burns set to a folk melody, it has been adopted across many cultures as a cheerful way to end a social event by joining hands, and singing (usually one of several different versions of the original words).

However, non-Scots may be less familiar with another quintessentially Scots expression: 'Here's tae us! Wha's like us? Nae mony — and they're a' deid!' (Tr. 'Here's to us! who's like us? Not many, and they're all dead.')

This somewhat immodest traditional Scottish toast is not confined to the annual festivals of haggis and hagiolatry of the National Bard. It will not have escaped readers that as well as the requirement to have been born in Scotland, and influential outside it, there is a third criterion for inclusion in this book. The people featured are all dead. Only then is it safe for Scots to revere them and view them through the rosy spectacles of hindsight. To proclaim a Scot to be a saint in his lifetime is not only an impossibility in canonical terms, it is to invite a dozen other Scots to point out that he has feet of clay. In a moment readers will be introduced to this peculiar facet of the Scottish psyche as the principle of 'I kent his faither', but here it is used to illustrate the argumentative nature of the Scots. Scots are fighters. Their belligerence may or may not take a violent or military form. It might simply be the wish to fight for rights or a principle. But whatever form it takes, we are proud of being fighters.

This is illustrated by the patriotic song written by Robert Burns which was quickly adopted as the unofficial anthem of Scotland. He wrote it in the period when declarations of the Rights of Man were being proclaimed and his own poems celebrated Universal Brotherhood. But his anthem harks back to an earlier era. It draws, for its mythology of the wee man fighting off the big bully, to the last drop of blood, on the period when Scotland fought to assert its independence from England.

> *Scots wha hae wi' Wallace bled*
> *Welcome to your gory bed or tae victory!*

The warlike tone is continued in a later verse, which asks rhetorically:

> *Wha would be a traitor knave? Wha would fill a coward's grave?*
> *Wha sae base as be a slave? let him turn and flee!*

Certainly such bloodthirsty imagery is present in other songs from the same period, such as 'La Marseillaise', but even as recently as the 1960s, the Corries folk duo looked for inspiration to this same period, and to the great battles with the English armies of invasion, when they were composing 'Flower of Scotland'. Their song, far from seeming out of date, was seized upon and adopted as the official anthem sung before rugby internationals.

> *O Flower of Scotland, when shall we see your like again?*
> *That fought and died for, your wee bit hill and glen.*

The words of these songs, still widely sung as an unofficial national anthem, seem more than a touch bloodthirsty, and anti-English. They carry echoes of the Declaration of Arbroath, sent in 1320 by the nobles of Scotland to the Pope asking him to exert pressure on England to allow them to live in peace (and independence). One oft-quoted sentence sums up the patriotic feeling of the time:

> *For as long as a hundred of us remain alive we will never allow ourselves to fall under the dominion of the English. We do not fight for glory, or wealth, or honours, but for liberty, which no man will give up while he has his life.*

The fact that Scots still write songs and sing about battles from so long ago tells us another thing about the Scots psyche — Scots are proud of being fighters, but they are also sentimental. Ironically some of our best songs are about monarchs who were failures (e.g. Mary Queen of Scots and Bonnie Prince Charlie) or about battles which we lost ('The Flowers of the Forest' and 'The Battle of Flodden'). But in order to understand why Scots fought battles and why they loved or hated certain monarchs, we need to gaze into the Scottish soul. That is why we need to look a little closer at Scots religion. For in its religion we see the best and worst of any nation.

The man most associated in the popular mind with Scots religion in the past five hundred years is John Knox. There is some irony in this, since Knox spent most of his active life outside his native land. He returned from exile as the catalyst of Reformation in 1560 rather in the way that Ayatollah Khomeini sparked the Iranian revolution in recent times, but unlike the Islamic leader, Knox did not exercise power in the new nation he helped create. Sidelined within a few years, he lived out the remainder of his life an embittered man. The period from the Reformation to the Enlightenment is dominated by conflicts in which the monarch tried to bring the Kirk under his control. These sapped much of the nation's strength; arguably Scotland's golden era might have come sooner but for these tensions and conflicts over religion. They left their scars on the Scottish psyche, and gave Scots a reputation for being quarrelsome over religion.

To illustrate this aspect of the Scots psyche, it is worth telling an apocryphal tale added to the saga of Robinson Crusoe. The character of Crusoe is based on the true story of a Scotsman, Alexander Selkirk from Lower Largo in Fife. But the following story does not appear in Daniel Defoe's novel. In this version, the Scots castaway builds himself a church in which he worships. As the boat which has rescued him pulls away from the beach, the captain spots another church building on the promontory of the bay. He turns to the castaway: 'I thought you said there was no one else on the island?' The castaway confirms that this is so. 'Then how did that other church get there?' asks the captain. 'Ah,' the Scotsman replies, 'I built that one as well. That's the church I *don't* attend.'

The image of the Scot as a fighter (whether with a sword on the battlefield, or with the pen in pursuit of some principle) is an enduring one, and summed up in the motto beneath the royal arms of Scotland, the lion rampant. The Latin text reads, 'Nemo me impune lacessit', but in Scots the pugnacity is more neatly captured in the phrase 'What daur meddle wi' me?' (in plain English, 'Who dares meddle with me?'). There is more than an echo of this phrase in the motto 'Who Dares, Wins' adopted by the crack troops of the Special Air Service (SAS), founded by a Scot, David Stirling.*

There is a Glaswegian version of this motto. As a city, Glasgow enjoys a reputation for toughness even today. The shipyards may have vanished, and many of the worst social problems. However, an echo of those tough times is left in the Glasgow accent. Perhaps it was the need to make themselves heard over heavy machinery in the factories, but the lilting intonation of the West was, over the years to become, at its gruffest and most Glaswegian, something between a cough and a bark. The Glaswegian version of 'Nemo me impune lacessit' is 'See you, Jimmy', a phrase which if pronounced by most people sounds like a friendly goodbye, similar to 'au revoir', 'ciao', or 'auf Wiedersehen'. But when a Glasgwegian growls 'See you, Jimmy' then beware. It is a prelude to conflict. He is about to point out that he has been traduced in some way.

We have encountered all kinds of fighters in the course of telling our story, but few hooligans. It often puzzles Europeans that Scottish and English football supporters are so different when they follow their team to away games on the Continent. On the surface the Scots look fierce, dressed in their kilts, some of them with the blue and white flag of Scotland painted across their faces like ancient warriors daubed with woad. Yet this 'Tartan Army' has an exemplary record and has not featured in any of the football hooliganism which has blighted the name of England's national team. Underneath his kilt, the Scotsman is not as fierce as he seems. His fighting instincts are defensive rather than provocative, and he is at his best when fighting to defend a principle than to enlarge his power or dominion.

It is this quality which has enabled the Scots to co-exist with their English neighbours in a political union for three hundred years, and also to emigrate around the globe and fit in with the vastly different cultures in which they found themselves. Unlike some ethnic groups, they have refrained from importing the kind of issues which have led to sectarian or civil strife in their history or homeland. This has made them welcome as immigrants who remained proud of their origins yet were able to integrate successfully into other societies. Perhaps because the Scots are a mixed ethnic group themselves, there has never been any suggestion of asserting Scottishness as a racial characteristic. There is a sense in which Scottishness is like Jewishness or Irishness — it is distinctive and has produced many distinguished people throughout history — but thankfully Scots have never desired to preserve that identity in a biological or theological way. Even the wildest and woolliest proponents of Scottish nationalism have never dared to suggest that there is a Scottish race.

Nevertheless, there is a curious phrase in the Declaration of Arbroath, the patriotic charter of 1320 referred to above, which states that the Scots were originally from 'Greater Scythia' and that 'though they lived in the furthest parts of the world [Our Lord Jesus Christ] chose that they be persuaded to faith by none other than the brother of the blessed Peter, the gentle Andrew, first called of the apostles though in rank the second or third, who he wished always to be over us as our patron'.

Scythia was, in the time of the apostles, around the northern end of the Black Sea, roughly where Ukraine is today, and was traditionally thought to have been evangelized by St Andrew. The passage above is the first official mention of Andrew as the patron saint of Scotland, but it also appears to identify the Scythians with the Scots. There is no evidence that a tribe of Scythians trekked across Europe and settled in Scotland (although some have speculated that it might have been possible via the Baltic states). The story appears to be on a par with the legend of St Regulus, who is alleged to have sailed with the bones of St Andrew from Patras in Greece, to have been shipwrecked and to have brought them ashore in Fife near the spot which became St Andrews.

The reality is that the Scots are not a single 'lost tribe' but a mixture of different tribes, some indigenous to north Britain and others who came via Norse invasions, trade with the Low Countries or even the Spanish Armada. From afar, Scots may seem to have a definite identity but anyone more familiar with Scotland will know what an extraordinary variety of types, cultures and accents exist across a very small territory. Those who are familiar with the vast distances of North America, Russia and Australia and how homogeneous the culture and speech patterns are, must be bewildered when they come to Scotland and hear citizens of Glasgow and Edinburgh, who live less than fifty miles apart, talk of each other as if they had an ocean between them.

Despite these parochial passions, it is not surprising that in such a small country, people know a great deal about one another and use this information to keep one another from getting too big for their boots. In order to understand this facet of the Scots psyche it is necessary to introduce the reader to another puzzling expression. It is the phrase, 'Och, I kent his faither.' This should not be translated simply as 'Oh, I knew his father.' The 'knowing' is rather more subtle than the recognition of kinship or social acquaintance. It is a kind of *gnosis* which renders the possessor able to put even the most powerful or famous person in his place, once his origins have been established. To savour this effect, it is necessary to pronounce the phrase with emphasis on the 'Och', just short of clearing the throat as if to spit. Then the necessary element of absence of awe or respect will have been introduced. The statement which follows ('I kent his faither') thus becomes the reason for which the lack of respect is evinced. Knowledge of the father is sufficient to place the person under discussion in the realm of ordinary mortals. His birthplace, his ancestors, his life up to that moment can safely be fitted into the known categories .

This essential parochialism is summed up in the apocryphal headline in an Aberdeen newspaper after the sinking of the *Titanic*: 'Aberdeen man drowns at sea'. 'I kent his faither' shrinks the world, but it also shrivels reputations, and it has been called the 'hiss from hell'. But the process is not always lacking in generosity, paying due tribute to the achievements of the person concerned, especially if their origins were humble. Thus Robert Burns was the Ploughman Poet or Hugh Miller the Stonemason, James Hogg the Ettrick Shepherd and so on. A more contemporary example might be Sean Connery the Milkman, based on the fact that nearly all biographies of the most famous living Scotsman begin with his career as a milk-delivery man in Edinburgh — not so much 'I kent his faither' as 'I kent him when he was only a milkman'.

Connery — despite his high-profile support for the Scottish National Party — is now a tax exile and therefore runs up against another Scots trait, the wish to count the pennies in other people's pockets. It is not so much envy, as a kind of moral disapproval that people should be rich at all. Perhaps it has its origins in a severe form of Bible reading, highlighting what happens to rich men when the Last Judgement comes, but it is more likely to be the reflection of another principle dear to most Scots — the idea that everyone is equal.

This is, of course, now regarded as a universal principle and forms part of the Declaration of Independence: 'This truth we hold to be self evident, that all men are created equal ...' The Scottish version of this principle can be expressed in two different ways. The first is 'We are all Jock Tamson's bairns'. This emphasizes the inclusive side of equality by what we have in common with others. It is a folksy version of the theological principle that we are all made in the image of God.

The variant is slightly more subversive. It states 'Jock's as guid as his maister' (i.e. Jock is as good as his master). Like 'I kent his faither', there is a nuance here which goes beyond the principle of egalitarianism. It seems to be saying 'Now, don't you be getting any ideas about yourself — you're one of us, and what's more, don't think you have the right to tell us what to do.' This aggressive egalitarianism is presumably what has made Scotland such a fertile ground for socialist ideas. The founder of the modern Labour Party, Keir Hardie, was a Scot, as was the first Labour Prime Minister, Ramsay MacDonald,* and although many of the modern heirs of the Red Clydesiders (John McLean, Jimmy Maxton and Manny Shinwell) seem pale pink in comparison, Scots continue to dominate the modern Labour Party, and the Cabinet.

Yet despite their egalitarian sentiments, Scots are different. Not better, nor worse than other nations, but distinctive. Being distinctive means being able to be recognized easily and thus to be caricatured, yet we would contend that the caricature of the Scots as mean is wrong. We are not mean (the high per capita giving to charities is one of many indicators that this is a false picture) but we are 'canny'. We do not like money to be wasted, nor do we admire those who have it in abundance. 'The Scots keep the sabbath and anything else they can lay their hands on' is a true statement but it requires a little exegesis. The first part says we lay stress on religious values and the second says we seldom miss opportunities. Here in a nutshell is the paradox of being Scots. Moralistic and materialistic at the same time, one moment we shout a slogan and then whisper it down with the next breath. 'Here's tae us, wha's like us — nae mony and they're a' deid' is not a cry of superiority or triumph. It is an expression of divine discontent, a declaration of being different, but doomed. Read again all these quintessentially Scottish expressions and you will find that they are all capable of being read in different ways. We may not be from Scythia but we have learned a little from the oracle at Delphi about making our declarations in the form of a paradox.

'What daur meddle wi' me?' is an assertion of independence, whereas 'We're all Jock Tamson's bairns' shows how interdependent we are. 'I kent his faither' brings someone down but 'Jock's as guid as his maister' restores him to an equal footing with the rest of us.

Being distinctive does not mean being superior. The conclusion of this book is not a claim to be the master race. Quite the contrary, our form of power operates from below. On the starship *Enterprise*, our representative is Scotty the engineer (despite the fact that his accent is Hollywood Irish), who gets extra power from the engine so that Captain Kirk can boldly go where no man has gone before. The last thing a Scot would like to be called is a hypocrite, but, like it or not, — we are quite capable of being both aggressive and servile at the same time. How else could we have co-operated in running the British Empire for so long? One cynical explanation is that whenever the sins of Empire had to be accounted for, we were happy to acknowledge that it was England's Glory but when the medals were being handed out, we wanted to be seen as Scotsmen. Don't think this is a specifically Scottish trait. Viewers of sports programmes in the United Kingdom are used to hearing that 'England' has won a gold medal, but when it fails to gain any, it is 'Britain' which has done badly.

Robert Louis Stevenson wrote eloquently in 'From Scotland to Silverado' about these traits of the Scottish character:

> *The old land is still the true love, the others are but pleasant infidelities. Scotland is indefinable, it has no unity except upon the map. Two languages, many dialects, innumerable forms of piety, and countless local patriotisms and prejudices, part us among ourselves more widely than the extreme east and west of that great continent of*

America. When I am at home, I feel a man from Glasgow to be something like a rival, a man from Barra to be more than half a foreigner. Yet let us meet in some far country and whether we hail from the braes of Manor or the braes of Mar, some ready-made affection joins us on the instant. It is not race. Look at us. One is Norse, one Celtic, and another Saxon. It is not a community of tongue. We have it not among ourselves; and we have it, almost to perfection, with English, or Irish, or American. It is no tie of faith, for we detest each other's errors. And yet somewhere, deep down in the heart of each of us, something yearns for the old land and the old kindly people.

The contradictions involved in being Scots — being a fighter without wanting to own up to having started the fight — or being proud of our famous sons while reminding them of their humble origins, are not unique. The eastern philosophies which mix Yin and Yang would be sympathetic to a nation which produces famous men and insists on making them humble, or which sings about bloody battles with the English and has lived at peace with them for over two hundred years.

When Scotland Ruled the World depicts a way of controlling events without needing political power. While power without responsibility has been the prerogative of the harlot throughout the ages, responsibility without power was the way that the Scots chose to run things.

Index